GEORGE JACKSON CHURCHWARD
1857–1933

For Melinda

My Devon Belle

GEORGE JACKSON CHURCHWARD
1857–1933

His Life, Leadership and Locomotives

TIM HILLIER-GRAVES

AN IMPRINT OF PEN & SWORD BOOKS LTD.
YORKSHIRE – PHILADELPHIA

First published in Great Britain in 2025 by
Pen and Sword Transport
An imprint of
Pen & Sword Books Ltd.
Yorkshire - Philadelphia

Copyright © Tim Hillier-Graves, 2025

ISBN 978 1 39904 691 6

The right of Tim Hillier-Graves to be identified as author of this work has been asserted by him in accordance with the Copyright, Designs and Patents Act 1988.

A CIP catalogue record for this book is available from the British Library.

All rights reserved. No part of this book may be reproduced, transmitted, downloaded, decompiled or reverse engineered in any form or by any means, electronic or mechanical including photocopying, recording or by any information storage and retrieval system, without permission from the Publisher in writing. NO AI TRAINING: Without in any way limiting the Author's and Publisher's exclusive rights under copyright, any use of this publication to "train" generative artificial intelligence (AI) technologies to generate text is expressly prohibited. The Author and Publisher reserve all rights to license uses of this work for generative AI training and development of machine learning language models.

Typeset in Sabon LT Std 9.5/11.5
by SJmagic DESIGN SERVICES, India.

The Publisher's authorised representative in the EU for product safety is Authorised Rep Compliance Ltd., Ground Floor, 71 Lower Baggot Street, Dublin D02 P593, Ireland. www.arccompliance.com

For a complete list of Pen & Sword titles please contact

PEN & SWORD BOOKS LIMITED
George House, Beevor Street, Off Pontefract Road,
Hoyle Mill, Barnsley, South Yorkshire, England, S71 1HN.
E-mail: enquiries@pen-and-sword.co.uk
Website: www.pen-and-sword.co.uk

or

PEN AND SWORD BOOKS
1950 Lawrence Rd, Havertown, PA 19083, USA
E-mail: uspen-and-sword@casematepublishers.com
Website: www.penandswordbooks.com

Contents

Acknowledgements 6

Chapter 1 A Victorian Childhood 7

Chapter 2 Fledgling Engineer 27

Chapter 3 Making a Start 41

Chapter 4 A Commanding Presence 73

  Churchward's Life and Work in Colour 105

Chapter 5 Picking Up the Pace 121

Chapter 6 Changing Times and Competing Expectations 148

Chapter 7 A Passing Age 182

Chapter 8 Drawing to a Conclusion 207

References Sources 239

Index 242

Acknowledgements

To say I was pleased to be asked to write about George Churchward would be something of an understatement. When researching many different aspects of engineering history his shadow and reputation loomed large over all I read. At one end of the scale, we have the words and recollections of men of equal status, such as Nigel Gresley and William Stanier, to guide our thoughts. At the other end, there are the memories of office staff, railwaymen, shop floor workers and many others to consider. Some worked closely with him in a variety of roles, while others simply glimpsed the great man as he wandered through workshops, sheds or along platforms. Each in their own way has added something of value to his fascinating story.

All these accounts, no matter from where they came, testify, most eloquently, to Churchward's skill, his intelligence and the astute way in which he set about his business. For the historian all this is a godsend, because the material this has generated illuminates all aspects of his life and his achievements. And if any of them allowed criticism to enter their vocabulary, they did so in a carefully considered way, paying due regard to the problems Churchward faced and the time in which he lived.

In tracing the life and work of this exceptional man I was also helped in my endeavours by researching Kenneth Cook and William Pellow, who knew Churchward personally and recorded much about him. Then there are my two old friends, David Neal and Phil Atkins, late of the NRM, whose help and advice was always given so generously.

In Britain we are lucky to have many institutions that have meticulously preserved as much material as possible for all to see and research. But sadly, much was destroyed by British Railways in the 1960s during a regrettable bout of 'good housekeeping'. However, more by luck than judgement, a great deal was saved by concerned individuals and this now exists in public and private collections. There are significant gaps and where these exist many people have committed time and energy to seek out information and publish the results of their work wherever possible. And by this diverse means an important part of our social and engineering history has been preserved to illuminate our understanding of the past.

In writing this book I was greatly assisted by three institutions in particular. First and foremost, there is the National Railway Museum and its extensive archives, then 'Discovery' at The National Archives and, finally the library of the Institution of Mechanical Engineers in London. The staff who manage these collections do so with great skill and always proved friendly and co-operative when answering my many questions, despite their busy schedules.

To all the people who helped me to research and write this book I give my thanks and hope I have done justice to all that they have contributed. Ultimately though, all an historian can do is sift and consider all material and reach a judgement that he or she thinks honestly reflects past events. There will, undoubtedly, be alternative views or conclusions, but that is as it should be. I don't think there's ever a final word and new material may be found to allow fresh interpretations to be made.

Chapter 1

A Victorian Childhood

In 1950, Kenneth Cook, who had recently become the Western Region's Mechanical and Electrical Engineer, was asked to write an appreciation of George Churchward, his most famous predecessor at Swindon, for the Institution of Locomotive Engineers. After much thought he offered this well considered evaluation of his life and work:

> He was above all else a tactful administrator and a leader of men. He gathered about him a careful selection of technical staff of diversified talents, many of them with fine academic distinctions. These he inspired with enthusiasm and drew from them the best, and then he created the conditions for the growth of good teamwork and esprit de corps.
>
> The eminence attained by Churchward was due to his personality as much as anything. His depth of vision, wonderful grasp of essentials, logical thinking and the intuition by which he seemed to sense what was at the back of the minds about him, ensured that the best was always forthcoming. Such items as the taper boiler barrel, Belpaire firebox, long-travel valves, top feed and the firetube superheater had first appeared elsewhere, while the domeless boiler, with internal steam collecting pipe and regulator in the smokebox was a revival of broad-gauge practice. It was from the recognition of the goods points in these details and careful blending of them into his own designs that success was attained, rather than the originality of ideas.

When Cook wrote these words, the outcomes of Churchward's life were well known and there for all to see. His reputation was secure and his achievements celebrated within his profession. But, as is always the case, much is left unsaid in such evaluations. It is almost as if the person in question just dropped from the sky fully formed ready to begin work. What went before is barely mentioned and there is little to say how that person acquired their skills, the

George Jackson Churchward when in his prime. Kenneth Cook, his eventual successor at Swindon, wrote on the back of this print, 'the great man in 1902 when promoted to replace William Dean as Locomotive Superintendent at Swindon. On that date the GWR truly began to come of age' (KC)

The mid-Victorian period, when George Churchward was growing up in rural Devon, was an age of great extremes. If you had an ample income, as only a minority did, life could be good. If not, extreme poverty and a short, unhealthy life were the most likely outcomes. In 1851 there was the Great Exhibition in Hyde Park for everyone to enjoy. (top) At the same time the work of men such as Isambard Kingdom Brunel (above left) and one of his greatest achievements, the soon be to completed *Great Eastern* (above right), reflected an age of great engineering advances but, sadly, minimal social change. These were two key issues Churchward would have to embrace during his career. (DN)

influences that played on their adolescent minds, the importance of what they did when first entering the workplace and much more. For the historian, all these things are important if we are to truly understand cause and effect.

For George Churchward there appears to have been little in his background to suggest that an engineer might result from many generations of farmers. Yet in the mid-nineteenth century, with Britain still in the middle of a long industrial revolution, such an outcome was always possible. In such a quickly developing world, engineers of many descriptions multiplied in number then merged into professional groups with their own institutions, absorbing those who, in the past, would simply have become artisans or tradesmen.

As this happened, these developing professions were given a huge boost by the pioneering work of such men as Isambard Kingdom Brunel, George and Robert Stephenson, James Thomson, William Boulton, Joseph Gibb and many more. It was they who were able to develop cutting edge solutions encouraged by the rapid growth of Britain's industries, supported by the country's enlarging rail network and its maritime fleet, where metal and steam were replacing wood and sail. Such were the advances made that in 1851 Britain held its historic Great Exhibition – a celebration of the country's empire, global power and its ever-growing scientific achievements – all housed in a huge, state of the art, metal and glass structure in Hyde Park.

Yet, despite these positive signs, a Britain of nearly 28 million people was, when Churchward was born, still a country where the vast majority lived in poverty and few rights of any sort

The Industrial Revolution, coupled to a severe depression in farming, led to a mass migration of millions from countryside to towns and cities where they hoped to find better paid work. With no plan to provide housing for all these people, the supply of accommodation was rarely more than a ramshackle affair soon resulting in overcrowded, disease ridden slums. As the century progressed the situation grew even worse, as this contemporary lithograph demonstrates. (Author)

existed. Even though some ardent reformers were pressing for change, progress towards a more humanitarian society, where liberty and riches were spread more evenly, was painfully slow in coming. In the 1850s, for example, no woman and only one in six men had the vote, with full emancipation more than three-quarters of a century away. In addition, newly introduced laws to protect workers' rights in the country's burgeoning industries were as yet having little effect. This legislation may have reduced working hours for children and women to 10 hours a day and made it illegal to send anyone under the age of 21 up chimneys to sweep them clean, but it barely scratched the surface of the problems that existed in society. It would remain this way throughout Victoria's reign, ensuring that working conditions for most remained extremely and unnecessarily poor. So, it is little wonder that workplace deaths ran into tens of thousands each year, as did the number of avoidable industrial illnesses and injuries.

If working conditions were bad, life in most homes was probably even worse. As industrial towns grew, they quickly became overcrowded. The government believed in a laissez-faire approach to many social problems and believed that politicians should not interfere in people's lives. This meant that public health schemes were not considered of any great importance until the latter part of the nineteenth century when the clamour for change grew louder. In the meantime, no basic standards for housing, sewerage and the supply of water existed, as a result the accommodation provided for the working classes was usually of the poorest kind – rat, cockroach and lice infested, no sanitation and with open sewers becoming breeding grounds for many illnesses. In the slum areas of towns and cities, diseases such as cholera, typhus, smallpox and diphtheria were endemic and there was always the ever-present threat of tuberculosis to contend with.

Literature of the time records, in graphic detail, the extent of the burden simply existing and surviving that fell on the shoulders of those in urban areas in this dark period. One anonymously written account, though probably authored by a social reformer, hints at the problems they faced and the hopelessness this must have engendered:

> Streets are narrow with little air or sunlight. Families often share houses, so overcrowding is common. In cases I have witnessed there can be as many as five or six people per room and 50 or 60 per house. There is no clean running water and families usually share standpipes, which often run dry in hot weather. Families commonly share 'privies' – too basic to be called toilets. These often overflow into the street or into wells from where people draw their water. There is no refuse collection so rubbish piles up, attracting rodents.
>
> Houses are 'jerry-built', with the aim of making money for landlords rather than providing warm and healthy accommodation for workers. They are damp inside and hard to heat. Roofs and window frames often leak. Worst of all were the cellar dwellings where some very poor families live in squalid conditions. These are very damp and sometimes flood with rain or sewage.
>
> The diets of the working population are of the very poorest standard and they cannot afford fresh food and there are few vegetables to be bought. People rarely wash themselves or their clothes and become infested with lice and fleas as a result.
>
> In all these communities around Britain, and they existed in all towns and cities, early death was a daily feature of life. For example, in 1860, 26 per cent of children died before the age of 5 and the average age when adults died was slightly over 33.

For those who were destitute there were workhouses to give them support of a kind. Here life could be, if that were possible, even harsher, but at least they offered shelter and food, though the living conditions were of the most basic kind with married couples separated, as were children from their parents. Life might just be sustained in these places but at a terrible cost for those caught in this trap who were rarely regarded, in such a society of extremes, with anything but scorn, indifference or, at

A Victorian Childhood 11

THE POOR PICKING THE BONES TO LIVE

Workhouses and Poorhouses were set up deliberately to gather in the most deprived in any community with most towns having at least one. Life in these institutions was uncomfortable, basic and often cruel. These buildings sat brooding austerely near the centres of towns offering a reminder of the fate that might befall anybody if they fell on hard times and were unable to work or care for themselves. (Top) This lithograph shows the typical sleeping quarters provided in Poorhouses for the huge number of inmates they held. (Above) Food, if provided at all in these institutions, was of the poorest quality and often included leftover bones usually destined to be ground up and used as fertiliser. This occasionally resulted in complaints as shown here that reached the press. However, any protest was likely to end in eviction and an even worse existence. (Author)

best, pity. And in Victoria's reign the numbers passing through the gates of these grim institutions were indeed huge, reflecting the depth of poverty that existed across the country.

Once inside such an institution, simply sustaining life became a perilous business. Mortality rates, which were already high amongst the poorest in society, increased still further, with many illnesses, such as smallpox and measles, able to spread more quickly. Conditions were cramped, poorly lit and poorly ventilated. Beds were squashed together leaving little room to move and when it came to meals the food was of the most basic type. 'Hard tack' if you were lucky or, as reported in *The Penny Satirist, a* 'diet of bones which should have been used as fertilizer' if you were not.

When they were not sleeping, the 'inmates' were expected to work though not as a means of improving their lives in any way, but simply to provide the unscrupulous with cheap labour. And the numbers caught in this trap were not small with 100,000 or more places available, with many more crammed in as demand soared. With so much poverty it isn't surprising that those who could manage to scrape together the cash chose to emigrate. In the 1860s, for example, it is estimated that nearly 2.25 million people living in the USA had been born in Britain and nearly 50,000 were migrating to Australia and New Zealand each year, encouraged to leave by the promise of better lives.

For the masses who remained, the prospects were not good with education and acquiring a trade being the only realistic means of escape from impoverishment and penury in a society

When Churchward was born only children of upper and middle classes received an adequate education, though hardly of a modern standard. So by 1850 it is hardly surprising that only 60 per cent of men and 30 per cent of women had the barest knowledge of reading or writing. The rest were deprived of education for the most part. This began to change, albeit at a painfully slow pace in the 1850s through church founded schools and the 'Ragged Schools' movement, as shown here, which offered some children a most basic education. It was a start, but it wasn't until 1870, with the Elementary Education Act, that the need for a system that educated all to a better standard began to be realised. (Author)

In the 1850s, Britain's farming community was undergoing a transition from manual to mechanised labour. For workers this was often a painful process, with many long established jobs lost. (Above) Agricultural Shows, as advertised here at Exeter, captured a flavour of these changes, with the railway thrown in as a sign of modernisation. (Below) Newspapers and journals of the time were quick to show how steam engines aided mechanisation on farms as well as the transport system. The young George Churchward, as a country dweller, would have witnessed these changes taking place and their effect on farming. (Author)

seemingly short on compassion. But in the absence of even the most basic form of State sponsored education or national curriculum, the prospects for all but the upper and middle classes were poor. However, there were some interesting initiatives at this time that tried to improve matters, such as 'Ragged Schools', as they were called, which were opened in some slum areas – 'ragged' being derived from the description 'raggedly dressed'. But this movement tended to remain within the confines of London, leaving the rest of the country to struggle on as best it could. Here a reliance on church based schools had grown up, while some factories occasionally provided the most basic level of schooling as did the Workhouses, but this was hardly progress, although better than nothing.

So much for the towns and cities, but how were people who remained in the countryside faring? Here the divide between rich and poor was just as great. Although serfdom had long been abolished, the nature of a master and man, some might say slave, relationship had hardly been broken despite social and scientific advances. Farm workers were beholden to large local landowners for most things, more so since various Enclosure Acts had handed 6 million acres of common land, much of it used by smallholding peasantry to make a living, for them to manage.

(Above) Most farming work in the mid-Victorian period remained seasonal in nature with landowners recruiting men, women and children to work their fields or flocks when necessary. In market squares across the country people needing work would gather on market days, at 'Hiring Fairs' to be sold as though animals to the highest bidder. It was a lucky person who was taken on permanently. (Opposite above) Many rural schools, usually linked to churches, were often the only means of learning to read and write, but the standard of education was poor and the discipline brutally applied, if contemporary accounts are to be believed. (Opposite below) A typical labourer's cottage as it appeared towards the end of the nineteenth century. In this case, the occupants are luckier than most and appear to enjoy a weatherproof, well-kept property. (DN)

Their labourers would be given accommodation of sorts, undoubtedly of the poorest kind, though probably slightly better than that available to town and city dwellers. Wages, with employment sometimes being on a seasonal basis, would have been meagre at best and only paid if a person worked, there being no requirement for sick pay or pensions for the elderly who couldn't labour.

To make matters worse, the food available would have been of the most basic kind, barely sufficient to sustain life and limb. However, some may have been lucky enough to have small strips of land on which they could grow vegetables and keep chickens to supplement their paltry diets. Yet to counterbalance these 'privileges' you could be hired and fired on the whim of a landowner, with no recourse to law or the prospect of compensation. So, it was a wise man or woman who remained silent in the face of any injustice, because starvation or the Workhouse would surely follow a challenge to the established order. When protests did take place, most notably when men were brave enough to demonstrate against the growing use of machines by breaking them up, the offenders could face the death penalty or penal transportation to Australia for life as convicts. It was indeed a harsh age in which to live in either town or country if you were poor or simply working class.

This then was Britain when George Churchward was born to a farming family. It was a country with a massive Empire that was taking giant strides both scientifically and industrially. But all the advances made tended to benefit the rich and affluent, who simply grew wealthier on the backs of workers and their families who had few rights or assets. All they could do was provide cheap labour and suffer in doing so. For the better off there were schools, decent housing, a living wage and status. For the poor, who were the vast majority, there was very little except a pitiable standard of living, few prospects of betterment and the strong likelihood of an early death brought on by a plethora of poverty linked illnesses and the appalling conditions in which they were forced to live.

By any standards, it was a society of extremes, but, through the effort of social reformers in the 1860/70s, when Churchward was being educated and about to enter the working world, this was slowly changing. Nevertheless, as a descendent of landowners and farmers, there would be many more opportunities for him to enjoy than those on offer to most of his fellow countrymen. In Victorian Britain, wealth, birthright and social position counted for all in determining whether you succeeded in life or not, with the poor suffering dreadfully as a consequence.

Stoke Gabriel, in Devon, where George Jackson Churchward first saw the light of day on 31 January 1857, at Rowes Farm, was a village that had grown up on the banks of a small creek leading off the River Dart. Fishing is recorded as being the reason a settlement was first established here, but with Devon's rich arable land all around, farming soon came to dominate life in this slowing expanding village. And for many centuries the Churchward family were an important part of its life, with parish records suggesting that they had settled in the area well before the coming of the Tudors in the late fifteenth century.

The description that might describe the Churchward family best is that of gentlemen farmers or squires, although they probably fell well short of being regarded as major landowners in the well-established Devon hierarchy. Here the Rolle estate, which covered 55,000 acres, the Duchy of Cornwall's 48,000 acres and the Earl of Devon's 20,000 acres would have been at the top of the social chain. 'Manors' that ranged in sizes from 1,000 and 10,000 acres, although large, were simply regarded as a second tier in the world of property. And behind these came estates of up to 100 acres which were then simply regarded as small-holdings. George Churchward's family, with 266 acres to their credit, attended by 'six labourers and two boys and three indoor servants', would have been seen as privileged by their neighbours in Stoke Gabriel, but probably not by those nearer the top of Devon's society.

George's father was 32 when he was born and his wife Adelina, who was the daughter of a wealthy corn and cider merchant hailing from Paignton, 24. As was the custom of the time, it appears to have been a home birth, attended by a local doctor or midwife. And with no apparent

A Victorian Childhood   17

Stoke Gabriel, on the banks of a creek leading off the River Dart in Devon, as it appears today. If Churchward returned to view the place of his birth, he would recognise much that was familiar to him as a child, with the Church of St Mary and St Gabriel and its ancient yew tree at the centre of this tight knit community. The house in which George Churchward was born is situated on rising ground above the village. (Author)

medical complications to contend with, Adelina went on to produce four more children – John a year later, James in 1861, Mary in 1864 and Adelina in 1873.

Around them in the village other Churchwards dwelt, including Frederick, George senior's cousin, who lived, with his wife Hannah and family, in a very substantial property called Hill House. Having been educated privately in Paignton and Totnes, Frederick went on to become a banker in Cardiff, where he also served as a commissioned officer with the 10th Glamorganshire Rifles. Rapid promotion followed and he rose to become Joint General Manager of the National Provincial Bank in London, lived at Clarendon House on fashionable Blackheath, while retaining Hill House as his Devon retreat. However, such was his impact on West Country affairs, though only living there part-time, that he was appointed Justice of the Peace for Devon, a post he held until nearly the end of his life in 1922. He was, by any standards, a man of substance and chose to use his assets and influence for the benefit of his wider family including George Churchward's children.

In 1919 a press report appeared describing Frederick's life and personality. It is an interesting and revealing assessment, especially in its brief description of the wider Churchward family and inherited character traits:

> The sons of the house of Churchward have for the most part followed three callings. They have been able diplomats, gallant soldiers and efficient and influential men of business. Frederick Churchward has never found time to try his hand at diplomacy, but he has been a soldier and a man of good business habits, combining two of the family traits. And there is no doubt that had he elected to share the fortunes of the Foreign Office, his strength of character and strong personality would have won him just as conspicuous a success there.
>
> He was appointed Justice of the Peace in 1886, and his service in this office has been of the same firm, but never unkindly character.....At the time of his retirement he enjoyed, to

an extent that few men ever have, the confidence, respect and esteem of the financial world. It is doubtful if any single man ever wielded more influence in the same sphere....

Although they undoubtedly learnt much from their parents, and were guided by them in many important matters, Frederick's role in their lives cannot be over-estimated, for he seems to have provided the funds and some impetus in furthering their education and careers.

(Left) Rowes Farm, where George Churchward was born in 1857, as it is today. (Below) Stoke Gabriel's church, of St Mary and St Gabriel, where George was christened and later worshipped with his family, is little changed from those times. The church walls, and the surrounding cemetery, hold many graves and relics of the Churchward dynasty. Today, it seems, no member of the family resides in or near the village and so a connection going back many centuries has been broken. (Author)

Frederick Churchward, Esq., J.P.

(Above left) Hill House in Stoke Gabriel was passed down through many generations of the family to Frederick Churchward (above right), a cousin of George Churchward senior. Frederick was a wealthy, influential man who took great interest in the lives of George's children and encouraged them in their education and may well have sponsored them more directly at some stage. Bearing this in mind, young George and his siblings would have been frequent visitors to Hill House and probably his second, substantial property on Blackheath in London as well. (Author's collection)

We will never know the depth of his influence on their young lives, of course, and so much remains speculation, but in his book *G.J. Churchward – A Locomotive Biography* H.C.B. Rogers hints at the impact this may have had:

> To help the education of the Churchward boys [George, John, James plus his own son Charles and their cousin Paul], Frederick Churchward arranged instruction by a private tutor at Hill House during the school holidays. Charles in due course went to Harrow – where Winston Churchill was his fag – George Junior was studying to make engineering his career and Paul was cramming for Sandhurst. Many years later Paul Churchward [by then a Brigadier-General] told his son how brilliant George had been at mathematics.

With five children to raise, and the ups and downs of income inherent in farming to cope with, George senior and Adelina may have struggled to provide the high standard of education Frederick was able to give his own son. If so, did he sponsor more than private tuition during the holidays for George, John and James? The answer is possibly yes, especially as George attended the King Edward VI's Foundation Grammar School for boys in nearby Totnes, until he was 16 years of age, which would not have been undertaken without the burden of fees or other costs.

Other than this short reference to the Grammar School and tuition in Hill House, no other record of George's education seems to exist. One wonders, for example, whether he, in his earliest years, attended a local elementary school, as Frederick did in Paignton before him, or was he tutored at home? Either way, he seems to have been a bright boy who had the ability to absorb knowledge like a sponge, displaying a gift for mathematics and science along the way. And being a farmer's son, and a confirmed countryman, he would have developed an understanding of his father's work and observed the gradual mechanisation of all that was happening around him. There would also have been hunting and fishing, which became lifetime passions for him, to fill his days – not surprising with the River Dart so close and vast acres of land on his doorstep over which he and his brothers could roam when time and other duties allowed.

With science appearing to dominate his life, George was lucky to be living in an age where so many advances were being made in engineering, in particular – as symbolised by the Great Exhibition. By 1854 the 'Crystal Palace', as it was called, had been moved to Sydenham Hill where it continued to attract huge numbers of visitors each year, perhaps even George and his brothers. With Frederick having a home within a short train ride of the 'Palace' the draw of this exhibition would have been strong one indeed, especially for someone with scientific leanings. And there was also the new Science Museum in London, which opened in South Kensington in the year George was born, to enjoy.

Sadly, this openness of mind to new ideas was not a practice carried over into schools in the 1860s and '70s, where the study of sciences was barely covered even in the most rudimentary way. This was not surprising in schools for the poorest in society, where simply learning to read and write was all that mattered, but in well-established grammar and public schools such an omission was unforgiveable. Despite the works of many emerging scientists and engineers, school teachers remained strongly resilient to the study of such essential, life-changing things.

For George Churchward and others of his class, their education would have been based on an almost slavish devotion to such things as English, Latin, Greek, History, Geography, French, Natural Sciences and Mathematics, with no place for such things as physics or chemistry. It was a regime enforced by a strict code of discipline and the liberal use of the cane. With many in Victorian society still believing in the ill-conceived, biblically derived concept of 'sparing the rod

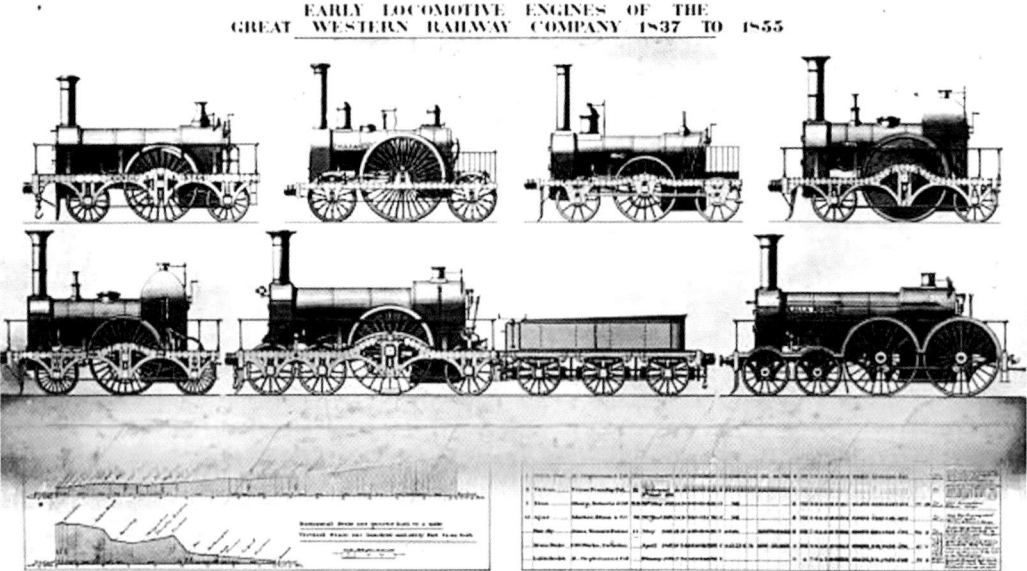

By the time Churchward was sixteen years of age and making ready to begin a railway apprenticeship, the Great Western Railway had been in existence for thirty-eight years since Parliament passed an enabling act. The company chose to use 7ft 0¼in. broad gauge track and the picture above demonstrates how the design of their engines gradually evolved to run on such a system. However, by 1855, due to a series of amalgamations with other companies, the GWR had also began to operate a 4ft 8½in standard gauge network as well. (DN)

and spoiling the child', this is hardly surprising. There were some influential reformers in teaching who looked to improve standards, such as the Marlborough headmaster Frederick Farrar. He was one of a small but growing band of educationalists determined to implement modern teaching methods, hoping to influence other leading schools of the time, including the grammar school in Totnes, in the process. However, even this forward thinking man still had a propensity for flogging, gaining the distateful nickname 'Mr Thwackham of Marlborough', even though he was not thought to be a sadist or a poor head.

Although 'Thwackham' Farrar was reaching the end of his career when George Churchward attended grammar school, many of these ideas were beginning to have an effect on teaching methods elsewhere and the range of subjects being taught at places such as Churchward's school. Despite this, old habits died hard and Farrar continued to voice his criticism of a system that still tended to focus almost exclusively on the history, philosophy, literature and archeology of the Greco-Roman world. In 1869, in a widely read and influential pamphlet, he wrote that:

> A boy would be terrified of such incubi and succubi as 'quid-quale', 'gerundive attractions', 'subolique clauses', 'spirants'…. And I know not what. A public school curriculum was exclusively designed to fit boys for an academic future….. Even these boys had been taught in ways which produced parrot-like repetition and sing-song knowledge, to the abeyance and destruction of intellectual powers.

So, when attending grammar school, George Churchward would have found himself studying subjects that were unlikely to encourage his growing interest in science, except mathematics, of course. And his interest in such things seems to have been profound indeed, leaving one to wonder how deeply his desire to become an engineer ran and when this ambition first took root. The

A class of engine that would probably have been familiar to George Churchward in his early years, one of twenty-nine Iron Duke 4-2-2 engines constructed between 1847 and 1855 under the guiding hand of Daniel Gooch (here represented by the 1851 built *Lord of the Isles*) These famous engines were built to pull fast express trains, including the Flying Dutchman service, and one of them, named *Great Britain*, is believed to have attained a speed of 78.2mph in May 1848. Some of the class remained in service into the 1880s, with two rebuilds *Great Britain* and *Prometheus* – carrying on until 1892. (DN)

thought processes that lay behind these issues can only be guessed at, though he seems to have been, as many talented engineers are, born for this purpose. However, his choice of pursuing a career in railway engineering is, perhaps, easier to fathom because all it could offer was so readily apparent to any clever young man in the 1870s, none more so than in the work of Isambard Kingdom Brunel.

By the time Churchward was old enough to begin his grammar school education, the work of the great man, though now long dead, was well-known and much admired – whether it be his ship building, his architectural projects or his work in developing the Great Western Railway (GWR) All around him in the West Country, Churchward would have seen and been able to study Brunel's work very closely. In addition, he would, undoubtedly, have travelled fairly regularly on the GWR's 7ft 0¼in broad gauge railway network, plus the linked Bristol and Exeter and South Devon Company lines, in his formative years. For a child such as Churchward, who was beginning to show a clear preference for scientific subjects, exposure to such a dynamic business, and the work of such an inspirational man as Brunel, would surely have influenced his choice of a career. And by 1873, when Churchward left grammar school, railway companies around Britain were eager to take on and train the best young men they could find to further enhance their business.

By this stage the railway industry had been growing rapidly for nearly 50 years. During this time, it had developed effective recruitment and training programmes to provide the skilled labour it needed to operate successfully. High amongst their priorities was the need for technically competent men to oversee the design and maintenance of locomotives and rolling stock, in particular. To do this they required young people who were fairly well educated for the time and capable of developing mechanical engineering skills to a high standard. To do this they fell back on the long established principals of the apprentice training schemes that had produced craftsmen for many industries over many centuries. So, the railway companies set up their own schemes. On one level this provided men with a range of workshop skills to do manual tasks – metalworkers, carpenters and so on – and on another level drew in and nurtured highly competent, ambitious men who would, in time, become supervisors and managers. But to prove himself suited to this life, George first had to graduate successfully from school.

Although he was better placed to do so than many in society it wasn't a foregone conclusion that he would succeed. The main stumbling block was the school itself, which in 1868, shortly after George arrived, was inspected by a Government Commissioner, who in a most critical report wrote:

> Twenty-one boys, principally sons of shopkeepers with a sprinkling of some of professional men, were present on my visit, all very young…The senior boy, said to be reading Xenophon and Horace, was absent, 12 boys showed some acquaintance with an elementary book of Latin exercises….They were not good in English, History or Geography. In dictation, out of fifteen boys the best had two mistakes…Their knowledge of arithmetic was very elementary, but several of them did simple sums correctly. French, which only three boys were learning, had just commenced.
>
> The external appearance was that of a ruinous building. The narrow approach down an alley, the noise of the children below, the smells around the entrance, where all sorts of abominations abounded, made the situation most unfit for schoolrooms. The scanty playground was used as a place for drying clothes.

And yet one of George's near contemporaries, Edward Windeatt, later recalled his time there with some affection:

> Many old boys have pleasant memories of the old school buildings, quaint and dilapidated though they were – the long narrow room approached by a flight of stairs, with the desks on each side and the Master's at the top of the room. At the top of the stairs hung the rope by which the old bell was rung just before nine and two, to call us to school.

A Victorian Childhood

George Churchward attended the King Edward Vl Foundation Grammar School for boys between 1868 and 1873. During his time there the school's master was the Reverend James Powning BD (right), a graduate of St John's College, Cambridge. By the standards of the age it provided a barely adequate level of education, following a model based on teaching the Classics. The school (below) occupied quite basic quarters which were much criticised by a Government Commissioner in the year Churchward started there. In 1887 these poor standard buildings were finally evacuated and the school, now simply called the King Edward VI Grammar School for Boys, moved to a newly purchased building called the Mansion. (DN)

The old desks had suffered much from the generations of Totnesians who had cut out their names on them and the draughtiness of the old windows rendered it necessary to stuff up the crevices with old copy-books when Winter was approaching. Our only playground was the paved yard outside, now known as the Guildhall Yard, and there we had many a good game of Prisoner's Base, and many a tussle with the inhabitants of neighbouring cottages, who would hang their clothes out to dry, a trespass we would never allow, which often led to us cutting the lines. With awe, on days that the Magistrates sat in the Guildhall, we ventured in and heard prisoners sentenced....

To this E B Stoyle added:

I can still visualise the room in the old Grammar School in which I spent four years from 1872 to 1876. On each side there were three rows of desks, seating five boys at each. When I left, there were twenty-five pupils in the school and a box-room served as the master's private room.

However, R Huxham Watson, another contemporary, provided a less savoury memory of his schooldays when recalling that:

> Lessons were held in a rather shady room, very badly ventilated, with forms and desks, and the centre occupied by a large oak table on which were engraved the initials of most of the boys. The particular use of this table was to 'stretch' boys upon, and as they had a particularly 'peppery' master who believed in flogging, it was often in use....The principal instruction was in Latin and Greek, and, for a change Greek and Latin.

With so few boys to teach there were only sufficient funds to pay for one full-time master which, from 1853 to 1886, was the Reverend James Powning BD, a graduate of St John's College, Cambridge. In his endeavours he was assisted by two of the older boys who acted as monitors and a master who came twice a week to teach French and a visiting drill instructor to help instill some military discipline into the boys lives. Charles Rea, who was a later successor to Powning, recalled that the older man was, 'full of intellectual and physical energy, resolute of purpose, strong of will, public spirited, animated by lofty motives, genial in manner and a centre of social influence'. However, even with such an energetic man in charge, it was difficult for him to overcome the dilapidated condition of the school and teach a group of boys, aged between 10 and 16 with such diverse educational needs, effectively.

So, whilst George Churchward enjoyed an education better than most of his contemporaries it was still of a most basic, unimaginative kind. Worse still, it was applied with iron discipline, with little true regard for the well-being of a child or the development of their minds. If toughening up a child for the adult world was their sole intention, the school may well have succeeded, but, inevitably, the joy of learning was probably lost along the way. And yet there were some,

OPENING OF THE SOUTH DEVON AND TAVISTOCK RAILWAY.—FROM A SKETCH BY T. V. ROBINS

In 1873 George Churchward became an articled 'premium' apprentice with the South Devon Railway, choosing this local company over much larger, more famous businesses such as the GWR at Swindon. Like the GWR and the adjoining Bristol and Exeter Railway it ran over a broad gauge network between Exeter and Plymouth. The line to Plymouth opened in 1849 and was extended to Tavistock ten years later. This later event is depicted in this contemporary print and was an occasion attended by great celebrations and reports in the national press. (RH)

like Churchward, who survived this ordeal to prosper, which probably says more about their intelligence and resilience than the standard of the education they received. In the circumstances the extra coaching Frederick generously provided was undoubtedly a godsend in preparing them for the adult world.

As his time at school drew to a close, it seems certain that young George's future would have been much discussed at home with his parents, and possibly his influential Uncle Frederick. Seemingly a strong-minded young man, he had probably already reached some firm conclusions about the direction he wished to go in his career. Perhaps his father wanted him to take up farming and assume responsibility for the family estate as he approached old age; as the eldest son there would probably have been a natural expectation that this might be so. But it wasn't to be and at some point in 1873, a decision was taken that George would become a railway apprentice. So, all that remained to do was choose a suitable company and seek a training billet where he could begin to learn the principals of his chosen profession.

In the 1870s there were many good, well established companies to choose from around the country. However, caring parents might think twice before committing a child to live far away from home in an industrial town or city at the tender age of only sixteen, especially one grown used to living in the backwaters of rural Devon. So a local posting, where George might be observed and supported more closely, might well have been an important factor in the decision

By the time Churchward began his apprenticeship with the SDR in 1873, most companies had well-established workshops. Leading the way was the GWR with their extensive, state of the art facilities in Swindon, as portrayed here in this 1842 lithograph. To populate these facilities, each of the major companies offered a range of apprenticeships to ensure they had sufficient trained specialists available to keep the railways running effectively. Some, like Churchward, would be deliberately selected to become design or production engineers, the best of which would then groomed for senior management positions. As such they might, for example, become pupils of Locomotive Superintendents or other senior managers and be tutored directly by them. (DN)

the Churchwards made. There may also have been the issue of expense to consider. The better, 'premium' apprenticeships came at a cost to the student's family, offering, as they did, a greater depth of education and, potentially, entry into work at a higher, non-industrial grade when completed. There would also be an additional cost for food and accommodation to bear in mind, though often a company might pay the student a small wage to cover this outlay.

If these were indeed factors in deciding young George's future, the choice finally made seems to have been an inevitable one, because in 1873 he was interviewed by John Wright, the Locomotive, Carriage and Wagon Superintendent (LCWS) of the South Devon Railway (SDR), passed muster and was successfully enrolled as his articled pupil. There has been some speculation that his Uncle Frederick may have played a part in this process, or, at least, paid some or all of the training and living costs involved. Being a man of great affluence and some influence, especially in banking circles, which most railway companies at the time drew heavily upon to raise capital for new projects or simply to service their debts, such speculation isn't without foundation. It is certainly an interesting thought, though not one supported by any document that I have seen so far. Nevertheless, bearing in mind Frederick's well established altruistic, even philanthropic, interest in his cousin's children, it remains a distinct possibility.

So ignoring the competing claims of other larger companies, such as the GWR, Churchward left the narrow confines of school and began work in the SDR's Newton Abbot offices and Works in late 1873. And so his rise to the top of his profession began and with it a string of successes that still resonate with us today.

Chapter 2

Fledgling Engineer

Rules of this Office

1. Godliness, cleanliness and punctuality are the necessities of a good business.
2. This company has reduced the hours of work and now staff will only be present between the hours of 7am to 6pm.
3. Daily prayers will be held each morning in the main office. All staff will be present.
4. Clothing must be of a sober nature. Staff will not disport themselves in raiment of bright colours.
5. Overshoes and top coats may not be worn in the office, but neck scarves and headwear may be worn in inclement weather.
6. A stove is provided for the benefit of staff. Coal and wood must be kept in the locker provided. It is recommended that each member of staff bring 4lb of coal each day during cold weather.
7. No member of staff may leave the room without permission. The calls of nature are permitted.
8. No idle chatter is allowed during business hours.
9. The craving for tobacco, wines or spirits is a human weakness and as such is forbidden to all members of staff.
10. Now that the hours of business have been drastically reduced the partaking of food is allowed between 11.30am and noon, but work will not on any account cease.
11. Members of staff will provide their own pens or any other equipment they require to do their jobs.
12. The company expects a great rise in the output of work to compensate for these near Utopian conditions.

(Above) Many businesses at the time held their employees, particularly office staff, to very high, even pedantic standards of behaviour. This particular set of rules, issued by the General Manager of the SDR, would have been very familiar sight to young George especially as it would have been posted on walls, with personal copies being handed to each new employee on arrival.

The step up from school to working life presents many challenges, but for Victorian children, more used to an iron discipline enforced by the cane, the change would, at least, see an escape from this particular terror. In its place there would be a strong emphasis on rules and regulations, many of them seemingly pedantic in nature, designed to get the best out of a workforce and ensure obedience. And when arriving at his new place of work, Churchward's freshly prepared apprenticeship articles would have set out what was expected of him during the four years of his training. Added to this he would have been handed a set of rules governing his day-to-day behaviour in office and workshops – godliness, cleanliness, how he dressed and behaved at all times, avoiding distracting 'chatter' and much more. Everything they did was managed with a critical eye with any indiscretion punished harshly, with instant dismissal without a reference being a possibility for even the mildest of misdemeanours.

For the well-behaved, conscientious and committed apprentices there were rewards, of course, not least of all learning a respected trade and the chance of a life-long career of substance. Then there would have been the promise of a gradual progression to better quality work, higher pay and even promotion. All this would have been particularly and quickly apparent to premium apprentices, especially to men such Churchward who had the added benefit of the tutelage of a senior and highly experienced engineer plus the staff in his immediate entourage.

Later in life, when seeking to join the Institution of Mechanical Engineers, Churchward wrote, simply and without embellishment, of these early years of his career:

> I was articled for 4 years to Mr J Wright, Locomotive, Carriage and Wagon Superintendent of the South Devon, Cornwall and West Cornwall Railway. I served under him from 28th July 1873 to 1st February 1876 and then completed my pupillage on 27th July 1877 first under Mr Joseph Armstrong and then Mr William Dean, both Locomotive, Carriage and Wagon Superintendents of the GWR. I was subsequently engaged in the Drawing Office at Swindon upon the design of plant in connection with the construction of the Severn Tunnel etc etc.

As Churchward would soon realise, the training course he was now beginning involved a great deal of practical work carefully supervised by craftsmen on the shop floor. Such was the level of skill they attained in various trades that many, who later rose to senior rank, would proudly boast of their ability to work many of the workshop tools and machines they now managed in

Newton Abbot at about the time that George Churchward began his apprenticeship at the Works of the SDR in 1873. (DN)

Fledgling Engineer 29

The three senior engineers under whom Churchward would serve during his four-year apprenticeship. (Above) Between 1873 and 1876 the young apprentice was directly tutored by John Wright, the SDR's LCWS based at Newton Abbot. If the caption hand-written on the back of this print from the 1870s is to be believed this photo is of 'Mr John Wright esquire standing in front of the 1874 built engine named Lance in the early 1880s'. In 1876 the SDR became amalgamated with the Great Western and Churchward spent the last year of his apprenticeship at Swindon under two influential LCWS. (Below left) Joseph Armstrong, who died in 1877, and (below right) William Dean who succeeded Armstrong that year. (DN/Author)

producing well-engineered and crafted items. Quite simply they were learning their business from the bottom up, so when they qualified, they did so with a keen appreciation of a craftsman's life. But of course their apprenticeship was much more than this, because they were learning to become very competent railway engineers and in so doing would specialise in the separate but complementary disciplines of production and design engineering. Early in their careers this would not have been readily apparent, but as their training progressed, and the nature of their talents became clearer, the separation began.

Bert Spencer, Nigel Gresley's very talented assistant, later described this process of selection and the skills a good tutor might look for in his pupils when deciding which specialisation might suit them best:

> It was, quite simply, a matter of aptitude. A good production engineer needed to understand and be able to manage the flow of work through a variety of associated workshops. To do this they needed a detailed technical knowledge of the locomotives and rolling stock in their charge and apply all necessary test and maintenance routines to ensure sufficient numbers were always available to meet the railway's needs. All this required strong organisational skills and extensive experience of how to manage a team of men and women often in very difficult conditions. From my earliest days as an apprentice it was very clear who amongst my fellow trainees had these particular skills and those best suited to become draughtsmen and designers.
>
> For the premium apprentices' selection began in the first year or two of the course, with tutors assessing each student's performance as they worked their way around the workshops learning the different trades. This was supplemented by technical classes, of one sort or another, which taught much more precise engineering skills, such as mechanical design and construction, technical drawing, advanced mathematics and so on. For those at Swindon there was the Mechanics Institute to impart these lessons, usually, I'm told, through evening classes, and at Doncaster we had access to courses run by the local Technical College. Then there was time spent in Drawing Offices being coached by the Chief Draughtsman and his staff, and many hours of private study with the results of your work being carefully scrutinised and assessed by senior managers. Woe betide anyone who did not pull their weight or pass muster, but the rewards of hard work were many, including a job when qualified and, if you were lucky the respect and patronage of the Locomotive Superintendent, in my case Sir Nigel.

Although Spencer's apprenticeship did not start until nearly forty years after Churchward's had ended, the pattern of work and the selection of a specialism remained virtually unchanged. In Spencer's case, and late in his apprenticeship, he chose to enter the Drawing Office and became a designer, a path that Churchward also took, with the help of John Wright and Peter Margary, the SDR's Chief Engineer, then, later on, assisted and directed by Armstrong and Dean at Swindon.

In 1873, having Wright and Margary as their tutors, Churchward and his fellow students, which apparently included the 29-year-old Cambridge graduate Robert Neville Grenville, were extremely lucky. More importantly, Wright, who was only 41, had been trained at Swindon and then rose to become the Locomotive Superintendent at Newton Abbot when still in his twenties. If anything, the 53-year-old Margary had an even better pedigree having been articled to William Gravatt, Brunel's chief assistant and a civil engineer of great note. Subsequently, he assisted Brunel in developing the atmospheric railway, then the SDR as it gradually expanded. His success here ensured that, when the time came, Brunel felt able to recommend his assistant to the directors of the line when the company were seeking a Chief Engineer, and soon the Cornwall Railway Company was added to his brief. In these posts Margary led in completing the extensions to Launceston, Moreton-Hampstead, Ashburton and St Ives.

Even though the SDR had only fifty or so locomotives by the 1870s, it was still a company of some standing, more so because it acted in partnership with the GWR and the Bristol and Exeter Railways in much that it did. This collaboration allowed the company to expand its broad gauge network across Devon into Cornwall, making it, by the time it enlisted Churchward as an apprentice, a key component of the service that ran from Paddington, via Bristol, deep into the West Country.

For a promising engineer, the SDR's workshops and running sheds, plus Wright and Margary's tutoring, would have provided much of interest to study, but was not a manufacturer of locomotives itself and had to look elsewhere for ways of populating its fleet. As a result, apprentices were unlikely to have had direct involvement in design and construction, only maintenance, unless they were able to visit the supplier of engines or the GWR's Works at Swindon.

In 1851, the SDR enlisted the services of Charles Geach, co-founder of the Midland Bank, and Edward Evans, who owned and ran the Haigh Foundry, to provide its motive power. They, in turn, contracted Daniel Gooch, the GWR's Superintendent of Locomotives, to design the broad gauge passenger and goods engines the company needed. Some of these were built at Haighs, but others came from Fairburn and Sons of Manchester, Longbridges, the Vulcan Foundry and Stothert and Slaughter of Bristol (later becoming the Avonside Engine Company) When the Geach and Evans contract came to an end it was superseded, in 1859, by a new partnership, in which Evans

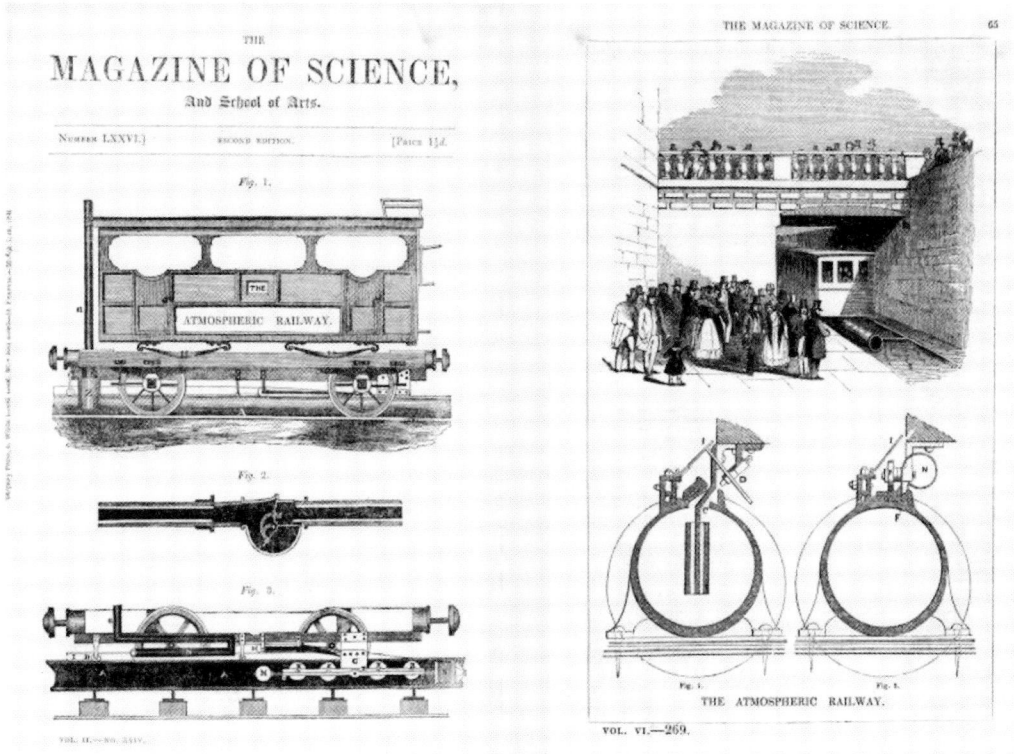

As a local man and a budding engineer, Churchward would have been only too aware of Brunel's abandoned Atmospheric Railway project. As a child, then young man, he would have seen for himself the last vestiges of this experiment and possibly pondered the nature of invention and how cutting edge science can often go awry when a desire to experiment runs counter to the practicalities of everyday life. However, at the time, as this science magazine demonstrates, it was much studied and analysed project which seemed to offer some commercial benefits. (Author's collection)

When Churchward began his apprenticeship at Newton Abbot, the SDR's locomotive fleet was well-established, but, perhaps surprisingly, all were tank engines and in various forms they covered passenger, goods or shunting duties. (Above) No. 2137 Prince was built by the Ince Forge Company for the SDR in 1871 and was employed mostly on branch line duties. She was converted to standard gauge in 1893 in which state she remained in service until 1899. (DN)

One more example of the engines acquired by the SDR shortly before or during Churchward's years with the company. One of four 4-4-0STs built by Avonside Engine Company of Bristol between 1872 and 1875, in this case No. 2129. (DN)

continued to play a central role. But he was now supported by Thomas Walker of Wednesbury, who had acquired many of Geach's business interests following Geach's death in 1854.

This new partnership was commissioned by John Wright to supply twenty-four new engines and Slaughter, Gruning and Company were contracted to build them all. These new locomotives consisted of sixteen 4-4-0 saddle tanks for passenger work and eight goods engines, all of which were delivered between 1859 and 1865. However, in 1866 this contract came to an end and the SDR's directors, led by Thomas Woollcombe, a Plymouth solicitor and founder of the Royal Albert Hospital in that city, felt able to buy all the stock then running on the line and then manage procurement more directly themselves.

For a time, this strategy worked and in the years leading up to Churchward's arrival, the company continued buying new or second hand engines when the need arose. There were six new passenger 4-4-0 saddle tanks and two goods engines all built by Avonsides by 1864, plus thirteen 'used' locomotives, some built by Slaughter, Gruning. To these were added an 0-4-0 shunting engine, named *Tiny*, built by Sara and Co of Plymouth, a 2-4-0ST called *Prince* constructed by the Ince Forge &Co of Wigan and an 0-6-0ST from Avonside in 1869. Finally there was 2-4-0 tank engine named *King*, that was originally built for the Torbay and Brixham Railway, which, it seems, they were unable to pay for when fresh from the works. As a result, by the time the intake of new apprentices gathered at Newton Abbot in 1873 there was a plethora of mixed locomotive designs to observe and consider. But more were to follow over the next two years and, of course, there were GWR locomotives passing by along the main line, as well as the Bristol and Exeter Railway engines, to view and assess.

Between 1873 and 1875 Avonsides were commissioned to build 22 'convertible' engines – ten 0-6-0s for goods traffic, four 4-4-0STs to pull passenger trains and eight 0-4-0STs for shunting duties. They were called 'convertibles' because by then the issue of a standardised gauge was under very serious consideration with all the other companies expressing a wish to see the 4ft 8½in gauge universally applied in preference to the GWR's broad gauge solution. This debate would run on for some time, but by the mid-1870s the battle had been virtually lost with 4ft 8½in being universally adopted. As a result, and to ease the changeover, new broad gauge engines began being designed so that when the time came they could be converted to standard gauge. In addition to the Avonside engines three 2-4-0STs were also ordered from Ince Forge and Co. However, before completion, the SDR, which was finding it increasingly difficult to survive, was absorbed by the GWR, with the bulk of the work undertaken at Newton Abbot being transferred to Swindon for completion.

With all this going on it is interesting to speculate on what Churchward thought and how these seminal experiences influenced the way he developed as an engineer, a manager and a designer. Kenneth Cook, in his 1950 paper to the ILocoE, briefly touched on this issue:

> His early environment was, no doubt, in two ways of strategic importance. The beauty of that part of Devon had its influence on the artistic externals of his engines. He was also fully aware of the diverse requirements of the locomotives he was to produce in negotiating the very difficult gradients in South Devon and Cornwall as well as the high speed possibilities elsewhere.

The reference to aesthetics is an interesting one and touches on the artistic appreciation often displayed by great engineers, although it is one which is hard to quantity, 'beauty being in the eye of the beholder'. The second issue, being rooted in something more scientific, is much easier to analyse. In Churchward's case, as Cook realised, the gradients found in South Devon in particular were very taxing for any locomotive. By comparison, much of the Great Western from London to Exeter, whether via Bristol or Westbury, was much flatter so faster running was the norm. All this presented an interesting juxtaposition of need for engineers to consider and seek to resolve, especially as locomotives grew ever larger, more powerful and refined.

Above all else much rested on the size, shape and capacity of a locomotive's boiler, a lesson that John Wright would surely have drummed home to his pupils at an early stage. And what better demonstration of this could there be than on the route to Plymouth and the high level of stresses and strains on the locomotive this created. So, it is little wonder, after such an early demonstration of the problem, that throughout his career Churchward made great play of this central issue.

With so much to learn from tutors there would have been little time to dwell on a detailed evaluation of boilers at this stage. But Churchward, as Wright and Margary must soon have realised, was a cut above the rest and had a talent that marked him down for great things, if he continued working hard and if his career was managed with some care. So it probably wouldn't have surprised either man when his creative powers found another outlet helped by a growing friendship with fellow engineer, Robert Grenville.

Grenville, who hailed from nearby Glastonbury in Somerset, had already begun to display highly inventive creative skills. Having graduated from Cambridge in 1869, before working for Easton and Andersons of London, this isn't surprising and being aged 29 meant that he already had quite wide experience of life, especially when compared to the 16-year-old Churchward. Yet, despite the age difference, Grenville clearly saw in the younger man someone with great potential and enlisted his help in a private enterprise that would see a horseless carriage powered by steam developed. It was a project on which Churchward could focus his keen mind and his developing ideas. And, as such, it was probably the only design and development work he had at the time on which his imagination and creativity could dwell, there being no direct involvement for him in the SDR's locomotive building programme.

How and why they came together to work on this project is open to speculation, as is John Wright's involvement – was he simply their tutor or did he deliberately facilitate the whole scheme as an aid to their development? As Grenville clamed ownership of the carriage, it is probably safe to assume that the concept was his and so was the funding. He came from a wealthy, landed family for whom the costs of such a venture would not have been excessive. With such a gifted young engineer, full of ideas and energy, close by, enlisting Churchward's help would have made sense in a very practical way. And so the two of them began work sometime in 1874.

This vehicle had as its base a 4 x 2in steel girder which gave the nearly 12ft long, 6ft wide structure strength and rigidity. In the middle of its wooden body sat a boiler producing 120psi, taken from a Merryweather fire engine, which, coming from such a well-known London based company, was probably a wise choice, although its purpose in creating wheel motion rather than

(Above left) Robert Neville Grenville in old age (he died in 1936 in his 90th year) was a man of many parts – engineer, 'squire', Justice of the Peace and High Sheriff of Somerset and philanthropist. In building a steam powered horseless carriage with Churchward he helped the young man spread his engineering wings. It seems they remained friends until the end of Churchward's life. (Above right) The Greville/Churchward horseless carriage in operation possibly with Grenville in the driving seat. (Author/DN)

simply providing power to a water pump would have required some modification. To do this, they initially chose a single-cylinder design to provide drive, but trial and error showed its weaknesses in this role, so they replaced it with a 236in^3 side-valve twin-cylinder version. However, in operation it was found that this boiler, cylinder arrangement needed careful handling and so it was necessary for an experienced fireman, who could constantly stoke the fire and maintain the boiler's water supply that ran from a 50 gallon tank, to be on hand when running.

Satisfied that this arrangement generated sufficient power to move a vehicle that weighed slightly more than 2.3 tons, they turned to other elements of its design. Here a single steering wheel, turned by a tiller situated at the front of the carriage was chosen and beneath they elected to fit three wheels – one up front and two much larger ones at the rear, which were connected to the driving axle. In composition, as was the custom at the time, these wheels were made up of sixteen teak sections held together by an iron tyre. It was decided that its maximum carrying capacity would be seven people, including the driver, who would occupy two parallel seats up front, with the brake controls on the left of the front bench. The fireman sat at the rear next to the boiler.

Records suggest that it ran for the first time in 1875, though continued to undergo occasional modifications for the next fifteen years, and despite its fairly basic design was found that it could reach 20mph on level ground, but this came at some cost. In 1911, during a much publicised 7 mile run between Glastonbury and Wells, it consumed 500lb of coal and 200 gallons of water. So, an interesting experiment and one on which Churchward could begin to demonstrate his developing talents, but not one that could ever be considered a serious commercial proposition.

After their time together at Newton Abbot, it appears that Grenville went on to work for Easton and Andersons in London and was involved in tasks relating to the GWR. Then in 1886 his father died and he inherited the family estate of Butleigh Court near Glastonbury, taking the steam carriage with him to live there. With no further need to work as a professional engineer he took on other local roles becoming a Justice of the Peace and then the High Sheriff of Somerset in the process. And for a while he drove his horseless carriage around Glastonbury, adapting it in 1898 for use as a stationary engine to drive a cider mill. Then, in time, it was restored to near original condition and can now be seen on display in the National Motor Museum at Beaulieu – an interesting witness to the aspirations of its owner as well as being the earliest known example of Churchward's work.

As he approached the end of his apprenticeship, the long-expected takeover of the SDR finally came to fruition. If members of staff were surprised by this change, the directors and senior managers would have been less so. Anyone able to read a balance sheet would have seen how difficult it had become for the company to remain as an independent business. While the GWR had for a time struggled financially, being a much bigger concern with greater assets, it begun to grow more rapidly as market forces improved. So in 1876 the SDR and the Bristol and Exeter Railway company, having toyed with the Midland Railway as a potential partner, were leased to their long term ally. And so Newton Abbot lost its premier status and became subordinate to senior managers at Paddington and Swindon.

For John Wright and Peter Margary, any uncertainty over their futures was soon resolved. Wright appears to have remained in charge of the facilities at Newton Abbot for a time, but now as a regional manager with fewer responsibilities than he had once enjoyed. At some point he seems to have left the company and set up a steam sawmill business in Devon and then become the proprietor of a wood case manufacturing business. Retirement followed and he is reported to have died in about 1910 at 78 years of age. Meanwhile Margary was appointed by the GWR to be Resident Engineer of their Western Division, which considering his leading role in developing much of this network is hardly surprising. In this capacity he led in the construction of the docks at Plymouth and the reconstruction of the Moorswater and St Pinnock viaducts before he too retired in 1891. Sadly, he didn't have long to enjoy his hard earnt pension, dying in London five years later aged 76.

For any admirer of railways in Devon, the line from Exeter to Newton Abbot, passing through Dawlish, will always be of great note. It would also have been of particular interest to George Churchward personally and professionally. Here it is captured in its full broad gauge glory as he would have seen it regularly on his travels. As an example of an all-encompassing project for a student to follow it had much to commend it from a civil as well as a mechanical engineering viewpoint. (Author)

For most craftsmen apprentices at Newton Abbot, life after amalgamation would have gone on much as before – there always being a need for their skills in the workshops there. But for premium apprentices such as Churchward, where expectations were much higher, there was little to keep them in this backwater of GWR activity. So, the centre of their world moved to Swindon and this is where he transferred to in 1876 to complete his training under the watchful eyes of Joseph Armstrong and William Dean.

By this stage it had probably become apparent that this gifted pupil favoured design engineering, although such a clever, diverse personality would undoubtedly have easily moved into the complimentary production engineering world if required to do so. As events would show, he was indeed a master of both disciplines, but for a man beginning to show a talent for invention it would have been a short-sighted employer who didn't exploit this potential to the full. Not surprisingly, when he arrived in Swindon, he was assigned to the Drawing Office to begin the final part of his training. In this he would have been assisted by attending evening classes in the Mechanics Institute which had been set up in the 1850s to provide a wide range of services for GWR employees.

During the final year of his training Churchward would have seen something of Armstrong, but although only 61 years of age he was failing fast and died in June 1877. In the situation, it is probably more likely that the final stage of Churchward's education fell to Dean, his Principal Assistant and successor, and Samuel Carlton, the Locomotive Works Manager, to oversee. Between them they helped coach their student and probably recommended his permanent employment when successfully graduating. However, this was rarely a foregone conclusion, with many promising students being 'let go' because all available posts were filled. But Churchward was probably too good to release and so became a permanent employee assigned to the Drawing Office where, in his own words, he was "Engaged in the Drawing Office at Swindon upon the design of plant in connection with the construction of the Severn Tunnel etc etc."

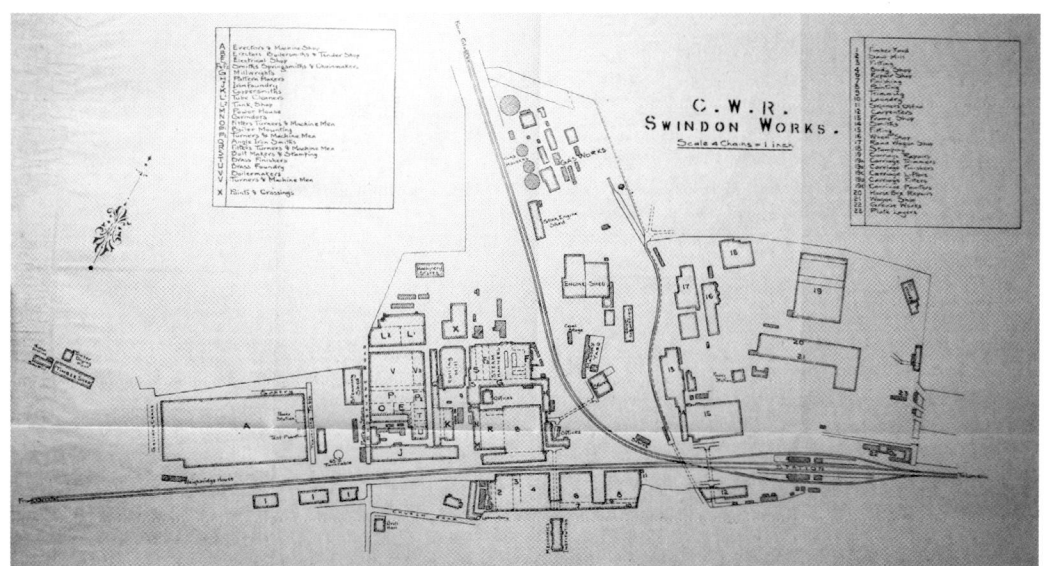

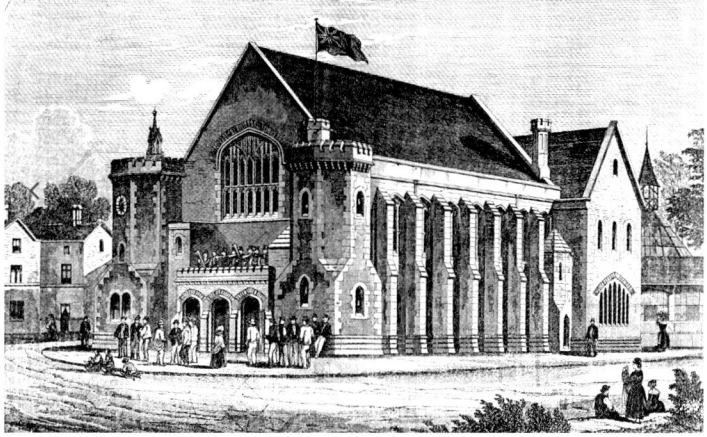

(Above) The Works at Swindon in the years following Churchward's arrival there as an apprentice in 1876. By the time he retired in 1922 the Works had expanded considerably – a development he oversaw with skill and an eye to the future. (Middle right) The Mechanics Institute in Swindon, shown here when it opened in the 1840s, fulfilled many roles in support of GWR employees, with training courses a key part of its work. Churchward would have attended some of these as an apprentice and then became a key advocate of its continuing role in the company's life. (Below right) The Administration Offices in the Works, which became the focal point in Churchward's life for 46 years. (DN/Author)

For a man who will forever be linked to locomotive design and development this was an unusual start to a career and may reflect the fact that he had begun to demonstrate a gift for civil as well as mechanical engineering. But it was a project of the greatest importance to the future of the company because it opened up a quick and easy route to and from the lucrative coal mines of South Wales. With demand for Welsh coal increasing each year as home and overseas markets

A view of Swindon Works that would become only too familiar to Churchward during his career. West Yard as seen from the tower of St Mark's Church, situated on the south side of the mainline. (Lower) A rather pristine looking Locomotive Paint Shop shortly after it was opened in the late 1870s. (DN)

The Severn Tunnel was an ambitious and costly project by any standards and could so easily had ended in failure if flooding problems not been corrected. As a junior draughtsman at Swindon, Churchward was involved in designing plant and machinery to ensure the ingress of water was controlled. As chief architect of the project (top left) Daniel Gooch took an active interest in its progress using personnel directly employed by the company to do the work. (Above left) Sir John Hawkshaw as consulting engineer saw the project through to a successful conclusion relying on the GWR to produce the funds and staff to do the work, including George Churchward. (Below) A simple diagrammatic sketch of the tunnel that underpins the complexity of the work to be undertaken. (Above right) As this contemporary print suggests, the problems the GWR faced were multifaceted and required great effort and imagination to resolve before success could be assured. (DN/Author's collection)

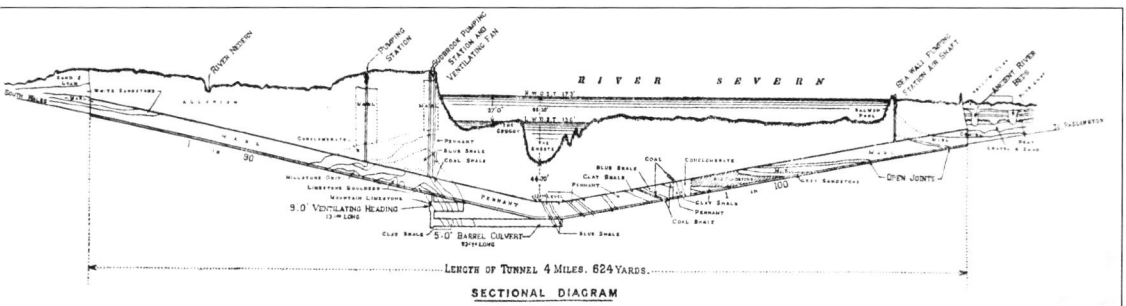

expanded, any company able to move a huge tonnage would reap many financial and political rewards. So it is little wonder that the GWR's Board of Directors, led by its Chairman, Sir Daniel Gooch, were prepared to speculate on this expensive project.

Serious planning for the tunnel commenced in the early 1870s in the hands of Sir John Hawkshaw, the noted civil engineer, then just turning 60, who had also actively advocated a tunnel under the English Channel. He was employed by Gooch as consulting engineer for the Severn Tunnel project and oversaw its development, using GWR employed labour from the day work started in March 1873. However, the rate of construction proved painfully slow and by the time Churchward became a permanent member of the Drawing Office team only the shaft and 0.93 miles of the tunnel had been excavated.

In late 1879, when the tunnels from both sides were within 130 yards of each other, the workings were overwhelmed with water from what became known as the 'Great Spring'. Faced with such a serious problem, all Hackshaw could do was arrange for the spring to be re-routed and held in check, which was only achieved when new pumping plant was installed and ready for use in January 1881. This allowed the spring to be temporarily sealed off, enabling excavation work of the tunnel to be completed later in the year.

However, this wasn't an end of the problems that continued to bedevil the project and it wouldn't be until October 1884 that track could finally begin to be laid; an occasion that Daniel Gooch himself chose to celebrate by being the 'first person to pass through the small hole in the heading between the English and Welsh sides of the tunnel'. With so many years of hard work and problems to be overcome, all costing, it is said, some £2 million, such a celebration was hardly surprising. In the meantime, a railway bridge between Sharpness and Lydney had been built by the company, presumably as a fall-back option and by the time the tunnel was completed had been operating successfully for five or so years.

For Churchward this was an interesting project on which to 'cut his teeth' and one from which he could observe Gooch, the driving force behind the tunnel, from close quarters. Undoubtedly, the plant the young man helped design played an important part in resolving the many flooding problems that had afflicted the project from the first, even before the 'Great Spring' did its worst. However, it was work that distracted him, for a time, from the main business of Swindon's drawing office – the design and construction of new engines and rolling stock. With his apprenticeship over, and his involvement in the tunnel coming to an end, he could now focus wholeheartedly on this area of work and begin to establish his reputation as a designer of note.

Chapter 3

Making a Start

Although the GWR had advanced a long way since its inception, by the 1870s the company was finding it more difficult to ignore the increasingly vexed question of broad gauge over standard gauge. Their reasons for adopting a 7ft 0¼in based system were sound and many still agreed with Brunel's view that this gauge was a far better system operationally than the alternatives. But with the other major companies choosing to adopt the 4ft 8½in gauge the GWR, prompted by many forces including some in Parliament, were faced with having to take drastic and costly action if the matter was ever to be resolved satisfactorily.

To a certain extent, its managers had seen the writing on the wall when, many years earlier, an independent Royal Commission was set up by the Conservative Prime Minister Sir Robert Peel, to study the issue in some detail. In an age of laissez-faire government this was in itself unusual, but with an increasing awareness of the problems created by companies, particularly the GWR,

By the 1870/80s, when Churchward began his career as an engineer, the railways were still undergoing a rapid period of growth, much of it speculative in nature as many looked for ways to make a quick profit. As a result, there was no centrally controlled plan to govern this work and so each railway company took their own path, not always with reference to others. This cartoon sought to convey the sense of confusion that then existed in the minds of people and the apparent mayhem that followed, in this case at Paddington Station. It also comments on the role of railways in Europe and how they were becoming central to all that happened – in trade, in politics, in economics, in society and more. So we have that symbol of Britishness, John Bull, talking to the German Chancellor, Bismarck, with a tiny Kaiser at his feet, Queen Victoria in a central position, while amongst the crowd we have other leading figures of the day including Disraeli, Gladstone, Charles Dickens, the French President and so on. By setting his scene at Paddington from which a broad gauge network spread, the artist was also having a sly dig at the GWR's desire to be and remain an entirely separate entity. By the 1870s change was coming, to Europe and the Board Room at Paddington. (DN)

using the gauge issue to achieve exclusivity and stifling competition, something had to be done. And so the Commission tried to establish an impartial and equitable way forward.

After much debate, their report was accepted by the newly elected Whig government, led by John Russell who, one source suggests, was a relation of Charles Russell, the one-time Conservative MP for Reading and the GWR's Chairman from 1839 to 1855. In due course the Commission's findings emerged as the Regulating the Gauge of Railways Act in 1846, which directed that standard gauge be used for all new railway construction. However, crucially, there was one exemption that might be deemed to apply, undoubtedly added at the behest of Brunel and Gooch, who campaigned strongly for broad gauge. In simple terms this allowed 7ft ¼in track to be laid for a new line but only if the proposal was supported by Act of Parliament. In theory a rather difficult path to follow, but one that the GWR successfully negotiated for a time. And so, broad gauge continued in common use in the West of England, Wales and even up to the Midlands for many more years to come. This, of course, wasn't an end of the matter and led to what became known as the 'Gauge War', which only served to postpone the inevitable unification of Britain's entire network under one gauge or another.

Armed with this exemption, the GWR, with the selective support of Parliament for each new project, kept up their expansion plans and pushed northwards into the Midlands, putting the company in direct competition with the Midland and the London and North Western Railways. As a result, in 1852 they reached Birmingham, via Oxford, then Wolverhampton two years later, but in each case they did so by laying mixed gauge track presumably to placate the government. However, this was the furthest north that broad gauge development was allowed to go.

Churchward would have seen for himself, very early in his career, the problems created by running a two-gauge system, the GWR being determined to continue with broad gauge when most companies had gone for standard. The national press and satirical cartoonists were quick to pick up on this strange arrangement with its double handling and the frequent, time consuming, but unavoidable transfers from one gauge to another it necessitated. In 1892, with Churchward by then a senior engineer at Swindon, the GWR finally discarded its broad-gauge stock in favour of standard gauge. (RH)

As a company that was growing ever larger by acquiring smaller businesses through amalgamation, the GWR found its broad gauge strategy gradually being diluted by the standard gauge lines they acquired. In the case of the SDR and Bristol and Exeter Railways this wasn't a particular problem because they mostly operated on broad gauge lines anyway. But in 1852 the Shrewsbury and Birmingham Railway and the Shrewsbury and Chester Railway were secured by the GWR, companies that ran their trains over standard gauge lines. So as time passed, the two-gauge issue grew increasingly more controversial. In the light of this it was probably inevitable that some in the GWR began to question the logic of a two-gauge network, but probably baulked at the cost involved in converting the existing broad gauge system to standard.

Gooch being one of the most vocal advocates of broad gauge was – as witnessed by his most robust, well-argued presentation to the 1846 Royal Commission – more than likely to resist such a change taking place. But this proved not to be the case and by 1865, when he became the GWR's Chairman, his views had become tempered by a growing awareness that he was fighting a losing battle, his opposition had largely dissipated. As a result, mixed track gradually became a feature of the GWR's operations. Nevertheless, it would take until 1892, three years after Gooch's

It is interesting to consider how the GWR's determination to continue with Brunel's choice of broad gauge, strongly supported by Daniel Gooch, played out when the company was faced with accommodating the gradual spread of standard gauge. This drawing, which was produced in the *Gazette* at the time, highlights what this meant in reality and hints at the extent of operational problems this created. (DN)

death, before broad gauge disappeared and the company finally joined the rest of the country, embracing, albeit reluctantly, in the eyes of some diehards, standard gauge.

The multitude of operational problems the GWR faced while this happened was made only too apparent in 1866 when a report to the company's General Meeting confirmed that of the lines they worked, approximately 600 miles were broad, 230 mixed and 420 standard gauge. To service the needs of such a diverse system meant that the fleet of locomotives and rolling stock developed by the company was becoming an unwieldy mix of designs. However, by the time Churchward made his first appearance in the Swindon Drawing Office, much thought was being given to the way locomotive and rolling stock fleets might be developed to meet the railway's current and future needs more effectively. All this is, of course, part and parcel of a designer's day to day life, but in the position they found themselves the company's convoluted operating system made it much more difficult for them to develop a clear, economically sound plan for the future.

As an ambitious young draughtsman, Churchward must have been only too aware of this. So it is perhaps unsurprising that this clear-minded man, having seen the muddle created by the gauge issue, would strive throughout his career for simplicity and standardisation whenever he could. And when standard gauge became the only choice for the companies operating the network, this undoubtedly helped release his creative energy, unconstrained by past creeds and loyalties.

In the meantime, there was certainly much he could learn from studying the work of Gooch, Armstrong and Dean. And to this could be added the work of other designers in Britain and overseas where engineers were taking significant steps in furthering locomotive design. In times past word of their achievements would have spread slowly, if they spread at all, but now, with the help of learned institutions, and their ever-growing membership, this was changing rapidly. As public forums these bodies actively encouraged the development of ideas then offered individuals an opportunity to present them to fellow members - at meetings and through published papers.

The debate over the comparative merits of broad and standard gauge is an open ended one with the benefits of each still occasionally debated by historians. Whatever your view there is no doubt that the GWR broad gauge engines were aesthetically very pleasing, as this picture of the 1872/73 built Rover Class 4-2-2 engine, *Iron Duke*, constructed during Joseph Armstrong's tenure, shows. The engine, which had 8ft diameter driving wheels, is photographed at Newton Abbott in about 1890. She was one of a class of 23 built and remained in service until 1892 when broad gauge workings came to an end. (DN)

Making a Start   45

Another member of the beautifully designed Rover Class, this time the 1880 built *Emperor*. This picture is recorded as having been taken in 1889 at Exeter St Davids Station. (DN)

The debates that followed were, in effect, part of a growing creative dialectic that enabled new concepts to be considered and tried, so potentially widening and deepening the scope and reach of an idea.

The late nineteenth century was also a time when publishing for the masses took off in a big way with the number of newspapers and magazines growing rapidly in number. This was helped

An anonymous member of the Rover Class running at speed. A note on the back of this battered print records that the engine is hauling the *Flying Dutchman* service between Paddington and Penzance in 1892. If this is the case the photo might well have been taken during the final few days of the *Dutchman* and broad gauge services across the GWR network. All came to an end in May that year and the domination of standard gauge was complete after a long and often bitter battle. (DN)

in part by growing literacy rates, as the government's efforts at reforming the education system began to bear fruit, mass production printing methods being developed, distribution becoming much easier as the railway network grew and revenue from advertising growing ever larger. In truth, the published word was no longer the preserve of the well off, but something to be enjoyed by a much wider audience. And as the number of publications and their readership grew, so knowledge of many subjects, including the world of science and technology, found a ready audience. For those such as Churchward, who had to pass through an education system where only the classics and natural sciences were taught, this was a huge bonus. Now lively minds could find a ready outlet for their imagination by devouring the contents of the ever increasing number of newspapers and journals becoming available.

It was this, plus the privilege of working alongside some truly great engineers, that would influence Churchward's development as he sat in the Drawing Office at Swindon pondering the future. And it was through professional institutions and the press that he would become aware of events and developments outside Britain. This was particularly so with regard to the railways where a growing awareness of inventions and patents would prove essential to his own growth and success as an engineer – to which he would add many himself. But first and foremost he had the achievements of Gooch, Armstrong and Dean to study at close quarters.

By this stage, his knowledge of the engines he had seen running on the SDR line, which were mostly designed or specified by Gooch and his team, would have been fairly extensive. For such a progressive man, though, it is more likely that Churchward would have been more concerned about the future and only looked back to absorb any lessons learnt. So, while Gooch's achievements would undoubtedly have been of interest to him their relevance to current design

As an example of the way locomotives evolved on the GWR in the 1870s and '80s, No. 2001, captured here, makes an interesting case study. She was originally built in the 1850s as one of eight 4-2-4 tank locomotives by Rothwell and Co for the Bristol and Exeter Railway. In due course, four were absorbed into the GWR's fleet. Following an accident with No. 2001, at Long Ashton in 1876, the engine was scrapped, while the other three were converted into 4-2-2 tender engines, becoming in the process the first inside-bogie singles in the country. On completion of this work the last of them, No. 2004, was re-numbered 2001. In this guise they continued to give sterling service until withdrawn in 1885 as the need for broad-gauge engines slowly diminished. (DN)

Another engine with which Churchward would have been very familiar. In 1878 the first of ten standard gauge '157' class 2-2-2s, also known as *Sharpies* or *Cobhams*, appeared (the latter name carried by the engine shown here which was numbered 162) These engines differed from their predecessors in having sandwich frames of the open-slotted type. As built they did not carry domes, which were added later during one of a number of rebuilds, the last of which included fitting a raised, domeless Belpaire boiler. The last of the class, No. 165, was withdrawn from service in 1914. (DN)

work would have been muted to say the least. By comparison, Armstrong and Dean's work was very much of the present and the future and so commanded greater respect and attention.

Here a review of the locomotives they produced gives us a better understanding of the engineering questions Churchward might have observed being solved and from which he learnt most. And in turn, as he gained experience and was promoted to ever more senior positions in the hierarchy, those issues he may have helped resolve himself. In determining which projects may have influenced him the most, we are lucky that Kenneth Cook left us a preparatory draft of his 1950 presentation, some of which didn't make it into the final version:

> It has been said that when Churchward took charge of the locomotive department its stock was in dire need of development. I believe that this statement should be considered in context and in conjunction with the circumstances of the time. There is no doubt that the intense battle of the gauges had cast its spell over development until the issue was resolved. Nevertheless, there were some good standard engines in service or in production during the early years of Churchward's development, and it is surprising how easily many of these were able to be incorporated in the new standards.

Amongst this group are:

1. The extremely graceful Dean singles of which there were 80 engines.
2. The Dean standard goods, the whole class of which numbered 260, the last 200 of which were particularly a standard group.
3. The Duke, Bulldog, Albara, City and Aberdare group comprising 367 engines built between 1895 and 1910, which had many standard components running through the group.

In 1881 the first of twenty members of the 2201 Class 2-4-0s rolled out of the Works at Swindon. By this stage Churchward was an established member of the Drawing Office and was heavily involved in locomotive design. The two-cylinder passenger service 2201s were based on Joseph Armstrong's 806 Class of twenty which were built in 1873. Dean updated the design for the 2201s with a different style of framing and fitted them with cabs. Here No. 2203 is captured at Bath, according to notes with the print, in about 1892. These engines had a long life and some survived in service until 1921. (Author)

The main line passenger engine of the nineteenth century was in general a 'single-wheeler', but the four-wheeled coupled engine was developed in order to obtain greater adhesion and power. Dean had introduced the 'Dukes' or 'Devons' and the 'Bulldogs' in 1895 on account of the gradients west of Newton Abbot, and it appears that Churchward commenced his boiler development with the boiler for the 'Bulldog'. It was a bold step to plunge suddenly into a six-coupled fast passenger engine era (the large versus the small engine controversy is not dead yet!), and hence the third group of the Dean engines was built in quantities to fill this gap at the beginning of the twentieth century while the Churchward standard engines were developing.

The narrative of his great work briefly falls into two spheres viz., that of the development of a complete system of locomotive classes ('after the confusion of previous years', he added in a handwritten note) and, secondly, the introduction of new features which could readily be adopted throughout his programme of work.

Much has been made of Gooch's engines and the early work of Armstrong in furthering the design of broad-gauge locomotives. This was undoubtedly true, but by the time GJC arrived at Swindon these efforts were being dwarfed by the need to build narrow-gauge locomotives [for GWR men the word 'narrow' was used for a long time as meaning 'standard']. From this it should not be concluded that broad-gauge engines did not add something to the overall development of the locomotives that followed. So, a forward looking young engineer such as Churchward would naturally evaluate their strengths when looking beyond their demise to plan the next generation of engines. To all intent and purposes by 1880 the end was in sight for broad-gauge and no more would be built except, that is, where the need for replacements or renewal of worn-out engines had been identified.

A sight that would have become only too familiar to Churchward at Swindon as broad-gauge was finally abandoned by the GWR. Those engines that could be were converted to standard gauge, but this left vast numbers that were only good for scrapping. With hindsight it is quite remarkable that the GWR continued to perpetuate its 7ft ¼in network for forty-six years after the 1846 Regulating the Gauge of Railways Act had come into force. (DN)

However, there was one exception to this which GJC himself referred me to when I began my premium apprentice during 1912. His reason for doing so was, perhaps, best summed in a document I kept in which he wrote that:

Gooch's thirty-three 4-2-2 Iron Dukes were the mainstay of fast passenger workings from Paddington for many years. However, by the 1870s they were passed their best with all but one withdrawn by 1884. With no end in sight for broad-gauge running Armstrong was faced with producing sufficient renewals to maintain all the fast passenger services then greatly in demand. This he did by adopting the principle of 'eight foot singles' again. As a result, the 'Rovers', as they became known, began appearing in 1871, with twenty-three built by 1880, with a final one [appropriately named *Great Western*] added in 1888. During their lives three of them underwent modification to coincide with the appearance of the last engine of the class.

The 'Rovers' did their jobs well, with few mechanical problems occurring and coped with the steep gradients of South Devon far more effectively than their predecessors. In so doing they were able to keep to a schedule that allowed the GWR to compete favourably with the London and South West Railway's service from Waterloo to Plymouth. For this reason alone, they are worthy of close study. Much can be learnt from them.

Churchward was also keenly aware of the publicity value the premier express services produced. Having the fastest and the most glamorous trains running attracted much press attention and the locomotives that pulled these services became household names long before the 'Flying Scotsman' appeared in the 1920s. In the 1880s the 'Rovers' fulfilled this role and became the GWR's public face even though broad gauge would soon disappear.

Cook's final point is an interesting one because it touches on an underlying issue that is easy to overlook when considering the successful development of locomotives – the overriding

In 1891 William Dean began introducing his 3001 Class 2-2-2 locomotives. Thirty would be built in two batches over the next year or so, the first ten (though some sources quote eight) of which were constructed as 'convertible' broad gauge engines. After one derailed in 1893 it was decided that a front bogie was needed to take the weight of these engines more effectively and they were all rebuilt as 4-2-2s by 1894. In so doing they became the first members of the 3031 Class, to which were added a further fifty locomotives by 1899. Although capable of reaching and sustaining high speeds, when pulling passenger trains, the 4-2-2 configuration was deemed by the early years of the twentieth century to be obsolete and withdrawals began in 1908, with the last going in 1916. Kenneth Cook in his 1950 appreciation of Churchward's work sited these engines as a major influence on his career. (Above) 3015 *Kennet*, originally built as a 3001 Class, stands at Bath Spa Station. (Below) 3020 *Sultan* and 3011 *Greyhound* make a fine sight as they double-head through Uphill with a fast express. (DN/RH)

Another class of engine that Cook listed as having been of great interest to Churchward was the 0-6-0 2301 Dean standard goods locomotive the first of which appeared in 1883. By 1899 260 had been built and the last would remain in service until 1958 proving how successful the design was. (DN)

commercial imperative of selling goods and making a profit. As might be expected these are issues that will impact in a major way on any enterprise, not least of all on the work of railway engineers. In many ways it meant that directors and senior managers would prefer that safety first principles be adopted rather than anything too speculative in nature. And yet as the old saying goes, you need to speculate to accumulate, so they could not lose sight of the need to build bigger and better engines if an increase in demand were to be encouraged then met, no matter how restricted their budgets. As always it was and will always remain a matter of balance and in the hands of a designer, unencumbered by a strong sense of business reality, things could go badly awry. Churchward, when his moment came to manage these processes, demonstrated from the first a sure-footed approach whilst revealing that he was a man who understood the value of a good press when pursuing his ambitions.

These were issues on which Dean appears to have struggled at times. In his noteworthy book entitled *Great Western Locomotive Design*, John Gibson paints an interesting picture of his time as LCWS and the way he managed design tasks after a promising start:

> In the event, Dean's work was extraordinarily erratic. It reminds one of the little girl in the rhyme who 'when she was good she was very good, and when she was bad she was horrid!' In fact, the saga of William Dean was a sad one....In 1868 Joseph Armstrong brought him to Swindon (then only 28) as his chief assistant to help with the enormous task laid on him by the rapid changeover to standard gauge.
>
> But a career which had begun so brilliantly ended with complete failure of his mind by the time he was sixty. Some of his crazier designs he produced during his reign suggest that he must always have been a bit unbalanced. Eccentric genius is perhaps the fairest description we can find of him.

Under William Dean, 4-4-0 express passenger engine designs were pursued with some vigour and as Kenneth Cook made clear, Churchward was closely involved in the evolution and production of five classes of these engines. The pictures above highlight three of them which together covered a development period spanning the years 1895 to 1910 – an interesting review of the evolutionary nature of design and the way lessons are learnt and modifications are incorporated, hopefully, to make the engines better or simply to meet changing operational needs. (Top) Atbara 4100 Class No. 3378 *Khartoum* one of forty members of the class that first began appearing in 1900. (Middle) Bulldog 3300 Class No. 3339 *Marco Polo* at Didcot in 1902/03. This engine was one of 136 built at Swindon between 1899 and 1910, to which a further twenty were added when some Dukes were rebuilt as Bulldogs. (Bottom picture) A member of the City 3700 Class – in this case neither engine or location are identified. This was a class of 20 engines that appeared in 1903, ten were new and ten were rebuilt Atbaras. (Author)

(Above left) Churchward as he appeared when becoming established as William Dean's Chief Assistant in the late nineteenth century. By this stage of his career he had gained wide experience of management and design engineering and was ready to put his developing ideas into practice. However, to do this successfully you need some good people around you and in Frederick George Wright (above right) he found just such a man. Wright was five years younger than Churchward and served part of his apprenticeship at Swindon alongside his leader, then joined him as a draughtsman. He rose to become Chief Draughtsman in 1892, then Assistant Manager of the Locomotive Works to Churchward four years later and his Chief Assistant when appointed LCWS. He and Churchward shared an outside interest in municipal affairs and became, in turn, Lord Mayor of Swindon. Wright died in 1938. (Author)

> Until 1902, when he was formally appointed [to succeed Dean], Churchward was for all practical purposes in charge of the department, although Dean continued in office as a kind of figurehead…From Churchward's point of view this interim arrangement [which began when he was promoted to be Dean's Chief Assistant Superintendent in 1897] had one great advantage. It enabled him to make his early experiments and learn by his mistakes before he was officially in charge, which was good for his reputation. Once appointed to the top job he could go right ahead with his scheme for standard classes, of what were then quite revolutionary designs, with more or less instant success.

If this is true, and some may doubt it being so, we have a picture of a man with exceptional skills from which Churchward could learn much, but then, as his powers appeared to fail, was sufficiently skilled to take his tutor's philosophies and build on them by applying his own unique ideas and way of working. The only question that remains is determining exactly if and when Churchward took control of the design process and how this was managed as successfully as it had been when Dean still nominally in charge.

From what we know, his rise from simply being a draughtsman to very senior manager was rapid and, probably, unprecedented, reflecting the depth of the man's engineering talents, his understanding of political, economic and business issues, his leadership skills and his ability to put a case succinctly and with some authority. Nothing less than being an expert in all these fields would have been sufficient for the company, especially in the hands of its strongminded and ambitious Chairman, Frederick Campbell, Viscount Emlyn, who had succeeded Daniel Gooch. Here was a man who ruled the GWR with the surest of touches between 1895 and 1905, and before that as a director. In both posts this ex-MP proved to be a hard-driving man. Not for nothing was he described by Joseph Chamberlain, the leading industrialist and politician of the day, as 'the best chairman now living'. With a very wide field of effective chairmen across the railway industry to choose from, this was indeed a compliment. And in many ways, he and Churchward shared the same qualities, so it is not surprising that they appear to have forged a sound, even dynamic working partnership together.

Behind Campbell lay the equally talented and powerful figure of the company's General Manager, Sir Joseph Loftus Wilkinson. His obituary captures the essence of his personality and his achievements:

Wilkinson who died on the 16th June, 1903, rose by merit to a high position in the Railway world. He entered the service of the Great Western Railway in 1863 as a Junior Clerk, and,

The two men who ensured that Churchward became William Dean's Chief Assistant then the GWR's LCWS, and whose continuing support was key to the development of the many ideas he pursued so successfully in these positions. (Above left) Frederick Archibald Vaughan Campbell, 3rd Earl of Cawdor and Viscount Emlyn. This influential man was, in a very active career, an MP, Deputy Lieutenant of Inverness and Justice of the Peace as well as a director, then Chairman of the Great Western (1895 to 1905). Campbell's term of chairmanship was cut short by his appointment to the post of First Lord of the Admiralty. The Earl died in 1911 when aged 63. (Above right) Sir Joseph Loftus Wilkinson (1845 to 1903), who became the GWR's General Manager in 1896 and remained in this post until his death at the comparatively young age of 58. (Author)

with the exception of three years (1885 to 1887) when he acted as Manager to the Buenos Aires and Pacific Railway, his career was identified with that Company. In the spring of 1888 he returned to England to become Chief Goods Manager of the Great Western system, and in 1896, on the resignation of Mr. Lambert, he was appointed General Manager to the Company.

Among the difficulties with which Sir Joseph Wilkinson successfully coped were those in connection with legislation affecting railway rates and charges, and the threatened competition of new lines to the South Wales districts. The latter schemes he not only defeated, but made the Great Western route more popular by improving the train service and by introducing dining-cars. Under his advice a new line to South Wales is now being constructed by the Great Western Company, as well as a new route to the South of Ireland, by way of Fishguard.

He received the thanks of the King for the manner in which the difficult arrangements for the late Queen's funeral were carried out by the Great Western officials.

Sir Joseph Wilkinson was a Lieutenant-Colonel of the Engineer and Railway Volunteer Staff Corps, and a member of the Army Railway Council and of the Hon. Artillery Company. He took great interest in all that conduced to the welfare and happiness of his staff, and was an active Freemason. He was elected an Associate of the Institution of Civil Engineers on the 1st March, 1898.

It is difficult to establish exactly when Churchward first came to their notice and why this was so? But even before these two men took their leading roles in the GWR their protégé had already proved himself in a number of posts, as Kenneth Cook briefly recorded:

He was engaged on designing and inspection of materials in the Drawing Office until 1882, when he became assistant manager of the carriage works at Swindon. In December 1895, he was moved to the locomotive works as assistant manager, becoming manager of these works in March 1896, and in September 1897 he became, in addition, Chief Assistant Locomotive Superintendent and so William Dean's Deputy and understudy (which proved to be a most important and necessary role as Dean's health worsened and no amount of gentle urging could persuade him to give up his post).

In the event Campbell and Wilkinson appear not to have forced the issue, accepting that Churchward would have to pick up the increasing amount of slack in day to day management of Dean's department and in the design of new locomotives and rolling stock. In doing so, he had to add the role of nursemaid and diplomat to an already challenging list of duties, while playing lip service, at least, to the wishes of his ailing leader. It was an interesting position in which he found himself and one he managed with a degree of compassion and tact; to have been too forceful and ambitious in what he wished to do would, undoubtedly, have been taken amiss by Dean and so have proved counter-productive. It also helped that Churchward had discovered a worthy deputy, in Frederick George Wright, to assist him in these endeavours.

Wright, who was born in Bordesley, Warwickshire in 1862, began his apprenticeship with the GWR at Gloucester in 1876 and completed it in the works at Swindon six years later. He was soon posted into the Drawing Office where he undoubtedly came to Churchward's attention, as he himself rose rapidly through the ranks to senior positions. So strong did the link between them become that Wright was promoted Chief Draughtsman in 1892, then became Churchward's Assistant Manager in the Locomotive Works in 1896. Finally, in 1902/03, he was promoted to become Chief Assistant to the LCWS remaining so when Churchward's title changed to Chief Mechanical Engineer.

To understand how Churchward, assisted by Wright, managed to cope with the ailing Dean, if indeed this was the case, it is interesting to study one of the projects suggested by Cook in his 1950 paper – the gradual development of the GWR's 4-4-0 classes of passenger engines.

By the time Dean and Churchward began exploring the potential of 4-4-0 designs much work had already been undertaken with this wheel configuration in both North America and Britain. In fact, the first of the type was designed and patented by Henry Campbell, Chief Engineer for the Philadelphia, Germantown and Norristown Railway, in 1836. Construction of the prototype tender engine soon followed, just beating, by a few months, a rival Eastwick and Harrison Co 4-4-0 being built for the Beaver Meadow Railroad in Pennsylvania. So popular did these engines become that it was a proud boast that almost every major railroad that operated in North America in the first half of the nineteenth century owned and operated locomotives of this type.

With word of their success reaching designers around the world, examples were soon appearing in England, most notably in the West Country with Churchward's Alma Mater the SDR. In 1849, under Gooch's guiding hand, the GWR built the first of its broad gauge Bogie class saddle tanks for the company, specifically to tackle the steep gradients on the route to Plymouth. Then, in 1854 and '55 the GWR constructed some for its own use as well. And so the programme ran on with the SDR acquiring another six saddle tanks and the Vale of Neath Railway a further nine by 1876. In the meantime, the Bristol and Exeter Railway had procured several of the type as well and these, plus the SDR engines, would have become a familiar sight to Churchward, in the early years of his apprenticeship at Newton Abbot.

It was not long before tender versions appeared in Britain too, the pulling power of 4-4-0 engines being seized upon by engineers including Gooch with his Waverley Class, built by Robert

The first of the prototype Armstrong Class 4-4-0s, soon to be retitled Dean Class 7, captured at Bristol Temple Meads, according to notes on this print, in 1898. Engine No. 7 was first called *Charles Saunders* after the GWR's noted mid-nineteenth century Superintendent, but was renamed *Armstrong* with *Charles Saunders* being passed on to Dean Class 7 No. 14. (Author)

Stephenson & Co in 1855. Then there was Samuel Johnson who, between 1876 and 1903, produced 350 or so inside cylinder versions for the Midland Railway and six new classes of 4-4-0 designed by Wilson Worsdell for the North Eastern Railway.

It was in 1894 that the first of Dean's 4-4-0s were built. In this case they came in the form of four double framed four-coupled prototype locomotives which became known as the Armstrong Class and later the Dean 7s. Though seemingly a success, the GWR built no more, but Dean continued to develop 4-4-0 types with the 3252 Duke Class, the first entering service in 1895. Over the next four years, sixty of these two inside 18 x 26in cylinder engines, with Stephenson valve gear, were built at Swindon for use on fast passenger services.

In practice the Duke's overall design matched to this wheel arrangement proved to have good adhesion and could easily meet the growing requirement for heavier trains. To provide sufficient power, round topped boilers and fireboxes were fitted which generated a working pressure of 160psi and produced a tractive effort of 16,848lb at 85 per cent cut-off. The only exception to this were the last four which were fitted with Belpaire fireboxes in 1899. Although Alfred Belpaire's design had been in existence for more than thirty years by then, it was an idea that was slow to catch on, perhaps due to the expense involved. However, in the early 1880s two railroad companies in the USA, the Pennsylvania and Great Northern, successfully matched the firebox to boilers in its engines, which greatly encouraging others to follow suit, including Churchward.

To him the advantages were clear, there being a greater surface area for evaporation and, as experience had shown in the USA, a greatly reduced risk of priming. By this stage in his career he was only too aware of the problems this posed and the harmful effect on the valves and pistons if their lubrication was washed away by boiling, foaming water. If this, in turn, caused water to collect in the cylinders, disrupting compression, the cylinder head or a piston might fracture with expensive and, possibly, dangerous consequences. And so he investigated the concept further with Dean and it was decided to fit Belpaires to the last of the Dukes. However, in doing so he closely studied the original patented design and adapted it to his own needs. This work included 'maximising the flow of water in a given size of boiler by tapering the firebox and boiler barrel outwards to the area of highest steam production at the front of the firebox'.

The GWR 4-4-0s proved to be good interim designs as passenger locomotives, filling the evolutionary gap between the 2-2-2 'Singles' and the 4-6-0s that began to arrive in the early years of the twentieth century. The 4-4-0s generated good adhesion and a low axle weight so allowing them to haul heavier trains. The photo above shows a 4-4-0 Duke 3252 Class engine, in this case No. 3267 *Cornishman* fitted with a Belpaire firebox, at Leamington Spa. (DN)

In 1897, the Dean/Churchward partnership decided to take the 4-4-0 concept further forward with the Badminton Class. These new engines were built with domed, parallel boilers and raised copper Belpaire fireboxes – the first on the GWR to be so fitted. The locomotive shown here, No. 3295 *Bessborough*, was the fourth of class to be built and was one of eleven that rolled out of the works at Swindon between September 1898 and January 1899. (DN)

Both the Belpaire and non-Belpaire locomotives were deemed a success, if contemporary accounts are to be believed. Nevertheless, as is usual in any engineering enterprise, the evolutionary process to achieve some improvement went on in a perpetual creative cycle. So, over the years, and long after Dean had departed the scene, the Dukes underwent modification most notably in 1906 when tapered boilers and Belpaire fireboxes were fitted to eighteen more of the class. Then in 1911 Churchward decided to fit a two row, 12 tube/72 element superheated parallel domed boiler, with a Belpaire firebox, to a number of engines which increased their working pressure to 180psi. This had the effect of enhancing the tractive effort to 18,955lb, at 85 per cent cut-off. However, this increased the maximum axle loading to 14tons 12cwt, which restricted their route availability somewhat. But, as is always the case, it was a matter of balancing cost against operational need to achieve the best possible engineering outcome and a sound financial return.

With the Dukes proving to be a success Churchward, presumably with Dean's backing and Wright's support, pressed ahead with a new, modified version. So, in December 1897 engine No. 3292, in time to become the first of the Badminton Class, appeared, looking distinctly like a Duke but with a number of modifications incorporated into the design. The frames were curved over each driving axle, with the steam chest and slide valves being positioned below the two inside cylinders which were driven by Stephenson valve gear.

This inverted layout, as it was called, had first been tried by William Stroudley when Locomotive Superintendent of the London, Brighton and South Coast Railway in the latter part of the nineteenth century. He had discovered that by adopting such an arrangement he could reduce cylinder wear because it allowed the valves to drop away from the cylinder's steam ports when the regulator was closed. Dean and Churchward, ever eager to achieve economy of effort and extend the lives of component parts, followed suit, identifying, in the process, that the cylinders could benefit from having an increased diameter.

In addition, Dean and Churchward adopted another Stroudley idea, in this case placing the crankpins for the coupling rods in line with the connecting rods' inside crankpins. It was a solution they had tried when designing the prototype Armstrongs and now could employ it more fully. In doing so, they were undoubtedly hoping to test Stroudley's claim that this enabled the motion of the inside cranks to be transferred to the coupling rods as evenly and smoothly as it did on outside-cylindered engines. This, Stroudley believed, could lead to a doubling of the service lives of axleboxes, hornblocks, coupling rods and bearing services, so putting them on a par with outside cylinder locomotives. Churchward's continued use of this methodology suggests that he was confident that this was true.

Having proved themselves in service, the Badminton Class continued in production until twenty had been built, with one, No. 3297 *Earl Cawdor* soon becoming the subject of an experiment led by Wright, who was gaining something of a reputation as a designer by then. This was helped in part by his work in developing a large, experimental boiler with a particularly deep firebox. It is said that he undertook this task due to the planned opening, in 1906, of a direct line between Reading and Taunton, which was more challenging than the line from Reading via Bristol to Taunton. This new boiler, it was hoped, would allow engines to cope better when working over the more southerly route. To do this, its capacity was increased from 76.2ft^3 to 85.13ft^3. This, it was believed, would increase its working pressure to something nearer to 210psi and, at the same time, allow a thick fire to be built up. If this could be achieved it was hoped that it would 'increase the area of the firebox coming into contact with the fire, and, hopefully, reduce the temperature so cutting the risk that the firebox stays might be damaged, the slope along the firebox plates having

Two of the three stages of a Churchward/Wright experiment to improve the steaming characteristics of the Badminton Class to make them more suited to the new, direct line from Reading to Taunton that opened in 1906. Initially engine No. 3297, *Earl Cawdor*, was built in 1898 with domed parallel boiler and Belpaire firebox. (Above) As rebuilt in 1906 with a new larger capacity boiler with a very deep firebox and non-standard cab (often quoted as looking like those fitted to North Eastern engines. (Below) Now with this cab removed and replaced by a more typically Churchward design. (DN)

been reduced'. In this state the engine entered service in 1903, fitted with a cab of a distinctly non-GWR pattern with side windows.

Very soon, the engine was pulling some of the more demanding services so that the new boiler could be fully tested. Sadly, it soon became obvious that the engine wasn't all that it was hoped it would be, falling well short of expectations. With nothing more to be gained from this experiment, the engine was stripped down and fitted with a Standard No. 4 boiler in 1906, the cab having already been replaced by a more traditional GWR type two years earlier.

As the Badminton's established themselves in the day to day life of the GWR, the next stage of the 4-4-0's programme got underway. In late 1898/99 the first of the Bulldog 3300 Class engines, No. 3312, made its appearance. Initially it was conceived as a new variant of the Duke Class but in development took on a slightly different form, were built in far greater numbers and then were developed into the Bird Class. In total 121 Bulldogs and 15 Birds were built by 1910, in what proved to be a prolonged construction programme, and in time 20 Dukes would be rebuilt and added to the list of 3300s.

In developing the first Bulldogs (originally called 'Camels'), Churchward and Wright continued to use two inside cylinders, measuring 18 x 26in, with Stephenson valve gear and curved outside frames matched to a domed parallel boiler with a raised Belpaire firebox. However, in this case a wrapper style smokebox was used. For the first engine the boiler was, as with *Earl Cawdor*'s a few years later, a prototype. However, where one was discarded, after several years of testing, the Bulldog's evolved into Churchward's Standard No. 2 boiler, which then went on to be fitted to the other members of the class, though occasionally with some modifications. These included boilers tapered over the rear half of the barrel, later known as the 'half cone' variant, with later versions built with three-quarters of the barrel covered. In addition, some of the early engines appeared with a circular drumhead smokebox supported by a saddle curved to its shape.

In 1903, the first of the Bulldog 3300 Class of 4-4-0s appeared ostensibly as a Duke Class variant, but in development it became something more. Here engine No. 3355, *Camelot*, which entered service in 1900, is seen at Bath Spa Station. (DN)

A Bulldog in repose, in this case No. 3340 *Camel* at Reading. This locomotive was part of the initial batch of twenty engines built at Swindon in 1899/1900 with curved outside frames, a domed parallel boiler matched to a raised Belpaire firebox. This engine lasted in service until 1934. (DN)

By 1906 the construction of the Bulldogs was complete, leaving a three-year gap before the Birds appeared. In the intervening years, thought had been given to the size of the outside frames and the design of the bogie. The former, it was felt, needed to be made deeper and the latter changed in its entirety. Up to then all outside framed bogies on the GWR locomotives so constructed had been of the Dean centreless type. They had proved more than adequate, according to contemporary reports, but Churchward believed that a type used on a new class of 4-4-2 four-cylinder compound engines in France might give a better performance. These engines were the result of a collaboration between the English engineer Alfred de Glehn and Gaston du Bousquet, who were tasked with producing a new class of engine to be built by the Société Alsacienne de Constructions Mécaniques (SACM) for the Nord Railway.

Their work came to Churchward's attention very early in his tenure as Superintendent because in 1903 he was given approval by Campbell and Wilkinson to purchase one of the SACM's Atlantic locomotives. His reason for doing so was only too clear – it gave him the opportunity to evaluate very closely the advances in locomotive design being made in France. By doing this he could absorb the lessons they were learning, particularly with regard to compounding, test such an engine when running over the GWR's metals and apply whatever he could to projects he and Wright were then developing at Swindon. And so in 1903 a SACM built locomotive arrived at Swindon, then numbered and named GWR 102 *La France*, to begin evaluation.

All this will be dealt with in more detail later in the book, but for the moment it is the bogie issue, in relation to the Bird Class, which is relevant and the way Churchward applied what he learnt from de Glehn and du Bousquet regarding the design of these fifteen locomotives. In this case, the inside-framed bogie previously used was modified to produce a deeper outside-framed alternative, in this case described as 'a de Glehn bar-framed bogie'. The trials with No. 102 that followed, and later on with two other SACM engines procured in 1905, gave Churchward many useful pointers to consider when developing his plans for new locomotives. But initially, it was the new style bogie that caught his eye and which he was quick to exploit when designing the Birds and other classes that came later. And so successful did it prove to be that it was still being

A Bird Class locomotive, in this case No. 3444 (up to 1910 numbered 3734), *Cormorant*, which appears to be waiting between turns at an unrecorded location. This engine, as did all of the Birds, had a long life and was only withdrawn from service in 1951. (DN)

applied by other noteworthy steam locomotive engineers many years later, including the LMS's William Stanier and BR's Robert Riddles.

As the same time as the Bulldog's came into existence, Dean and Churchward began introducing their Atbara Class of 4-4-0s, so extending the Badminton Class design still further. In this case the outside curved frames were dispensed with and replaced by straight topped frames, which were thought less likely to fracture because they were, in effect, strengthened by having a greater depth of plate between the coupled wheels. However, in doing so, their length and wheelbase, when compared to the Badmintons, were cut back, resulting in the Atbaras being a foot shorter overall. Atop the frames sat a parallel domeless boiler of the Standard No. 2 type, and beneath the Stroudley inspired crank, cylinders, valves and valve gear arrangement.

Swindon built forty of the class in this form in 1900/01, their production running parallel with the Bulldogs. And soon they would be joined by the City Class which began development when Atbara, No. 3405, *Mauritius*, was fitted with a tapered domeless boiler coupled to a Belpaire firebox in 1902. In due course, this prototype boiler became Churchward's Standard No. 4 and would then be fitted to ten new City 3700 Class engines built in 1903. These were then followed by nine more rebuilt Atbaras in 1907 and 1909 to complete a class of 20.

Of all the 4-4-0s built by the Dean/Churchward/Campbell partnership the City Class has come to be seen as being at the pinnacle of their work. Kenneth Cook, who became very familiar with them when an apprentice, then junior engineer at Swindon, later wrote:

> The Cities when turned out in 1903 were most valuable and the best of the 4-4-0s in which Churchward's played a leading part. They were excellent performers no matter what the size of load and managed the Devon Banks with comparative ease. They were also capable of a fair turn of speed when required. For example, in July 1903 City of Bath [No. 3433]

Two views of Atbara Class engines at work. (Above) No. 3376, *Herschell*, gently simmers at an unidentified location with what appears to be an interesting polished pattern on the tender. The names of the first Atbaras reflected British military operations and generals at the time, but later engines were named after places with an Empire connection such as *Dunedin*. The name *Herschell* was removed in 1914 presumably because of its German connection. (Below) Engine No. 3460, *Montreal*, makes a fine sight as it passes Teignmouth at speed in 1908 heading for Plymouth. (Author's collection)

Atbara Class No. 3405 *Mauritius* first entered service in 1900/01. However, in 1902, following his promotion to Locomotive Superintendent, Churchward decided to take development of his standard boilers a step further by fitting a prototype of his No. 4 to this engine (as shown above) so that he could test its capabilities. This tapered boiler passed muster and was then fitted to the new City Class being developed and, later on, another nine Atbaras were converted in the same way as 3405. (DN)

The first 3700 Class locomotive was No. 3433 *City of Bath* which appeared in March 1903. This engine made a name for itself in July of the same year when she was recorded as having covered 240 miles from London to Plymouth at an average speed of 62-3mph. During this run she covered approximately 90 miles between Langley in Buckinghamshire and Chippenham in Wiltshire at an average speed of 72mph, reaching, at one point, 81mph. However, a year later her efforts were easily eclipsed by *City of Truro* when reported as having broken 100mph passing through Somerset on the way to Paddington. 3433 (later numbered 3710) survived in service until 1928. In the photo here she is being made ready for Royal duties.. (DN)

was recorded as having covered 240 miles, from Paddington to Plymouth, at an average speed of 62-3mph. And during this run it covered approximately 90 miles between Langley in Buckinghamshire and Chippenham in Wiltshire at an average speed of 72mph, reaching, at one point, 81mph.

Then there was 'City of Truro's' record breaking run of the 9th May 1904 when some sources recorded the engine breaking the 100mph barrier when dropping down the Wellington Bank in Somerset pulling an express from Plymouth to Paddington.

When I later spoke of this to GJC in retirement, he recalled making it known to the top link drivers that he expected, 'them to push the Cities whenever possible, and safe to do so, to see how fast they might go!

He also kept copies of newspaper reports describing this event and an article by Charles Rous-Marten, the writer on all things to do with the railways, on whose evidence the claim for 100mph rests. In this he wrote that:

On one occasion, when special experimental tests were being made with an engine having 6 ft. 8in coupled wheels hauling a load of approximately 150 tons behind the tender down a gradient of 1 in 90, I personally recorded a rate of no less than 102.3 miles an hour for a single quarter-mile, which was covered in 8.8 seconds, exactly 100 miles an hour for half a mile which occupied 18 seconds, 96.7 miles an hour for a whole mile run in 37.2 seconds; five successive quarter-miles were run respectively in 10 seconds, 9.8 seconds, 9.4 seconds,

One of the most famous of the City Class engines, and, perhaps, one of the most distinguished GWR engines of all time. No. 3440 *City of Truro*, the 2,000th engine built at Swindon, waits with her crew, as interested in the photographer as he is with them. This class had comparatively short lives with all being withdrawn by 1931. *Truro* was the last to go, in her case into preservation, undoubtedly saved by events on 9 May 1904 when the engine is believed to have reached 100mph, the first steam locomotive to do so, when pulling the Ocean Mail from Plymouth to Paddington. (Author)

9.2 seconds and 8.8 seconds. This I have reason to believe to be the highest railway speed ever authentically recorded. I need hardly add that the observations were made with the utmost possible care, and with the advantage of previous knowledge that the experiment was to be made, consequently without the disadvantage of unpreparedness that usually attaches itself to speed observations made in a merely casual way in an ordinary passenger train. The performance was certainly an epoch-making one. In a previous trial with another engine of the same class, a maximum of 95.6 miles an hour was reached'.

Other 'evidence' later emerged of this gallant effort and, in due course, the company made much of the achievement in its adverts.

Fine words indeed and an interesting comment on an important strand of Churchward's work, in the years before he succeeded Dean. During this period, he was clearly thinking deeply about the future and developing then testing various options before deciding which he would take forward and apply more broadly. The 4-4-0 engines seemed to have been the ideal vehicles on which to rehearse these ideas and he didn't stop working on them when finally promoted to the top job – they remained an ideal test bed for many things he was considering.

However, there is one other interesting development during the last years of Dean's time in office to consider. This concerned experiments with both 2-6-0 and 4-6-0 type engines. In some historians' eyes these projects were simply a brief distraction from the main thrust of locomotive development at Swindon and so play little or no part in Dean and Churchward's modernisation plans. This is a view to which Kenneth Cook, in his 1950 paper, seems to suscribe; neither type barely getting a mention. But there are others who see them as a part of this evolutionary process, though, perhaps, of lesser importance than the 4-4-0s and the soon to arrive Saint Class of 4-6-0s. So, where might the truth lie?

By the time designers at Swindon began getting to grips with the idea of a 4-6-0 type locomotive, the concept had already been widely adopted in the USA; the first, built by the Norris Locomotive Works for the Philadelphia and Reading Railroad in 1847. After that, demand for the type continued to grow across North America and from here seems to have spread to Europe,

The first GWR 4-6-0 locomotive, number 36, was a two-cylinder engine built in 1896 specifically to pull heavy freight trains through the Severn Tunnel. However, it didn't perform as well as expected and was then, it appears, treated by Churchward simply as an experimental engine and tested as such until its demise in 1905. (DN)

with the first in Britain, the Jones Goods Class, developed for the Highland Railway by Sharp, Stewart & Co, appearing in 1894. Being keen observers of engineering developments around the world, Dean and Churchward would have seen what was happening in other countries and considered how the lessons being learnt elsewhere might be applied to the GWR. Bearing in mind the way that 4-6-0s would become the cornerstone of all that happened on the GWR for decades to come, it is an inescapable conclusion that two prototype engines, numbers 36 and 2601 that appeared in 1894 and 1899 respectively were, indeed, the forerunners of what came later, whether successful or not.

Number 36 was, some historians believe, built to a design typical of William Dean's later years and included the only large boiler entirely conceived by him. If true, the assumption must be that Churchward's role in its development was a small one at best. This is a view given some credibility by the fact that he didn't become Dean's Chief Assistant until 1897 and was likely to have been entirely engrossed by his duties as Works Manager, perhaps even to the exclusion of all other things. Nevertheless, he would have overseen its construction which would have allowed him to assess the design and suggest modifications if he thought them necessary.

The engine was built to a specification that called for a freight locomotive capable of working the heaviest coal trains from South Wales to Swindon through the Severn Tunnel without the added cost that came with double-heading. To do this, the engine was constructed with double frames reaching down over the 4ft 7½in coupled wheels, ahead of which was an inside frame bogie. Drive was provided through two-cylinders measuring 20x24in, with steam generated by a particularly long boiler, producing 165psi, and a raised round-topped, wide firebox atop. The boiler was fitted with a French designed Serve internally rifled tubes which were thought to create more effective evaporation of water so allowing more effective heat transfer. The only trouble with

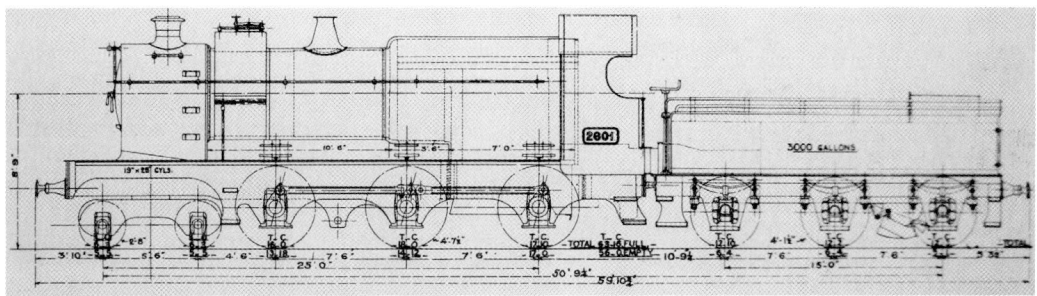

In 1899 Dean and Churchward's engine No. 2601, their second prototype 4-6-0 locomotive (above and below – in diagram form and in reality) appeared, taking the experiment a step further presumably to test the 4-6-0 concept more fully. However, its performance was disappointing and its solid crank axles proving to be prone to cracking. (DN)

this solution was its higher initial production costs and a more expensive maintenance regime to keep it in good order. To make matters worse, in service the Serve tubes were soon found to shorten the life of the boiler and, more critically, didn't produce the desired level of performance.

It has been suggested that the engine was not employed full-time on the duties for which she was designed, perhaps due to the boiler's fragility. So, Churchward, now Chief Assistant, chose to keep it close by at Swindon, reduce its workload and simply regard the engine as an experiment from which lessons might be learnt. In this state it remained in service and was finally withdrawn in 1905 having only completed 171,428 miles.

When it came to Dean's next 4-6-0 experiment in 1899, it is likely that Churchward played a more active role in its development and, in doing so, sought to include the lessons learnt when building No. 36. And in due course it appeared with two-cylinders, though slightly smaller at 19 x 24in, outside frames similar to No. 36 and wheels of the same size. However, this time a shorter boiler, without Serve tubes, producing 180psi coupled to a combustion chamber and wide Belpaire firebox, was attached instead. On this occasion a large saddle-shaped sandbox was fitted over the first ring of the boiler immediately behind the smokebox, and thus gave the engine, in Kenneth Cook's words, 'a very odd appearance, although the engine was rather ugly already'.

With the Boer War still raging in South Africa, when this engine was completed, some unnamed wag at Swindon captured the feelings of the age and applied the nickname Kruger to 2601 – Paul Kruger, the Boer leader, being a despised figure at the time. And when, three years later, a 2-6-0 version was developed it attracted the name *Mrs Kruger*, according to Harold Holcroft who joined the GWR as an apprentice at the Stafford Road Works in 1898, then became a draughtsman at Swindon in 1906. In so doing he became a key witness to the way Churchward pursued his locomotive policy and also the man's nature and way of working.

It is unclear why it was decided to build a 2-6-0 version of the Kruger, numbered 2602, in 1901, except that Churchward, having succeeded Dean, wished to experiment with this alternative wheel configuration and compare these two types of engine. However, by this time his thoughts on 4-6-0s designs had begun to take a large step forward, though in a different direction. In this he was helped by No. 2601 not being as successful as some had hoped it would be. Its overall performance was thought poor and there was the added problem that the engine's solid crank axles were prone to cracking, plus the combustion chamber was found to cause problems. With little to be gained in trying to correct these shortcomings, the engine's fate was sealed. Meanwhile, Churchward's attention had turned towards his own first true 4-6-0 design and the birth of his Saint Class was not long in coming.

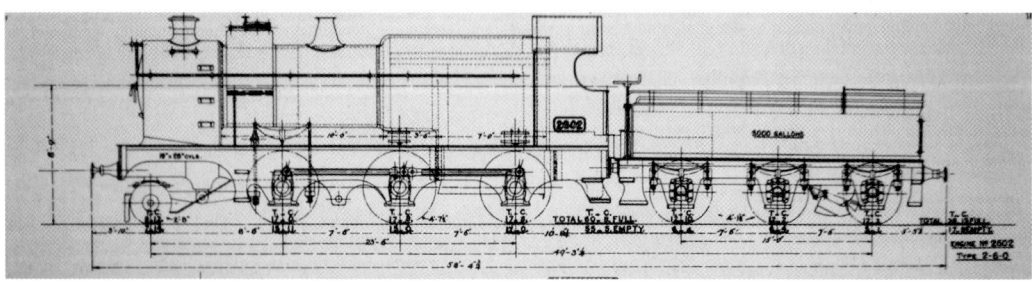

The 2-6-0 Mrs Krugers, as they became known in some quarters, simply followed the pattern of the 4-6-0 with a pony truck rather than a four-wheeled bogie and nine were built between 1901 and 1903. With such a large number for testing purposes and use it must have been hoped that the expenditure and effort might have proved worthwhile. Sadly, this proved not to be the case and all were withdrawn from service by 1906. Churchward did not lose sight of the 2-6-0's potential benefits and in 1911 introduced his 4300 Class mixed traffic engine, of which 342 would be built by 1932. (Above) An early diagram showing the 2-6-0s general layout. (DN)

In looks, at least, the Aberdare Class, that first appeared in 1900, seemed to be a far more balanced design that the Krugers. But their superiority ran much deeper than that and they simply proved to be far better, more cost-effective performers in the role for which they were designed. (DN)

The lone 2-6-0 engine carried on being tested and, presumably, proved sufficiently successful to justify building eight more by 1903. But as time went on, they too presented problems and were all summarily withdrawn in 1906, their number being replaced by ten new two-cylinder Aberdare Class 2-6-0 engines. These were a freight version of two proven classes of 4-4-0s – the 3300 Bulldogs and 4100 Badmintons, so came with a good pedigree. The prototype entered service in 1900 and soon proved to be far more successful in service than the Mrs Krugers. As a result, by 1907, eighty more had been built with some remaining operational until in 1949 having successfully served the company in peace and during two arduous world wars.

In many ways the Krugers and the Aberdares were a brave attempt by Dean and Churchward to find a better way of meeting the GWR's growing demand for bigger, stronger locomotives as traffic volumes increased. The Aberdares were chosen but this didn't mean that development work on the Krugers was wasted. Nothing is certain in engineering and speculation is something forward thinking companies must embrace. So the need to experiment, at some stage, is unavoidable. However, it takes a very astute manager to know when the return is unlikely to justify the outlay and the time has come to move on. So, the Krugers were tried and tested, in the process adding something to the accumulation of knowledge so important to a scientist's work. And these engines, in fulfilling this role, played an important part, even though rejected.

So, 1902 arrived and an inevitable promotion followed, the 71-year-old Dean heading into a well-earned retirement. For Churchward it must have seemed to have been a long time coming, but the years as Chief Assistant hadn't been wasted. During that time, he had been able to think deeply about the future, consider and test various ideas and reach certain conclusions about locomotive design in particular. And all the time he would have had, in William Dean, the wise council of a giant of the industry, even one who latterly seems to have been in decline due to

By the time Dean departed in 1902, much of the GWR's locomotive fleet was comparatively new, especially the 4-4-0s and his 0-6-0 goods engines, but to the casual observer they all looked distinctly Victorian in style. With a new monarch heralding in the Edwardian era that emphasized style and modernism, change was in the air – a mood best captured by Churchward and his designers in their post-Dean creative surge of work. However, there was still much to marvel at the efforts of those who preceded him, as shown here. (Above) The beautifully balanced lines of the 3300 Bulldog Class 4-4-0 No. 3393 *Australia* are captured in this photograph taken in about 1905 when the engine paused at Oxford. This locomotive appeared in 1904 five years after the first of the class was built at Swindon. (Below) The 1899/00 built 4-4-0 Bulldog No. 3326, *Laira*, making light work of its load (said to be the service from Newcastle to Bournemouth) (Opposite) An unidentified Dean 2301 Class 0-6-0 goods engine captured here on duty at Dawlish. These engines found favour with Churchward and the 260 built between 1893 and 1899 saw long service with the GWR, some lasting into the late 1950s. (Author's collection)

poor health. Churchward had been his student, his draughtsman then one of his senior managers since 1877 so the influence on the younger man had been long term and, generally, of the most positive kind.

So what did Churchward carry forward with him, in terms of locomotive design, when he walked the short distance from his old to his new office at Swindon to take sole charge of all that happened there? The list was a long and varied one, but within its core lay the main ingredients of what would result in a group of engines that would serve the company well for the next sixty years.

To achieve this Churchward, with Dean, had experimented with tapered, round topped and domeless boilers, ever higher boiler pressures, parallel barrels and varying lengths of barrel, Belpaire fireboxes, various tube configurations, superheating and much more. Most of these developments he was then able to test, post 1894, on the Dean 4-4-0 standard gauge engines and then with the Krugers. The results were carefully analysed, choices made and proven ideas then woven into a plan that would see a new set of standard, free steaming boilers introduced to power a fleet of what he hoped would be standard class locomotives. And from the first this appears to have been one of Churchward's key aims, having recognised that such a fleet would be easier and more cost effective to build, run and maintain than a plethora of non-standard designs. Not all agreed with him, preferring a 'horses for courses' type approach, Nigel Gresley amongst them. But Churchward was adamant and this remained the GWR's primary direction of travel for many years to come, though not to the exclusion of other options when the need arose; Churchward was far too clever a man to restrict himself by being too dogmatic or myopic in outlook or approach when it came to design.

The boilers and their associated parts, of course, were not all that mattered in Churchward's plans for the future. There was much else besides to be considered as his ideas on standardisation became firmer – types of brakes and axleboxes, various wheel configurations, lubrication, the type of bogies to be used, cylinder numbers and dimensions, inside and outside framing, the requirement for trailing wheels, the dimension of piston valves and bearing surfaces and so on.

Type	2-8-0	4-6-0	4-6-0	2-6-2T	4-4-2T	4-4-0
Engine No.	97	—	98	99	2221	3473
Date of first engine	June 1903	—	March 1903	Sept. 1903	Dec. 1905	May 1904
Boiler:—						
Length of barrel	15 ft. 0 in.	15 ft. 0 in.	15 ft. 0 in.	11 ft. 2 in.	11 ft. 2 in.	11 ft. 2 in.
Diameter of barrel	5 ft. 0 in.	5 ft. 0 in.	5 ft. 0 in.	5 ft. 0 in.	5 ft. 0 in.	5 ft. 0 in.
Length of firebox	9 ft. 0 in.	9 ft. 0 in.	9 ft. 0 in.	8 ft. 0 in.	8 ft. 0 in.	8 ft. 0 in.
Length of connecting rods	10 ft. 8½ in.	10 ft. 8½ in.	10 ft. 8½ in.	6 ft. 10½ in	6 ft. 10½ in	6 ft. 10½ in
Wheels:—						
Diameter of pony or bogie	3 ft. 3 in.	3 ft. 3 in.	3 ft. 3 in.	3 ft. 3 in.	3 ft. 3 in.	3 ft. 3 in.
Diameter of Coupled	4 ft. 7½ in.	5 ft. 8 in.	6 ft. 8½ in.	5 ft. 8 in.	6 ft. 8½ in	6 ft. 8½ in.
Diameter of Radial	—	—	—	3 ft. 3 in.	3 ft. 3 in.	—
Cylinders, one pattern for all types	18 in. diameter × 30 in. stroke with 8½ in. diameter piston valves					

When undertaking research for his 1950 paper, Kenneth Cook, who, as Churchward's pupil and then his successor when becoming Mechanical and Electrical Engineer at Swindon in 1950, was able to access all Churchward's papers. This allowed him to use important, primary source documents when assessing his leader's work. As part of this, Cook uncovered material that confirmed that his standardisation plans were well advanced by 1901 and did not begin when promoted in 1902, as one might have expected. The chart above, which Cook added to his paper, makes clear that there were six planned standard engines and outlines their basic specification. To this Cook has added dates when all but one of these engines appeared. (KC/ILocoE)

In fact, no part of the engines or tenders was not subjected to his analytical, astute gaze. And, as Kenneth Cook discovered, his ideas were well advanced even before he took the top job:

> The conception of the Churchward series of main line engines appears upon a drawing board dated January 1901. This is a very interesting document which provides the foundation for a comprehensive locomotive development plan, and it is amazing to ponder the extent to which later developments fitted into the general picture. This drawing outlined six projected engines, indicated common components and comprised the following types as shown in the diagram produced here.

When preparing for his presentation he added a scribbled note to his paper which on the day he did not use, but is interesting none the less:

> In time, and when Locomotive Superintendent, the list of standard classes would grow to eleven, the commonality of components increasing as did the number of standard boilers. To my mind he probably created too many variants of locomotives and boilers to truly reflect a minimalist standardisation suggesting that he too found this too restrictive or impractical at times. Nevertheless, his motives for pursing a standardisation programme were well-considered and ultimately sound.

Chapter 4

A Commanding Presence

In May 1902, at the age of 45, Churchward finally replaced William Dean in the LCWS post at Swindon, after twenty-nine years of careful preparation. However, it is quite likely that he had probably taken on the role much earlier as Dean's health began to decline. Either way, by 1902, he was a much respected figure in the railway industry and in Wiltshire's civic life, having become a councillor then, in 1900, Mayor. He had also been elected a member, then Councillor, of the prestigious Institutions of Mechanical Engineers (in 1894) and Civil Engineers (1897) And it was through these professional bodies that he began to give voice to his developing ideas on locomotive design and his wider interest in scientific matters.

Perhaps his most notable contribution came in 1906 when presenting a paper entitled 'Large Locomotive Boilers' to fellow members of the IMechE. His reason for writing were made clear in a meeting in London when he admitted that it was composed 'some time ago and as a means of promoting discussion'. However, in doing so, he has bequeathed us a unique insight into the way he thought and the way he managed change. Sadly, he didn't feel moved to write an autobiography or even a more detailed account describing the way he came to the conclusions

Churchward photographed when reaching the peak of his powers as an engineer and senior manager. (DN)

he did. So his 1906 paper is one of the few opportunities we have to see into his mind and understand how it worked. Having begun with words about the modern steam locomotive being 'principally a question of boiler', he then went on to underpin this declaration with a much wider evaluation of the key elements involved:

> The increase in the size of boilers and in the pressures carried, which has taken place during the last few years, has necessitated the reconsideration of the principles of design which had been worked out and settled during many years' experience with comparatively small boilers carrying low pressures. The higher temperatures incidental to the higher pressures have required the provision of much more liberal water-spaces and better provision for circulation. Locomotive engineers have now, apparently, settled down to the use of one of two types of boiler for very large engines, the wide firebox extending over the frames and wheels, and the long narrow box sloping over the axles behind the main drivers.

On the back of being home to the GWR's Works, Swindon had grown large on the business and employment it generated. By 1902, when Churchward became master of this giant concern, the Works employed more than 12,000 men and women of many trades, all drawn to the GWR as an employer of considerable standing and one that was continuing to grow. The three photographs here were all taken in the first few years of the twentieth century. The upper two pictures show a bustling, tram served town, while the lower picture captures exterior views of the Works as its employees make their way to and from work. (DN)

Institution of Mechanical Engineers.
ESTABLISHED 1847.

PROPOSAL OF MEMBER OR ASSOCIATE.

Name in full: *George Jackson Churchward*

Designation or Occupation: *Ass^t. Manager, G.W.R. Carriage Wks*

Business Address: *G. W. Ry Works Swindon*

being *37* years of age,* and being desirous of admission into the INSTITUTION OF MECHANICAL ENGINEERS, we the undersigned proposer and seconder from our *personal knowledge*, and we the three other signers from trustworthy information, propose and recommend him as a proper person to become a *Member* thereof. (*Member or Associate* to be inserted by the Proposer.)

Witness our hands, this *14th* day of *Mch* 1894.

FIVE Members' Signatures are required for the proposal of a Member or an Associate.

Proposed from *personal knowledge* by † *Wm Dean*
(See Note.)

Seconded from *personal knowledge* by *James Holden*

Supported from trustworthy information by: *Saml. W. Johnson.* / *W Adams* / *Patrick Stirling*

Signature of Candidate: *George Jackson Churchward*

Above and overleaf: By the time Churchward had succeeded William Dean in 1902 he was already a widely recognised figure in Britain's railway industry and, in due course, his reputation would spread beyond the confines of his country. To get some idea of the respect in which he was held it is fascinating to view his application for membership of the Institution of Mechanical Engineers in 1894. William Dean, as one would expect, proposed his assistant, but it is seconded by a veritable who's who of other leading railway engineers of the time – James Holden, Locomotive Superintendent of the Great Eastern Railway, Patrick Stirling, retired Locomotive Superintendent of the Great Northern Railway, William Adams Locomotive Superintendent of the London and South Western Railway and Samuel Waite Johnson Locomotive Superintendent of the Midland Railway. (IMechE)

Mr George Jackson Churchward was articled for 6 years to Mr Jno Wright, Loco. Carr. & Wagon Supt. of the South Devon, Cornwall & West Cornwall Rlys. Served from 28th July '73 to 1st Feby '76 and completed his pupilage 27th July '77 under Mr Jos. Armstrong, late, & Mr W. Dean present, Chief Loco. Carr. & Wagon Supt. of the G.W.Ry. Was subsequently engaged in the Drawing Office at Swindon upon the design of Plant in connection with the construction of the Severn Tunnel &c &c. From April 1882 to Dec: 1882 was employed as Inspecting Engineer, and in Dec: 1882 was appointed Chief Asst. Manager of the Carriage Works of the Great Western Railway at Swindon, which position he still holds, having under his supervision 1950 hands.

His age is 37.

Signature of Proposer ......

Example of the Information desired.

Mr. A. B. served his time from 18.... to 18.... in the................Works of C. D. at................;
was then engaged as Draughtsman from 18.... to 18.... in the................Works of E. F. at................;
superintended from 18.... to 18.... the execution of................at................;
was Assistant Manager from 18.... to 18.... in the................Works of G. H. at................;
and has been from 18.... Partner in ....His age is ....

Institution of Mechanical Engineers, 10 Victoria Street, Westminster, S.W.

A Commanding Presence

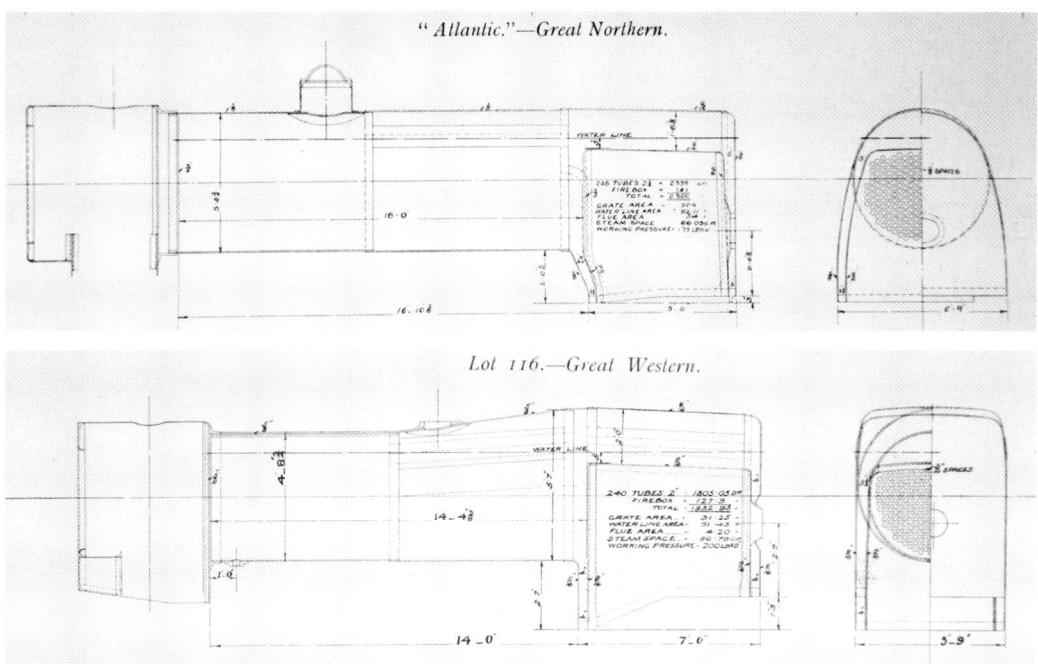

In presenting his paper 'Large Locomotive Boilers' to the IMechE in 1906, Churchward drew some comparisons with the designs he was pursuing as the GWR's Locomotive Superintendent with other companies in Britain and the United States. Two examples showing the way different designers met the need for larger, more powerful boilers are shown here. (Top) In 1898, Henry Alfred Ivatt, Locomotive Superintendent of the Great Northern Railway, introduced his C1 Class Atlantics with small boilers, then in 1902 his version with a much large boiler appeared. It is this development that caught Churchward's eye, especially when it became known that these engines could travel up to 90mph and pull 500 ton plus loads. (Above) When speaking in 1906 Churchward talked of his new boiler then being designed and its a distinctive tapered shape, a practice he had rehearsed fairly often with the GWR's 4-4-0s. (Author's collection)

In Great Britain the contracted loading-gauge prohibits the use of the wide firebox type over wheels larger than 4ft 6inches diameter, so that it is not being used so generally as in America where it has become practically universal. In America the great power of engines now employed renders the wide firebox a necessity, but in Great Britain, where the coal burnt per mile is very much less, few boilers of this kind have been built. On the Great Northern Railway Mr Henry Ivatt has provided his fine Atlantic Class with wide fireboxes and they are undoubtedly very successful. On the North Eastern Railway Mr Wilson Worsdell has also designed a wide box for the boiler of his new Atlantic type. Mr James Holden's boiler, on the heavy suburban engines for the Great Eastern is the largest of the type yet built in this country. For the Great Western Mr Dean designed and built some goods engines with wide fireboxes, and I have since designed, but not yet built, a modified form of the same type to be carried over 4ft 6inches wheels.

Much more experience has been gained with the wide box in America than in this country and, so far as I can ascertain, it has been found there that the poorer coals in larger quantities can be burnt with much greater facility and economy in this type than in the narrow pattern. This advantage is offset to some extent by the fact that, when standing, there is considerable waste in the wide grates as compared with the narrow, and this is, of course, serious when goods trains are kept standing about, as is often the case. This disadvantage has been found on the Great Western, but no doubt careful design and fitting of ashpans will keep this waste within bounds.

Having broadly outlined the position of boiler development Churchward then went on to highlight some of the issues that he thought crucial, addressing them in fairly simplistic terms, as good communicators do, beginning with the performance of boiler tubes:

> A much more serious trouble has been found in the leaking of tubes in these boilers. This seems to be quite general, and the Master Mechanics' Association has a committee specially investigating this question with a view to finding a remedy. All methods of tube making have been tried, and also much wider spacing, even up to I inch, without curing the trouble.
>
> The reduction of the depth of the fire-box, in order to get a long box sloping over the trailing wheels of coupled engines, certainly increased the trouble from leakage of stays, but the alternative of a wide fire-box entails a much heavier engine for most types, and then apparently tube trouble is then increased. The wide fire-box evidently requires a higher standard of skill in the fireman, for unless the grate is kept well and evenly covered, there is a tendency to have an excess of air, reducing efficiency and increasing tube trouble.
>
> With modern high pressures the temperature of evaporation is so much increased that the provision for circulation, which was sufficient for the lower pressures formerly used, is doubtless insufficient. Boilers in which this provision has been made have shown a very marked reduction in tube and stay troubles.
>
> It is probable that in the wider boxes the main mass of the fire being so much nearer the tube-plate will have a bad effect on the tubes, as the intensity of the temperature at the tube-plate must necessarily be increased. The extra width of the box has enabled the tubes to be put too near the sides of the barrel. When this is done, the water feed up to the spaces between the tubes near the back tube-plate has to be drawn almost entirely from the front of

As part of his presentation to the IMechE Churchward only briefly referred to his own efforts at producing new, more efficient boilers. However, by 1906 when he spoke much progress had already been made in constructing a range of new standard boilers. This had been achieved with the help of his Chief Assistant, Frederick Wright, and the man chosen to replace him as Chief Draughtsman in 1896, H.C. King, who remained in this post until 1902. He was then succeeded by F.N. Snell and then George Burrows in 1905. To help illustrate the development work undertaken at Swindon, Churchward presented several examples in drawing form, but only included a single photograph – the Standard No. 1 boiler shown above. Perhaps he was simply being modest or may have been trying to avoid any accusation that Swindon was far ahead of the opposition in these matters, so stifling the open debate he hoped to encourage. Either way, it is recorded that both William Stanier and Nigel Gresley, by then members of the Institution, were deeply influenced by all Churchward was doing and saying. (IMechE)

the barrel, and it is possible that in some cases the space left for this purpose is inadequate. It will probably be found that neglect of this consideration is the cause of three-fourths of tube trouble.

At this point Churchward introduced a drawing of the new boiler he was then developing and referred to in the introduction of his paper. This solution, he asserted, 'provides for this upward

Swindon Works at about the time Churchward took command in 1902. This sprawling mass of workshops, covering an ever increasing acreage of land north of the station, dominated the town ensuring that the company's influence spread beyond its geographic boundaries. To help gauge the size of the task the Works undertook in the first half of the twentieth century, one only has to point to the number of steam locomotives the company had built and were still maintaining in 1948. There were 3,857 in all, to which could be added 8,368 carriages and other rolling stock. These three pictures purely focus on the locomotives. (DN)

circulation near the back tube-plate by leaving a space between the tubes and barrel from top to bottom of a sectional area equal to the combined area of the vertical spaces between the tubes at all points....this is enough to prevent the necessary feed of water down the spaces of the fire-box that causes stay trouble as well as tube-trouble.'

He then moved on to the question of flow of water around the boiler and demonstrated how the improvements he and his team had made greatly improved performance. In so doing he touched on the level of research and experimentation they had undertaken in identifying problems and seeking solutions:

> By putting the clack-box for both injectors under the boiler barrel and providing an internal nozzle directing the feed-back towards the fire-box, considerable assistance is probably given in feeding 'solid' water back to the fire-box and the hottest part of the tubes. It is generally supposed that the circulation in a locomotive boiler proceeds along the bottom of the barrel from the front end down to the fire-box front and up the sides and back of the fire-box. Two or three years ago I fitted a number of vanes in a boiler with spindles passing through lightly packed glands to the outside, with indicators to show the actual direction of the flow of water.
>
> Observations showed that the circulation was generally as stated above, but a little alteration of the firing had the effect of materially changing the direction of the currents and of completely reversing them. These experiments suggested the desirability of bringing in a circulating pipe from the front of the barrel, bifurcated (divided) to each side of the fire-box at the foundation ring. However, the consideration of the possible danger from an outside pipe open to the boiler caused the experiments to be abandoned. This experiment has since been repeated in America, and it is reported that a great reduction of the trouble with the side sheets resulted."

Moving on from this issue Churchward then turned to the question of 'the gradual extension of the practice of making the top of the fire-box and casing flat instead of round'. Here again he refers to the experience he'd gained when designing and building locomotives:

> On the Great Western Railway less trouble has been experienced with the flat-top fire-box than with the round-top, although no sling-stays of any kind are used. The flat-top has the important advantage of increasing the area of water line at the hottest part of the boiler and so materially contributes to the reduction of foaming. This, combined with the coned connection to the barrel, has enabled the dome, always a source of weakness, to be entirely dispensed with and drier steam obtained. Some years ago I made an experiment to settle this much disputed point.
>
> Two identical engines and boilers were taken, one having a dome in the usual position on the barrel, the other having no dome, the steam being taken by a pipe from the top of the flat-box fire-box casing. The engine without the dome proved to be decidedly freer from priming than the other. The liberal dimension of 2 feet between the top of the fire-box and the inside of the casing no doubt contributed to this satisfactory result....On consideration of the great intensity of temperature at the fire-box plate, as compared to that at the smoke-box plate, the advantage of this arrangement is obvious.

More analysis followed concerning fire-box stays and water-tubes in fire-boxes, before moving on to the key issues of superheating and the essential business of correctly matching wheels and cylinder sizes to different types of boilers to achieve the optimum overall performance:

TABLE 1

Fig. Plates 19–32.	Engine.	Type.	Cylinders.	Fig. Plates 19–32.	Coupled Wheels.	Weight. On Coupled Wheels.	Weight. Total of Engine.	Total Heating Surface.
					Diameter. ft. ins.	Tons. Cwts.	Tons. Cwts.	Square feet.
1	Mallet Compound—Baltimore and Ohio	0–12–0 Articulated	20 } 32 } ×32	1	4 8	144 5	144 5	5,600
2	Lake Shore and Michigan Southern	2–6–2	20½ ×28	2	6 8	58 0	77 18	3,343
3	"Decapod"—Great Eastern	0–10–0 / T	18½ ×24	3	4 6	80 0	80 0	3,010
4	Baldwin Compound—Atchison-Topeka and Santa Fé	2–10–2	19 } 32 } ×32	4	4 9	104 15	128 0	4,796
5	Cole 4 Cyl. Compound—New York Central and Hudson River	4–4–2	15½ } 26 } ×26	5	6 7	49 0	89 0	3,446
6	Compound—Colorado and Southern	2–8–0	16 } 28 } ×32	6	4 9	79 8	90 8	2,966
7	Chicago and Alton	4–6–2	22 ×28	7	6 5	60 6	99 0	3,053
8	"Atlantic"—Great Northern	4–4–2	19 ×24	8	6 7½	36 0	65 10	2,500
9	Baldwin 4 Cylinder Compound—Chicago, Burlington and Quincy	4–4–2	15 } 25 } ×26	9	6 6	41 8	87 14	3,217
10	Great Western	2–6–0	19 ×28	10	4 7½	51 16	60 8	1,933
11	Do. Do.	4–6–0	20 ×24	11	4 7½	47 4	59 10	1,518 Distributing 2,388 Absorbing (Serve Tubes)
12	North Eastern	4–4–2	20 ×28	12	6 10	39 0	72 0	2,456
13	Do. Do.	4–6–0	20 ×26	13	6 8½	34 17	67 2	1,769
14	Great Western	4–4–2 4–6–0 2–8–0	18 ×30 18 ×30 18 ×30	14	6 8½ 6 8½ 4 7½	39 0 54 4 61 18	70 10 70 4 68 6	— 2,143 —
15	New De Glehn Compound—Great Western	4–4–2	$14\frac{3}{16}$ } $23\frac{5}{8}$ } ×$25\frac{3}{16}$	15	6 8½	39 0	73 6	1,617 Distributing 2,756 Absorbing (Serve Tubes)
16	"La France"—Great Western	4–4–2	$13\frac{3}{8}$ } $22\frac{1}{16}$ } ×$25\frac{3}{16}$	16	6 8½	33 7	64 13	1,446 Distributing 2,456 Absorbing (Serve Tubes)
17	Chicago, Burlington and Quincy	—	—	17	—	—	—	1,768
18	Illinois Central	—	—	18	—	—	—	2,461
19	Canadian Pacific	2–6–2	20 ×26	19	5 9	56 12	73 8	2,425
20	Great Eastern	4–4–0 0–6–0	19 ×26 19 ×26	20	7 0 4 11	33 19 43 14	51 13½ 43 14	1,630
21	London and North Western	4–4–0	15 } 20½ } ×24	21	7 0	37 0	57 12	1,508
22	Midland	0–6–0	18 ×26	22	5 3	43 16	43 16	1,403
23	Compound—Midland	4–4–0	19 } 21 } ×26	23	7 0	38 3	58 9	1,598 outside plain tubes
24	North Eastern	4–4–0	19 ×26	24	6 10	35 5	51 14	1,413
25	"Cawdor"—Great Western	4–4 0	18 ×26	25	6 8½	35 10	56 14	1,934
26	Great Western	4–4–0 4–4–0	18 ×30 18 ×26	26	6 8½ 6 8½	34 6 36 2	55 6 55 6	1,818
27	Water tube—London and South Western	4–4–0	19 ×26	27	6 7	37 2	53 19	1,550
—	Do. Do.	4–6–0	4 (16×24)	—	6 0	51 10	73 0	2,727

In summarising the various messages imparted in his 1906 presentation, Churchward produced this table. First of all, his intention had been to demonstrate how boiler design had advanced and with it an understanding of the fine balances that had to be achieved between boiler capacity, cylinder size and the diameter of an engine's driving wheels to produce the most effective and economical solution. His second objective was more subliminal in nature. He was, in effect, saying that we study very closely any advances made in design and absorb these lessons when we think it appropriate, taking what we observe, seeking to improve upon it where necessary or invent something new. (IMechE)

The employment of a superheater is having an extended trial in Germany and Canada. This affords the prospect of obtaining the same efficiency by the use of, say, 175lbs pressure, as by employing the pressures of, say, 200lbs to 225lbs. This, no doubt, offers some prospect of success, and it is attractive from the fact that the alternative of compounding necessitates the use of higher pressures, and consequently presents no hope of relief from boiler troubles.

The Great Western Railway are fitting one of their Standard No. 1 boilers with the Schmidt arrangement of superheater, with a view to seeing what advantage can be gained with the 'simple' engine. Formerly the power of a locomotive was estimated from the capacity of its cylinders and this led, occasionally, to the use of cylinders of such dimensions that the boilers provided were not capable of generating sufficient steam to enable them to be worked at their maximum economical power for any length of run. Today this is changed, and the first consideration is the capacity of the boiler.

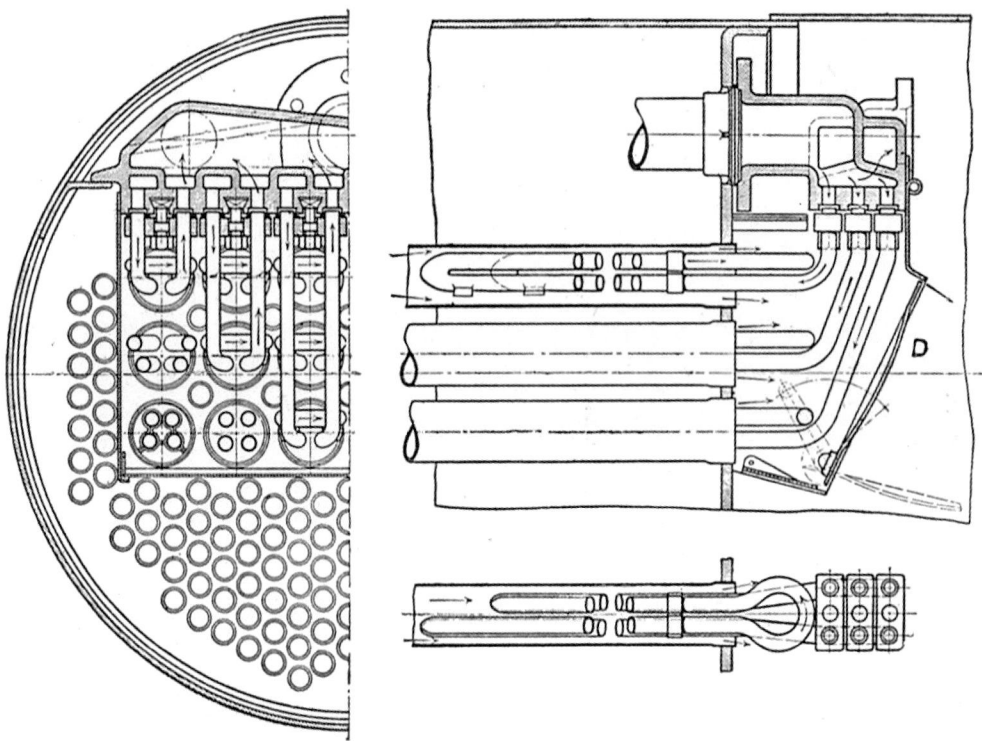

Churchward carefully observed work being undertaken in Germany where Wilhelm Schmidt had, by about 1890, developed a superheater for use in steam locomotives and steamships. Schmidt had invented a heater which, it was estimated, could raise the thermal efficiency of an engine by as much as 50 per cent. Later on, and in co-operation with Robert Garbe, Chief Engineer of the Berlin Division of the Prussian State Railway, he produced an effective superheater and a piston valve arrangement which then went on to be selected by that company, then soon found favour in the work of other engineers such as Churchward. (IMechE)

An examination of the ratios will show how much more heating surface is now being provided for a given area of cylinder than used to be considered necessary. The higher pressures now common have undoubtedly produced much more efficient locomotives in respect of handling power and coal consumption. This improvement has been very marked with every increment of pressure, right up to 227lbs carried by the de Glehn compounds. These have been the most successful compounds, and the high pressures carried is, no doubt, an important factor in this.

By employing 225lb per sq inch in the 'simple' engine, and making the necessary improvements in the steam distribution, enabling higher cut-offs to be used, corresponding improvements in efficiency and economy of fuel have been obtained. A great increase in the drawbar pull at high speed has also resulted.

Of course, the price for these improvements has to be paid in the matter of fire-box repairs and renewals, but it is probably better to submit to this expense than to employ the very much heavier and more-costly machines which would be necessary to give the same hauling power at high speed.

To a certain extent, by the time Churchward presented this paper his own work had moved on a pace. The need for a degree of secrecy in such a competitive commercial world, even when the audience was made up of fellow members of the IMechE, remained, which is probably why he chose not to update a paper by then already four or five years old. It served the purpose for which it was intended – to spark debate – but the information it imparted had already, for the most part, become a matter of public record. His Chairman and General Manager would not have wished it otherwise, but by 1906 his reputation was so well-established that he could have taken some issues further if he'd thought it appropriate. At root, though, he was an astute businessman who knew when to hold back or when let go. And so he gathered around him at Swindon many like-minded men who were able to do his bidding in a dynamic and reasoned way, but at the same time he encouraged them to display a creative independence that would complement their leader's skills. So, it shouldn't be lost on anyone that Churchward was a good judge of character, a motivator and an astute leader, which all who knew him and set pen to paper confirmed.

Perhaps most important was the way he was able to persuade his senior managers, based at the company's headquarters at Paddington, to accept his plans. This ensured he was able to get a fair hearing and, by doing so, could obtain permission to speculate and experiment where he saw fit. And with this strong support he was able to set his team to work on ideas long in the making, particularly when it came to locomotive design. First amongst them, as we have seen, was Frederick Wright, who after six years as Chief Draughtsman, succeeded Churchward as Works Manager, then, in 1903, took on the role of Chief Assistant. His place as Works Manger was taken by Henry Charles King, who between 1896 and 1902 had been Chief Draughtsman until replaced by F.N. Snell. And behind Snell came George Henry Burrows as the new CD in 1905, a post he would fill in the most crucial period of Churchward's reign and onwards into the stewardship of Collett.

Behind these main players came many talented junior engineers, whose recruitment and development suggests that Churchward was eager to surround himself with some of best minds available. In time this group came to be known as 'his bright young men' so important was their role in the organisation he led. One of them was Charles Collett, who was primarily a Production Engineer, and from this role was promoted to become Assistant Works Manager in 1900. From there he continued to rise under Churchward's guiding hand until eventually selected to succeed the great man himself in 1922. Then there was Frederick Hawksworth, who began his apprenticeship in 1898 and then became a draughtsman, another young engineer destined for greatness. Such was his skill that he was promoted in 1941, when Collett retired, to become the GWR's Chief Mechanical Engineer, as the Superintendent post had become during the Great War.

Others who rose to fame under Churchward included William Stanier, who having served his apprenticeship at Swindon became a draughtsman in 1900. He was then appointed Inspector of Materials – a post once held by Churchward himself – then in 1904 he went to London as Divisional Locomotive Superintendent. A return to Swindon followed in 1912 when appointed Assistant Works Manager, then eight years later he was promoted to Works Manager adding lustre to his growing reputation. Sadly, with Collett remaining CME for so long, his path to the top of the GWR was blocked resulting in his promotion to CME of the LMS and, perhaps, even greater fame. Beside him were two other noteworthy figures to recognise – G.H. Pearson and J.W. Cross – in each case Swindon apprentices who had both apparently worked as draughtsmen before becoming assistants to the Works Manager where their duties focussed on experimental tasks. Most unusually, these men, though working directly under Collett, ended up reporting on a number of issues to Churchward himself.

It is easy to forget when studying Churchward's work, that he did much more than develop the GWR's locomotive fleet in such a vibrant, energetic way. There was, of course, his day to day management of a department that spread far beyond the confines of Swindon with

Although the Works at Swindon was the heart of the company, its executive head was most definitely rooted in the GWR's Headquarters at Paddington where its senior managers sat and controlled all that happened, including allocating funds and then applying a tough audit regime to appease shareholders' eager for a return on their investments. Although Churchward astutely met their needs and pushed forward his ambitious plans it was often a difficult balance to achieve. It probably helped that, apart from being an exceptional engineer and leader, he appreciated the economic realities that prevailed and understood the politics of big business. These four pictures capture the world at Paddington in the early years of the twentieth century. (Above and below) Literally the corridor of power leading to the GWR's Boardroom itself. (Opposite above and opposite below) Despite the speed with which the railways were developing horse drawn transport was still the mainstay of most lives in Britain with few internal combustion vehicles around to disturb this ancient order. Rail transport for the masses was still very basic, but for those few who could afford it, as shown here, the standard was very much higher. (DN)

Mr. H. C. King, Wh.Sc., M.I.Mech

Some of Churchward's 'bright young men' as they became known – in this group of pictures we see them mostly later in life when fully established and in senior positions. (Above row left to right) Henry Charles King who became Works Manager at Swindon under Churchward and Charles Collett who began his career as a draughtsman, remaining so from 1893 to 1900. (Below row left to right) William Stanier who was apprenticed to William Dean and Churchward in 1892 and rose to become Collett's Principal Assistant then CME for the LMS. Frederick Hawksworth began his apprenticeship in 1898 and soon began specialising as a draughtsman in the Swindon Drawing Office rising to become Chief there in 1921 so being involved in all Churchward led locomotive design projects. With all the high profile developments in motive power it is easy to overlook the work being done to improve carriages and wagons. Here Frank Marillier, a specialist on the design and repair of rolling stock, since being apprenticed to the Bristol and Exeter Railway, reigned supreme more so following his promotion by Churchward to Carriage Works Superintendent a post he held, with some distinction until 1920. (Author's collection)

Mr. F. W. Hawksworth.

A Commanding Presence

Thought to be a photograph taken sometime between 1898 and 1900, of those Drawing Office staff at Swindon specialising in locomotive design. Identification of some of these men has proven difficult, but contemporary notes attached to this badly faded print gives us the following details (Left to right back row) ?, A.E. Leader,?,?,? and George Burrows. (Left to right front row seated) G H Pearson,?, F.N. Snell, Senior then Chief Draughtsman from 1902 to 1905 (sometimes listed as being Frederick Hawksworth who was only 15 years of age when this picture was taken. This is clearly a much older man), Charles Collett and ?. The young boy sitting at the front of the group is also unidentified. (DN)

its many workshops and thousands of employees of many trades. It was an empire that included workshops and sheds in Wales, London and across the West Country employing many thousands more to be added to his already large complement of staff at Swindon. But equally important was the substantial carriage and wagon task that was so essential to successful running of the network. Here he was lucky to have in Frank Marillier an expert designer and production engineer combined who could manage this task with great skill and presence of mind.

Having completed an apprenticeship with the Bristol and Exeter Railway, this Bristol born engineer was first employed as a draughtsman by the company. In 1876 he, like Churchward, joined the staff of the Drawing Office at Swindon, when the Bristol and Exeter and the SDR were absorbed by the GWR, it was then probably the case that being six years older, and an experienced draughtsman, he took the younger man under his wing, as he did later on with Stanier. So it is, perhaps, not surprising that when becoming LCWS, Churchward took the opportunity to employ Marillier's undoubted skills and promote him to be the Carriage and

Wagon Works Superintendent at Swindon, after a period managing the company's wagon works at Saltney. It was a move that neither man would come to regret.

All these men represented the tip of a very large iceberg that included many other, mostly now anonymous, people all striving to design and build ever more modern locomotives and rolling stock. Churchward sat at the top and the engines he led in building inevitably carried his name because he was the leader. But this recognition tends to run contrary to the realities of what was truly happening in the world of design as each new engine rolled off the production line. Here anyone amongst a large team of specialists could have influenced the development of a project in both large and small ways.

In this situation, who is to say where credit might truly lie and to whom the acclaim should rightfully go. Luckily in the autocratic world existing then, few if any would have questioned this way of working, preferring, one assumes, the satisfaction of a job well done and the private recognition of their leader. Nevertheless, in doing so, the actuality of who did what and when is forever clouded in mystery with only the occasional hint emerging, via memoirs or official documents, to provide some enlightenment. So when describing any creative process, it is important that we look more closely at the reality of team working and seek to highlight singular contributions from the plurality of a group whenever we can.

In terms of Churchward's personality and way of working we have an interesting assessment by Harold Holcroft which he recorded in response to Kenneth Cook's 1950 paper. Although tinged with a degree of hero-worship his words convey an honest appraisal of his leader:

> Mr King has eulogized Churchward's personality and depth of vision, but his words fail to convey the impression which he created by his presence. All those qualities which distinguish the true English gentleman were inherent in him. More than anything else it was as a tactful leader of men that he excelled. He collected around him by careful selection a technical staff of diversified talents, many of them having attained high academic distinctions. These he inspired with enthusiasm and drew from them their best, much as a conductor does from his well-trained orchestra.

Churchward (front row centre) as Superintendent surrounded by other senior GWR managers whose names, for the most part, have not been recorded on the very old print I was given. However, three have been listed as being Henry King (second from the left front row) who succeeded the new Superintendent as Locomotive Works Manager, Frederick Wright (third from the left front row), Churchward's Chief Assistant, and Frank Marillier (back row far right). (DN)

Churchward cast his net wide and had his scouts out to spot any likely recruits to fill any vacancies. Himself a Newton Abbot man, he did not restrict his catchment area to Swindon, but spread it over the entire GWR system. It was excellent team work that contributed so much to his success, and he saw to it that there was always a succession of suitable men climbing the steps to the highest positions and ready trained to step into a place when it fell vacant. The whole organisation ran like a well-oiled machine.

When some scheme was to be put in hand, Churchward would issue general directions to the Chief Draughtsman as to what he wanted done. As soon as the draughtsman detailed to carry out the scheme had something to show him, he would come along and settle himself on the high stool in front of the drawing board surrounded by the Chief and Assistant Chief Draughtsman, the chargeman of the particular gang (which would be constructing the item, probably the locomotive itself) and the draughtsman himself. He would then go into everything in detail. If any question of shop practice or manufacture arose the foreman concerned would be sent for to give his views, or an official of the Running Department would be summoned to express his opinion on questions of operation and maintenance. Churchward might say, 'What do other railways do in this matter, or the Americans or the French?' In a matter of a minute or two, bound volumes of technical publications or textbooks giving the information would be forthcoming from the Record Office through a highly efficient card indexing system.

His grasp and discernment were extraordinary, and when he viewed the subject in all its aspects and had heard what those about him had to say, Churchward would, by a process of logic and sound sense, come to a clear-cut decision. There was always an air of finality about it and one felt completely satisfied that the right solution had been reached. It was a positive delight to work for such a man. His method might be described in modern parlance as that of the working party, of which he was chairman.

This view of Churchward is shared by Cornishman William Pellow, who from 1912 to 1922 worked as a draughtsman at Swindon and came into regular contact with the Superintendent. I was privileged to meet him in the 1970s when he was retired and living near St Austell where he recalled that:

Churchward was a big man in looks and personality and stood out for this reason. He was large and heavy in build and wore tweed suits with a trilby hat always on his head, unlike most other senior managers who wore bowlers especially when touring the workshops to help stamp their authority on the workforce. With these clothes he presented a picture of a country squire, an impression reinforced by his full rich voice that still held hints of Devon. Although measured in speech he could, when roused, be blunt to the point of rudeness leaving someone in no doubt that they had incurred his displeasure. However, although quick to anger it was a mood that soon passed when a point had been made and the victim suitably chastised.

He had a broad mental outlook and realised that a carrot and stick approach would only work if applied proportionally with common sense and balance. However, he had little time for trade unions in particular and today would be considered an illiberal employer who dictated not discussed workers' rights or claims for better wages or improved conditions. This is not to say that he was deaf to their needs, but only that he would decide what was appropriate and dictate what was needed in a way typical of the times.

The 'old man' was a considerable presence in our lives and managed his vast empire with a sure touch. It always astounded me how he coped so well with all that he had to do, juggling competing claims on his time with great skill. The list of tasks he had to manage, whether they

Churchward at home. Before being promoted to be Superintendent he lived quite modestly at 160 Drove Road in Swindon with a manservant, a housekeeper and maid. In 1902 he was able to move into the house occupied by William Dean, which had first been built by the GWR for Joseph Armstrong, which sat just south of the works. It was given the name Newburn (above) and here Churchward, attended by four members of staff and driven about when necessary by Robert Northover, who lived in nearby Dean Street, remained a tenant until the end of his life, Collett choosing to live elsewhere when becoming CME. (Below) Churchward in repose at Newburn in a room filled with a great deal of Victorian/Edwardian chintz. As a master of a great industry, he seems somewhat out of place in such a room. For a man who seems to have avoided the camera's lens as much as possible, and when necessary only struck the most formal poses, this is quite a candid picture. (DN)

be the day to day running of all those workshops and an extensive modernisation programme, development of new locomotives or rolling stock, financial issues, day to day administration and much more, was indeed a very long one. He chose good deputies and senior managers, of course, but they all had to be marshalled and controlled to ensure all ran well.

In terms of staff in the Drawing Offices he had the gift of dealing with us as individuals and made us feel that our contributions and our opinions were valued. On one occasion I well remember I had been working on the design of outside pipes to supply steam to the cylinders, I had been told to produce a scheme whereby steam would flow from the regulator valve, out through the sides of the smokebox and directly into the cylinder chests.

One day I looked up to see GJC walking towards me with the Chief Draughtsman, George Burrows, in tow. This was not a surprise because he often visited me and the other draughtsmen to see what we were doing, displaying a very easy manner as he did so. On these occasions he would say, 'Now then, my son, get off that stool and let me sit down, you are much younger than I am'. He would then study in great detail what I was doing and question me closely on different aspects of my proposals. He was always quick to say whether he approved or not, adding the words, if the latter, 'That's no good – that cock won't fight'. It was a saying I felt he must have picked up as a child growing up in Devon when cockfighting was commonplace.

On this occasion Churchward began in a similar fashion and asked, 'Well, my son, how are you getting on with this contraption?' Burrows then began to explain some of the scheme, but Churchward stopped him abruptly with the words, 'Shut up and let the boy talk. He has done the job so far and knows what I expect'. The arrangement I proposed was then made a standard design for as many locomotives as it could be fitted to."

However, to manage so many different and sometimes conflicting demands placed on him, Churchward had to have a quick and active mind capable of storing and recalling a huge amount of information. This was essential if he was not to be caught wanting when questions were asked or a complex idea was being developed by his team. He also had to have a tough inner core to deal with such a large workforce and the burden of so many high priority tasks thrust upon him. In this he was helped considerably by the degree of unquestioning obedience practised in society at the time, probably best summed up by Alfred, Lord Tennyson's poetic words 'theirs not to reason why, theirs but to do and die'.

William Stanier caught a hint of what lay within Churchward when he recorded that:

I would like to tell the meeting something of the 'old man'. After the First World War a deputation visited Churchward to tell him of their wishes. Churchward had rather an autocratic way and used to tell his people what to do. The leader of this deputation, the district organiser, said, 'You know the time has come when we wish to be asked to do a thing and not ordered to do it'. 'Damn it all, it is time the 'old man' retired.' he replied.

In some ways his attitude to women also stood in stark contrast to the way the world was changing in the first two decades of the twentieth century with the women's suffrage movement gaining ground, to sit alongside the gradual spread of improved employment rights and working conditions. A brief exchange of words at a formal dinner in 1914 captures the flavour of a man grown used to a male dominated society and one who also chose, for whatever reason, to remain single. Pellow recalled that:

At an after dinner speech at a big, well reported, civic function Churchward's leg was being gently pulled by the main speaker about his bachelor status, when compared to the happier

Above and left: A drawing office will always be at the centre of the creative process in any engineering business. This is particularly so in the railway industry and at Swindon, in the early 1900s, a particularly talented team, led by Churchward, was assembled with remarkable consequences not only for the GWR, but also railway history. These pictures show the company's L shaped drawing office as it appeared post 1904, following refurbishment. It was a place where Churchward spent a great deal of time directing the efforts of his designers, approving or rejecting the results where necessary. This office sat on the top floor of the main building which allowed good natural light to stream down from the skylights that ran along the roof to help illuminate the rows of drawing boards below. (DN)

By the standards of the age the workshops at Swindon were set up and run to a model other companies might aspire to equal. The GWR, under Churchward's direction, were quick to invest in the latest production line technology and ergonomically sound shop floor layouts to boost flow rates and make the processes smoother and safer to operate. This was none more so than in 'A' Erecting Shop (seen above), which was designed and constructed on Churchward's watch and opened in 1904. (DN)

position of his married contemporaries. In reply Churchward, or so I am told, snapped back that, 'A lot of you are big men, important men and doing big jobs where what you say goes. But what are you when at home? Worms! Bloody worms!' Word of this 'friendly' encounter soon spread round the offices at Swindon, reinforced by a report that appeared in the press, with those who greatly respected him feeling that the witticism was uncalled for and lacked the respect Churchward was due.

For those who worked with him day by day, and were well-placed to judge these matters, there was an awareness that he preferred the company of men and relished the cut and thrust of their society – at work or following his fishing or shooting interests. Nevertheless, he relied heavily on his housekeeper and maids to keep his home in order and respected them for the way they undertook these duties. However, he did show less tolerance to women employed in and around the Works at Swindon, which during the Great War became a running sore with so many being employed to fill the gaps left by the many men serving at the Front.

He was a man who liked everyone to be at their desks or in the workshops when he started work. He abhorred unpunctuality and one morning observed a group of female clerks still on their way to work at ten past nine. On entering the office he was clearly angered by this and telephoned the Chief Clerk and demanded to know at what time his 'bloody hens' were supposed to start work! Although he treated women with the greatest respect and politeness it seems clear that he wished to avoid having them in the workplace whenever and wherever possible. It is noticeable that when the war ended the number of women employed at Swindon diminished rapidly even though there were insufficient trained men returning from the battlefield to fill the gaps. Inevitably, this created a number of problems whilst new recruits developed the necessary skills to do the work to the standard Churchward and the company required and expected."

If Churchward was indeed intolerant of women in an industrial environment, not a progressive in industrial relations and forthright when expressing himself on many issues, he was not alone in this. Britain was still a country where equality was rarely practised and when done, only very grudgingly. But these were far less sensitive times, with few, if any, statutory rights to offer even the most basic level of protection for workers, no matter what their trade. In the event no employee was likely to offer resistance or complain when treated poorly, because to do so could have meant disciplinary action or, at worst, instant dismissal without a reference.

So, this is the situation in which Churchward found himself when promoted to become Superintendent in May 1902. The demands on his time and energy were many and varied, with the need to build new more powerful locomotives, supported by modern rolling stock, high on his task list. To do this he had an established team who knew him well and how he worked and in time he would add many other 'bright young men' to their number as the years passed by.

He had a Chairman and Board of Directors determined, or so it seems, to support him and a period of peace and comparative prosperity in Britain that proved stimulating to business. Then, on a more personal level, he had a range of management and engineering skills that were second to none, all backed up by great ambition and a determination to succeed. It seems, with hindsight, to be a case of the right man being in the right place at the right time and

Although possessing cars from the early years of the twentieth century, Churchward tended to only use them for travel around Swindon and the adjoining countryside – for pleasure, when rough shooting or fishing on land he rented on the Wiltshire Downs, and on company or civic duties. For longer distance travel he preferred to go by train when visiting all parts of his empire, the Chairman and General Manager in London, or his family in Devon. By 1905 when this photograph was taken of the GWR's sheds in Exeter, Dean's dominating influence was still apparent in the types of engine on view but great changes were in store as Churchward's standardisation programme began to produce much bigger, stronger engines. (DN)

very quickly he flexed his creative muscles and began work unencumbered by any limitations imposed by being second in command. And his first job, when becoming chief, was to develop his standardisation plan to a successful conclusion and begin building the engines he believed the company needed to keep growing.

It was almost as if a starting gun had been fired when he took office and what followed was an explosion of ideas that he was determined to pursue with great vigour. However, it is one thing to have a standardisation plan, but it is quite another to implement it. First of all, there is the question of cost to consider and then, more significantly, the need to test theories and explore options to ensure what you do will work and, in so doing, better meet all the company's motive power needs. Without careful analysis of what is on offer and what is possible, there will always be a risk that what is produced, rather like the Kruger Class, will not prove effective or suitable.

It was in tackling such issues successfully that Churchward proved to be a such astute manager. He realised, as good design engineers do, that you do not have to reinvent the wheel each time you develop a new machine. Instead, you can build on what is known or is being developed and tested elsewhere. Nigel Gresley, who was a friend and great admirer of Churchward, caught this mood when, in words later recorded by Oliver Bulleid, he stated that 'when you run out of ideas then copy the best'. In Gresley and Churchward's case they did just this but then added their own distinctive ideas to this collective mix and produced their own engines in the process.

For any progressive design engineer at this time there was much to observe and consider in Britain and overseas. As we have already seen this covered development of boilers, fireboxes, smokeboxes, superheaters, motion, wheel configuration, materials and much more. For Churchward, all this helped inform his emerging plans which in February 1902, shortly before his promotion to Superintendent, resulted in the creation of his first prototype engine at Swindon – a two-cylinder 4-6-0 type locomotive given the number 100. Bearing in mind that Dean was still nominally in charge at this point, and could, if he had so wished, have objected to the direction Churchward was taking, this development, which some saw as a radical departure from established practice on the GWR, seems to have been given his seal of approval. However, there was certainly a need for such a locomotive as the demand placed on express engines rapidly increased, especially on the high profile Paddington to Bristol and Paddington-Exeter-Plymouth services. Here a weightier 4-6-0 engine would provide greater adhesion than the 4-4-0s then in use which would enhance pulling power, increase acceleration and allow these heavier trains to attain and sustain higher speeds.

To a certain extent Churchward was undoubtedly influenced in this choice by development work he had observed being undertaken in the USA by a number of companies in the second half of the nineteenth century. Most notable amongst them was the Pennsylvania Railroad which in Churchward's time had Alfred Wolcott Gibbs as its CME. He was a man most noted for his work in developing 4-4-2, 4-6-2 and 2-8-2 locomotives but he also took a hand in producing at least three classes of 4-6-0s – the G2, G3 and G4. In doing this he focussed on such things as superheating, improvements to valve gear and the use of cast steel frames. Also, it seems, he took a keen interest in developing a test and evaluation facility at the company's Altoona Works, to which a rolling road was added in 1905.

It is reported that Gibbs and Churchward became friends, though I could find no evidence that either visited the other's country during these active years. However, it isn't beyond the bounds of possibility that they did in fact meet at some stage. Either way, much that Gibbs and his fellow Americans designers were doing was regularly described in railway journals and by the IMechE, where much of interest was reported and discussed. So, in developing his locomotives Churchward had much to observe and consider in the States, as well as countries such as Germany. Here 4-6-0s were also making their presence felt, most notably with the Alfred de Glehn designed four-cylinder compound Class IVes, eighty-three of which were released from

When developing the first of his classic 4-6-0s, Churchward had much to observe in other countries to help direct his thoughts. Although 4-6-0s had proliferated in the United States since the mid-nineteenth century, it wasn't until the 1890s that the railway press widely reported the advances being made there and in other countries. As word spread a number of designs came under their close scrutiny, including the Pennsylvania Railroad's G3 and G4s, which first appeared in the mid-1890s (above) and the Baden Railway de Glehn designed Class IVe four-cylinder compounds of 1894 (below). It is impossible to say how much note Churchward took of this work when designing the first of the GWR's 4-6-0s, but the coverage they received would not have escaped such a clever man. More importantly, though, was the broader work being undertaken by the Pennsylvania Railroad's CME, Alfred Wolcott Gibbs, with whom Churchward seems to have shared ideas. (Author's collection)

1894, and forty-three Maffei-built four-cylinder compound Bavarian Railways CVs that began to enter service in 1899.

As Churchward developed his 4-6-0, the concepts explored in the USA and Germany would have been of interest to him, especially where de Glehn's work was concerned. Conversely, they may simply have offered him an object lesson in what to ignore or to avoid when deciding what he might want to do himself. After all, one person's failure, especially when the reasons for it are firmly established, can offer a valuable route map that the wise may follow as they seek their own path to success. In this, Gibbs' works in particular would have proved most useful. And Churchward could not have failed to take note of the test centre evolving at Altoona, which allowed locomotives to be evaluated in a more scientific way and be modified and re-tested when shortcomings were uncovered. Nothing like this existed in Britain at the time, but in Churchward's hands would soon do so.

Having studied what was happening elsewhere and having tested various theories, Churchward decided to fit his 4-6-0, soon be numbered 100 and named *William Dean*, with 6ft 8½in coupled wheels and a prototype Standard No. 1 boiler. This was rated to produce a working pressure of 200psi when married to a 9ft Belpaire firebox and would generate 20,525lb of tractive effort. In addition, it would carry two 18 x 30in outside cylinders that were served by a Stephenson derived valve gear. These drove 6½in diameter double-ported piston valves, set between the frames, through rocking levers; a solution that was only applied to this engine and then discarded as the design was refined.

A period of testing followed which resulted in, amongst other things, the piston valve diameters being increased from 6½ to 7 then 7½ inches. This, as Kenneth Cook reported, 'could be done within the cylinder casting as designed' before adding, 'it is interesting to note that these original cylinders lasted throughout the engine's life until it was scrapped in 1932' as proof of their success. But having observed No. 100 in service, Churchward was far from satisfied with his and Dean's creation. So, in 1903, a new, Churchward solely designed version, given the number 98, appeared.

So important was this engine to Churchward's emergence as a truly great designer, that Cook paid it particular attention in his 1950 presentation. In doing so, he highlighted the key issues that had influenced its designer in chief when first setting to work:

> Several features of American design were incorporated, particularly concerning the type of cylinders, which were cast in halves, bolted together in the centre and incorporated a cast saddle to accommodate the drumhead type of smokebox. In order to introduce this feature, while retaining plate frames, forged extension frames were bolted to the front ends of the main frames, which produced the equivalent, at the front end, of bar frames and enabled the cylinders to straddle these in a way similar to American practice.

Churchward's prototype 4-6-0, No. 100 (later re-numbered 2900), as it appeared when new and unnamed in 1902. This engine marked a massive shift in the direction the GWR was heading and reflected Churchward's progressive thoughts on design. It has been said that No. 100 heralded the dawn of the most exciting phase of locomotive development on the GWR and, in so doing, helped bring the company into the modern age. In due course this engine was named *William Dean*. (DN)

Churchward's second prototype two-cylinder 4-6-0 engine, No. 98, left the Works in March 1903. This design included modifications identified in the year when operating No. 100. As a result, this engine had a tapered firebox and a cone shaped taper boiler that produced 200psi of pressure, plus a modified front end, amongst other things. As such it became the model for the 2900 Saint Class which began appearing in 1905 and would, by 1913, become a class of seventy-seven locomotives and lead to the development of the four-cylinder Star Class in 1906. (DN)

The front-end was built up individually on each engine, but later developments have enabled them to be assembled on jigs, which have facilitated assembly and renewal to such an extent that even on a tank engine it has been possible to change a complete front end without removing either the boiler or tanks.

The cylinders were 18in diameter and 30in stroke, coupled wheels were 6ft 8 ½in as on No. 100, the grate area was 27sqft, the boiler pressure was again set at 200 lb per sqin and tractive effort slightly higher at 20,530lb. In this case the boiler introduced a tapered barrel but here only applied to the rear plate.

The original specification for this engine indicated 8½ inch diameter piston valves, but Mr Churchward became imbued very early with the importance of a very free exhaust which, it was stated, occurred to him from early motor car practice, and he maintained that freedom of exhaust was greater than admission. So, he went straight to 10 inch diameter valves with increased travel, and for large two-cylinder engines these have remained ever since.

The valve motion was again derived from Stephenson gear inside the frames being finally transmitted through rockshafts, which did not reverse the motion to piston valves above the cylinders. These valves had 5⅞ inch travel, 1⅝ inch steam lap and ⅛ lead at 25 per cent cut-off with nil exhaust lap."

Though No. 98 brought Churchward much closer to his target there was, he believed, still room for improvement and, a little later, in December 1903, another, slightly modified version, No. 171, appeared. In this case the boiler pressure was raised from 200 to 225psi and the tractive effort to 23,090lb. But during the construction of this locomotive it emerged that Churchward wanted to explore more closely developments taking place in France in the hands of Alfred de Glehn and Gaston du Bousquet for the SACM. In this case it was compound, four-cylinder engines. However, he didn't simply wish to obtain theoretical data or performance reports, but actually acquire a working model to analyse in detail.

So, in 1903, as we saw earlier, Churchward obtained financial approval to purchase one locomotive of this type, in this case a 4-4-2 configured engine of a type then becoming common in that country. On arrival at Swindon it was registered as No. 102 and named *La France*, and was joined by two more, Nos. 103 *President* and 104 *Alliance*, in 1905.

A Commanding Presence 99

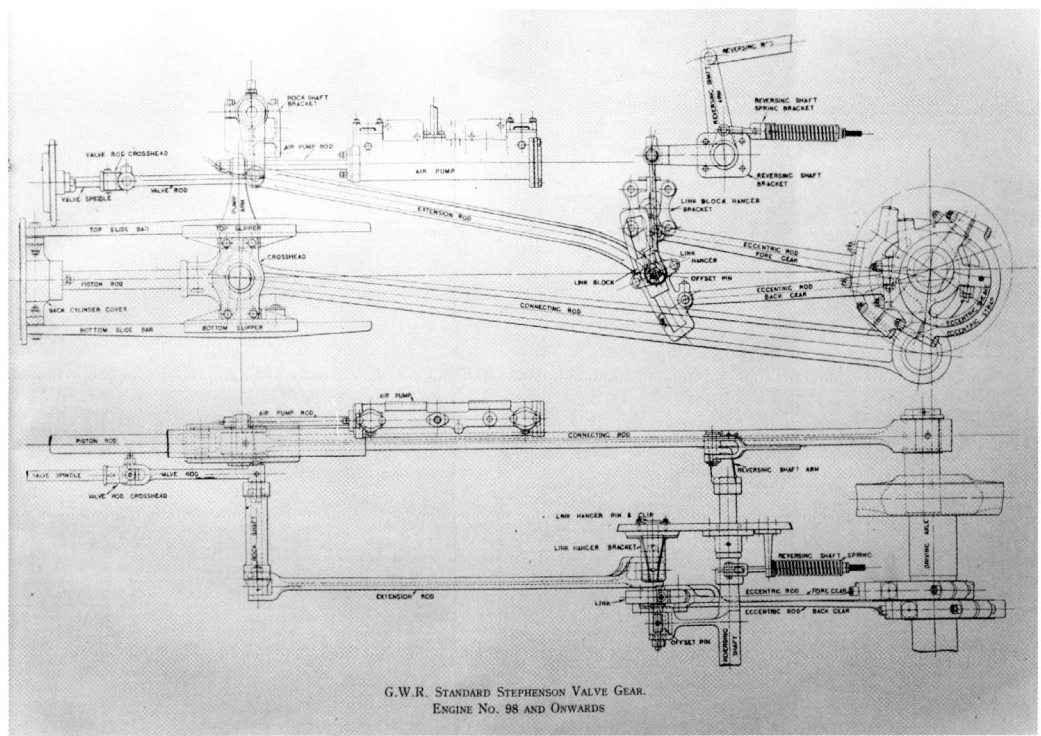

G.W.R. Standard Stephenson Valve Gear.
Engine No. 98 and Onwards

As part of the evolution to a standardised fleet of locomotives Churchward was prepared to experiment with different forms of valve gear. The scheme shown above was adopted for his second prototype 4-6-0, No. 98, and in this form, with 10in diameter valves, they remained the choice for large GWR two-cylinder engines. (KC/IMechE)

At this stage some may have wondered why these additional engines were purchased. One, it would seem, should have been enough for testing purposes, so did Churchward, or another senior GWR manager, wish to populate the fleet with more imports from France? This seems unlikely in the face of Churchward's grand plan for standardisation, so where might the truth lie? In a letter written by Kenneth Cook, late in life, we can find a clue to help us understand his thought processes. He wrote:[1]

> Numbers 103 and 104 were slightly different to No. 102 being based on the Paris-Orleans Railway's Class 3001 and so were larger than 102, which was seen as a copy of the Nord Railway's No. 2 641/2. They also produced greater tractive effort (27,000lb compared to 23,710lb) had slightly different cabs, modified bogies with inside frames and different diameter hp cylinders. As a man who wished to test and evaluate all the time these two types of compound engines were sufficiently different to offer Churchward the scope he needed to make the broadest possible comparison. So, there was so much more for him to think about when forming his own ideas.

After much thought, and having closely observed these three engines in action, Churchward rejected compounding as a concept as it offered little that could not be achieved by more conventional means. However, other elements of both designs clearly appealed to him – four-cylinders for one plus their bogie arrangement. But the list also included such things as their divided drive, balanced motion, fluted connecting rods and double slide bars.

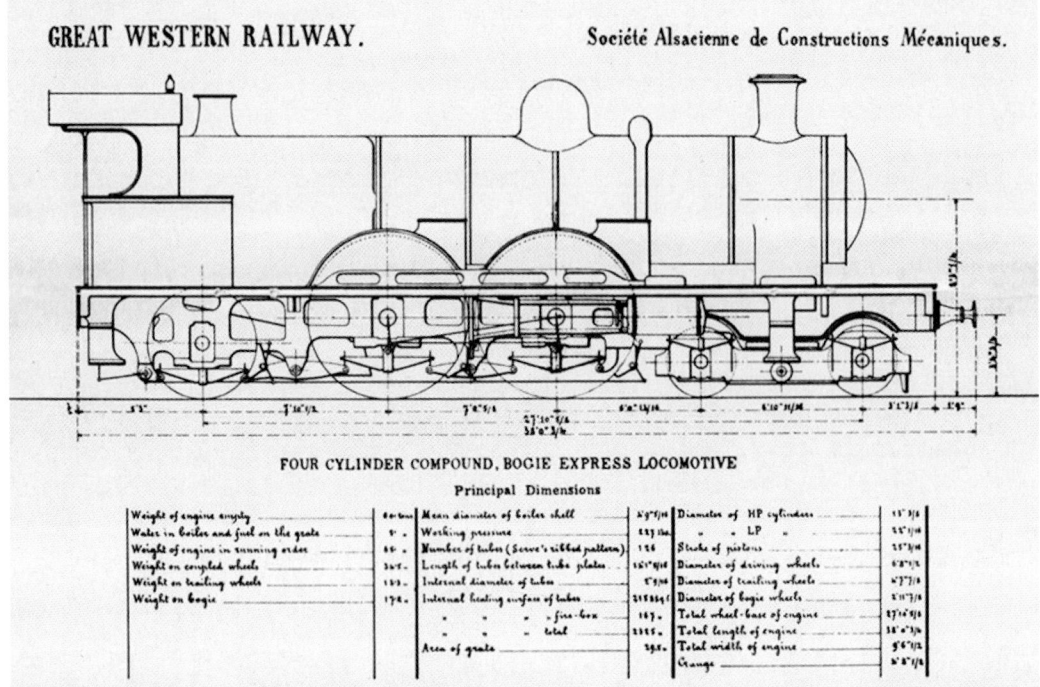

By 1905 Churchward had acquired three de Glehn/du Bousquet 4-4-2s from SACM (above picture shows the official diagram produced at the time). Perhaps one might have been enough for analysis and comparability testing purposes, nevertheless, all three found a regular home on the GWR and remained in service until 1926 having undergone various modifications in the meantime. (Below) No. 102 *La France* on shed at Old Oak Common in 1906. (Opposite above) No. 103 *President*. (Opposite below) No. 104 *Alliance* shortly to depart from Paddington with an express. Towards the end of their service all three engines were based at Oxford. (DN)

It is always important when undertaking comparability testing that it is done, as far as possible, on a like for like basis. So in this case, Churchward needed another 4-4-2 type engine to add to the equation. As a result, No. 171, now named *Albion*, lost its status as a 4-6-0 and was converted to 4-4-2 in October 1904, according to Cook. Subsequently, perhaps as a sign that he was content with this wheel arrangement, Churchward ordered three from a batch of nine new 4-6-0s be built instead as 4-4-2s in 1905, with ten more following in the same year. Once again, this as an interesting development if the conversion was simply a means of providing a fair

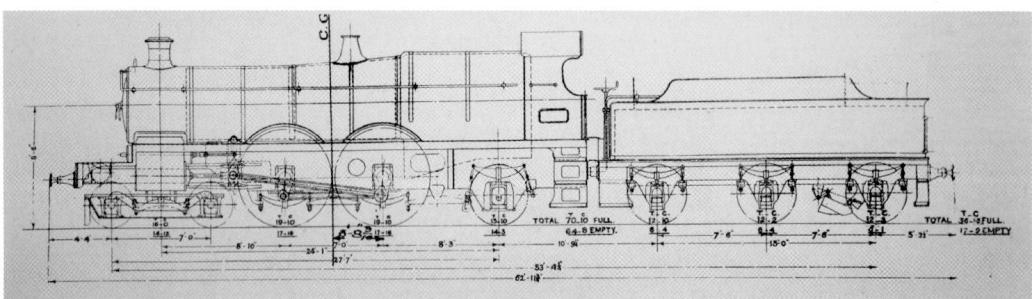

Engine No. 171 in its two guises in the early years of the twentieth century. First, it was built as a 4-6-0 (top picture), so developing the theme Churchward first explored with Nos 100 and 98. However, having purchased three SACM built locomotives from France in 1903/05 for experimental purposes, he needed to be able to compare like with like, as well as with the company's 4-4-0s and other two new 4-6-0s. And so he decided to have No. 171, *Albion,* converted in late 1904 to a 4-4-2 configuration (middle picture – the engine's post modification diagram and, above picture, in its new form). Comparability trials failed to convince him that the SACM locomotives offered any significant advantage over the alternatives on offer. However, there were elements of their design that appealed to him and found their way into his own work. No. 171, which was re-numbered 2971, was briefly re-named *The Pirate* in March 1907 before being rebuilt as a 4-6-0 five months later at which point her original name was restored. (DN/Author's collection)

means of comparison. Surely one or two would have been enough. So, this leads one to wonder whether Churchward believed there was indeed a future for locomotives such as these in his standardisation plans? Neither Kenneth Cook nor Churchward himself, it seems, left any clue to suggest where his motivation for doing this may lie, though the large number converted suggests they may have featured in his long term planning for a while.

With *La France* available, Churchward wasted little time in putting her to work on assorted duties, carefully assessing how she performed on a variety of tasks. Much of this work involved pulling the more demanding express trains, working in turn with well-established 4-4-0 classes such as the City Class and Atbaras then the new GWR 4-6-0s and 4-4-2s when they became available. These duties included the Cornish Riviera Express from Paddington to the West Country which ran for the first time on 1 July 1904, and then became, for a time, one of their regular turns. This demanding service included a non-stop run from London to Plymouth – a task that would, most probably, have tested any engine to their limit.

Although the de Glehn/du Bousquet engines proved useful, they didn't offer any significant improvement over GWR locomotives then in service or in development. In fact, in terms of economy and performance they don't seem to have rivalled or improved on No. 171, in 4-4-2 form, to any great extent, let alone as a 4-6-0. However, they still influenced Churchward in other ways, most notably their ride quality, their de Glehn bogies and the reduction of the load placed on the rods and axleboxes – which resulted from the drive being split between two axles. Then, of course, he could study the benefits of using four cylinders rather than two, although their compounding seems to have left him unimpressed.

So there were both plusses and minuses to consider when judging how useful these three engines were in informing Churchward's plans for the future. On the whole, though, there were clear benefits in pursuing this programme and, at the end of the day, the GWR had three good engines to boost their motive power fleet. However, their presence did act as a reminder, if one were needed, of the pressing need to pursue plans for standardisation to reduce the odd mixture of locomotives then in service and the heavy overheads this incurred.

Kenneth Cook, for one, believed that:

The need to procure and store a range of non-standard spare parts for such a plethora of locomotives then managed by the GWR was excessive and expensive. The French engines' different maintenance and servicing needs only made the problem worse. This wouldn't have held much appeal for Churchward - a man noted for his economy of effort and desire for greater efficiency. Nevertheless, being someone who would not waste any opportunity that arose to experiment with any engine in his area of responsibility, he played with their design occasionally to see if he could improve their performance in some way. To a certain extent he probably considered this a way of offsetting the higher spares and maintenance costs.

Churchward was indeed loath to discard these three engines, which outlasted him in service, and did take the opportunity on offer to undertake some modification work. For example, in 1913,

Saint Class engine No. 178, *Kirkland*, which was one of the first nine members of the class produced in 1905 and, unlike some sister engines in this group, was never outshopped as a 4-4-2 at any time. The arrival of these engines helped promote Churchward into the leading rank of engineers and undoubtedly added much to his growing reputation. However, much more was to follow this good beginning as he forged ahead, with great determination, to implement his standardisation plan. (DN)

No. 102 was fitted with a top feed and new steam pipes, then in 1916 had her boiler replaced by a Swindon Standard No. 1. Nos 103 and 104 both received un-superheated No. 1 boilers in 1910 and 1907 respectively with *Alliance* being further modified in 1914 when it was decided to equip her with a superheated boiler. So until withdrawn from traffic in 1926, they retained the air of being experimental locomotives and something of an anomaly for that reason. Despite this, the French engines proved to be of some worth as test vehicles and as fully operational locomotives, when the comparability trials ended. If it had been otherwise Churchward, the man of efficiency and common sense, would undoubtedly have sold or had them reduced to scrap. The fact that he didn't suggests a certain respect for their engineering and it was left to Collett, when CME, to withdraw them from service.

Although the comparability tests probably lasted into 1906 it is likely that Churchward had absorbed all he needed to learn by the end of 1903, as far as his first 4-6-0s were concerned anyway. All that was left to do was refine and modify their design to make the good even better. However, he was in no rush to build them in substantial numbers, probably due to the proliferation of 4-4-0s and a general satisfaction with their performance. This was no better demonstrated than on 9 May 1904 when engine No. 3440 performed so remarkably, and very publicly, when pulling the *Ocean Mail Express* from Plymouth to Paddington. But the 4-6-0s, although designed for the company's highest profile services, were only one part of Churchward's development plans. Goods traffic if anything was a far bigger earner and so demanded much more in terms of motive power if profits were to increase. And behind this lay a plethora of secondary passenger services requiring better engines. So, as the big express engines entered a new age, Churchward focussed his team's great talents on meeting these less glamorous but probably more pressing needs.

Churchward's Life and Work in Colour

DAWLISH.

For a child such as young George Churchward growing up in Devon in the mid-nineteenth century the railways were a dominating presence. This was especially so of Brunel's atmospheric railway that ran from Exeter westwards. The scheme was a failure and the line, which evolved into the South Devon and Cornwall Railway, became, like its neighbour, the Great Western, a broad gauge line with its most memorable section lying along the coast at Dawlish, as captured here in this contemporary print. Churchward would often have travelled along this line and studied its history and its engineering. Then, in time, he was apprenticed to the company itself. As such it played a key part in his life and undoubtedly influenced his choice of career. (Author's collection)

The Devon village of Stoke Gabriel became the home for many generations of the Churchward family. It was here that George Churchward was born in 1857 the eldest son of this traditional farming family. With a life of comparative comfort, by the standards of the age, he probably experienced few of the worries that beset the majority of people at the time where poverty and hardship were their daily lot. (Above) The village as it appeared in the nineteenth century and (left) the Church of St Mary and St Gabriel where the Churchward family worshipped and many are now buried. (Author's collection)

The broad gauge engines used by the railway companies that served the West Country from Bristol down to Cornwall – the SDR, the Bristol and Exeter and the Great Western - would have all been familiar to Churchward as a child then as an apprentice. In this case it is locomotive No. 2002, one of the Bristol and Exeter's four Pearson designed Rothwell & Co built 4-2-4 tank engines with 8ft 2inch driving wheels. Three were built in 1868 and the fourth five years later. In due course three of these locomotives were rebuilt by the GWR as 4-2-2 tender engines. (Author's collection)

Another type of locomotive that would have been familiar to Churchward would have been the Daniel Gooch designed GWR broad-gauge 4-2-2 Iron Duke Class (later known as the Alma Class) (Top) These are represented here by *Lord of the Isles*, the 23rd member of the class built in 1850/51. This class were noted for being particularly fast and were recorded at speeds in excess of 70mph when hauling the *Flying Dutchman* service. This particular engine was first given the name *Charles Russell* and was exhibited at the Great Exhibition in London in 1851. However, the following year, when hauling a director's inspection train from London to Birmingham, with both Isambard Kingdom Brunel and Gooch on the footplate, the locomotive ran into the back of a stopping train seriously injuring a number of people in the process. Although withdrawn from service in 1884, the engine was stored at Swindon having run, it is claimed nearly 800,000 miles. Permanent preservation should have undoubtedly followed but in 1906, with Churchward as LCWS, the decision was taken to scrap her along with Robert Stephenson's sole surviving member of the 2-2-2 Star Class, *North Star* (above and another locomotive Churchward would probably have studied closely as an apprentice), which had also been in store at Swindon for some time. However, three years after Churchward retired, a decision was taken to build a replica of this engine by Collet suggesting that he may have disagreed with some of his predecessor's actions. (Author's collection)

The Grenville/Churchward steam powered horseless carriage as it appears today on display in the National Motor Museum at Beaulieu. In helping build this vehicle Churchward was able to rehearse his developing ideas on boiler design, linkage to drive and steaming capacity. This photo captures the simplicity and compactness of the carriage's mechanical parts with a dome that would have been a credit to Great Western locomotives. (Author)

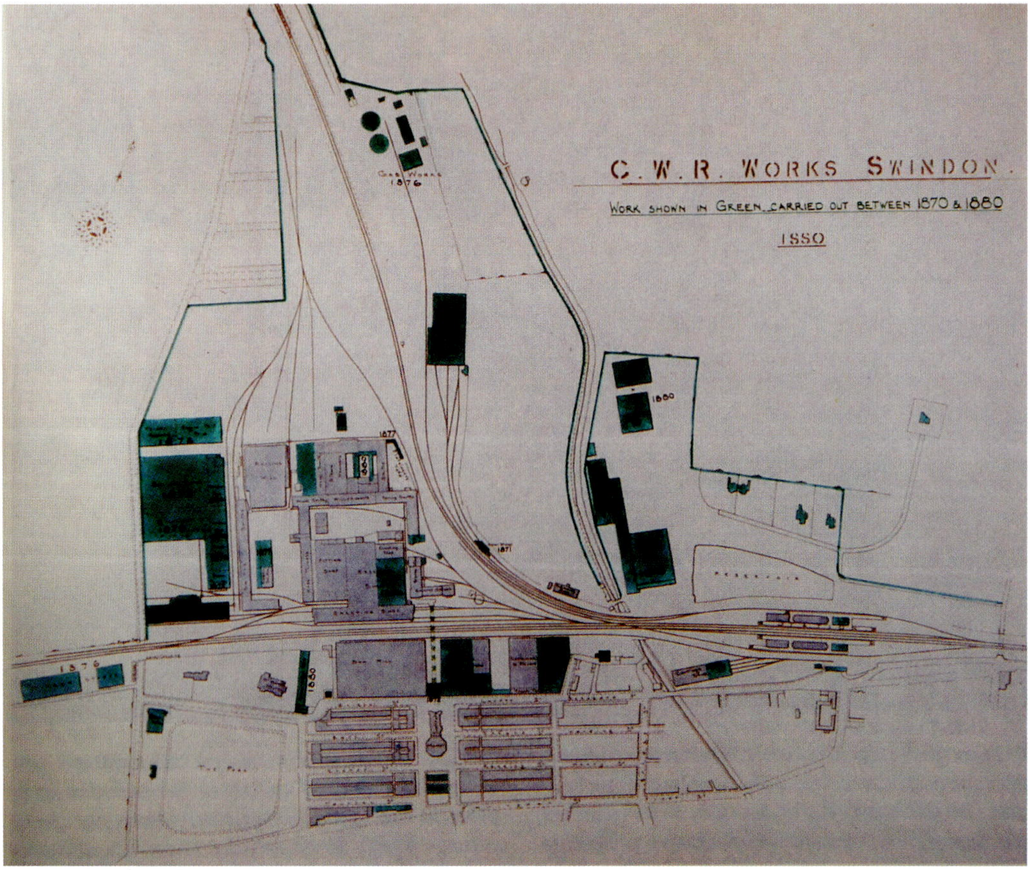

The Swindon Works at the time Churchward arrived there to complete his apprenticeship. Although already substantial in size, and employing many thousands of people, it continued to grow, exponentially, each year so becoming one of the great railway works in Britain if not Europe. (DN)

Churchward's Life and Work in Colour 109

As always, civic leaders and politicians become the butt of satirists and cartoonists as captured here in this 1903 drawing which was carried by the local press in Wiltshire. The selection of a Mayor and Aldermen each year was regarded by many as a 'job for the boys' – a reward for patronage and past services – and drew much criticism for that reason. Here we see a queue of councillors waiting patiently for selection to these posts. Here a diminutive Councillor Cook anoints the 1903 choice for Mayor – the large and rotund figure of J.A.S. Hinton – while to one side George Churchward, who was Mayor in 1900/01, stands arm in arm with a uniformed Mr Wheeler who for some reason carries a postman's sack. Why this pose caught the cartoonist's eye is now lost to time, but when men choose to live alone and they express, as he did, quite vehement views about the institution of marriage, they will inevitably invite all sorts of comment and speculation, then as it does now. Hinton was a leading member of the Swindon based Gooch Lodge of Freemasons, re-named after Daniel Gooch and a movement he had been introduced to by Brunel. It is rumoured, but not confirmed that Churchward, amongst others of senior rank in the GWR, was also a Mason. (DN)

In 1892, broad gauge services on the GWR finally came to an end after a battle for survival lasting many decades. Churchward would have been only too aware of the complexities of running a two-gauge system and the costs involved. While regretting its loss, he probably welcomed the focus that could now be given to developing standard gauge locomotives and rolling stock to carry the company forward. The final broad-gauge services from Paddington to the West Country were much celebrated events and resulted in many newspaper reports and this painting of the last train, which left Paddington for Plymouth at 1700hrs, and is captured passing through Sonning Cutting on 20 May of that year. The locomotive selected for this duty was Rover Class 4-2-2, 1880 built, *Bulkeley* which took the train as far as Bristol. The following morning, she steamed back into Paddington pulling a special 'Up service' from Penzance after which she was withdrawn from service. (Author's collection)

In the years before succeeding Dean, Churchward played an active role in developing various classes of 4-4-0 passenger locomotives. On these he was able to rehearse many ideas that he would implement more fully when becoming LCWS in 1902 – different types of boilers leading to the development of a new standard range, superheating, modified frames, the use of the Belpaire Firebox, the de Glehn bogie and much more. The first of the type appeared in 1894 with the Armstrong Class and development continued through the Dukes, Birds, Badmintons, Bulldogs, Atbaras, Cities and, as shown here, the Flower Class (represented by No. 4107 *Cineraria*, one of twenty built between 1910 and 1913). (Author's collection)

As the GWR turned its attention towards building their large fleet of 4-6-0 engines, Churchward became increasingly interested in development work being undertaken in France by Alfred de Glehn and Gaston du Bousquet on four-cylinder compound locomotives for the SACM. As a result, he used the bogie the French team had developed on the new 4-4-0s, then when becoming Superintendent he sought closer scrutiny of these compound locomotives in their entirety. The easiest way to do this was to purchase some examples for comparative trials and detailed evaluation and in 1903 Churchward obtained financial approval to do so and the first engine No. 102 (above), soon named *La France*, joined the fleet in 1903 and the other two, named *President* and *Alliance*, in 1905 being numbered 103 (below) and 104. While rejecting compounding as a concept, other elements of their design clearly influenced Churchward – the bogie, as already mentioned, but also, amongst other things, a divided drive, balanced motion, fluted connecting rods and double slide bars. (Author's collection)

GREAT WESTERN RAILWAY EXPRESS LOCOMOTIVE, No. 171.
DESIGNED BY MR. G. J. CHURCHWARD, LOCOMOTIVE SUPERINTENDENT.
DRIVING WHEELS, DIAMETER, 6 FT. 8½ IN.   CYLINDERS, DIAMETER, 18 IN.   STROKE, 30 IN.
HEATING SURFACE, 2,142·91 SQ. FT.   BOILER PRESSURE, 225 LBS. PER SQ. IN.
WEIGHT OF ENGINE AND TENDER IN WORKING ORDER, 113 TONS. 7 CWTS.

Having played second fiddle to Dean for so long, Churchward's promotion in 1902 to Superintendent allowed him to put into practice ideas that had been forming for many years. As a result, two new types of engine, each with two outside cylinders, were soon in production each emblazoned with the trademark name 'Churchward's engines'. These were the 2900 Class 4-6-0 passenger engine that first appeared as a prototype in 1902 and, a year later, a 2-8-0 2800 Class freight engine. In delivering these two classes, Churchward took the GWR a giant step forward in locomotive design and firmly established his reputation in the railway world. The third prototype of the 2900 Class was engine No. 171 (later renumbered 2971) which was originally constructed as a 4-6-0 engine then rebuilt as a 4-4-2 for nearly three years so that it could undergo comparative tests with the SACM built compound engine *La France*. (Author's collection)

The first 2800 Class 2-8-0 engine, numbered 97 initially before becoming No. 2800 in 1912, entered service in 1903 and would be joined by another eighty-three of these locomotives by 1919. In so doing, Churchward introduced 2-8-0 type engines to Britain's railway network. This picture, which was published in 1912/13, shows engine No. 2840, one of ten built at Swindon in 1912. (Author's collection)

Churchward's Life and Work in Colour 113

Churchward's outpouring of new engines and new designs continued into 1903 with his prototype 3100 Class 2-6-2 two outside cylinder tank engine, numbered 99 (later number 3100 then 5100). Over the next two years he and his team extensively tested and evaluated this engine and when satisfied that it was effective, and having modified the design, began producing them in greater numbers. By 1906 forty more had been built, including the engine above, No. 3120, which appeared in 1905. In 1906, Churchward considered that the design would benefit from being fitted with a Standard No. 4 boiler and in doing so created the larger more powerful 3150 Class of which he built another forty by 1908. But these were the last produced during his time in office. Under Collett, the 5101, 6100, 8100 and another 3100 Class types appeared and by 1939 the total number of all these related classes totalled 306 engines, none of which have been preserved. During 1904, a new, lighter variant of the 2-6-2T appeared (the 4400 Class) primarily for use on branch lines where the heavier engines were prohibited to go. Eleven of these were built by 1906. (Author's collection)

During Churchward's years as LCWS, and later CME, trade on the railways continued to grow. This was particularly so of the Edwardian Period when, even though poverty was rife and hardship was the lot of the majority in Britain's many poor areas, the emergence of a middle class, and the aspirations this engendered, contributed in no small measure to an increase in passenger traffic. For most this might simply have been day trips to the seaside, for the better off it meant stay away, hotel holidays. At the same time industrial traffic was on the increase, as consumption increased and the export market grew, so for a time business ran at a healthy level which helped fund Churchward's ambitious development plans. (Above left and right) The GWR's advertising campaign at the time, though muted by today's standard, was, nevertheless, beginning to make an impact, aided in part by *City of Truro's* record breaking run on 9 May 1904, when she is said to have broken the 100mph barrier for the first time. (DN)

Having successfully introduced the 4-6-0 Saint Class in 1902, beginning a production run that would last until 1913, Churchward went one step further and developed the four-cylinder 4000 Star Class 4-6-0 the first of which appeared in 1906. It was a building programme that would last until 1923, a year after Churchward's retirement. The Stars are considered by many to be Churchward's masterpiece and were developed following a long period of analysis – aided by the construction of a test facility, which included a rolling road, at Swindon which opened in 1904. Having carefully observed the compound four-cylinder divide drive 4-4-2 locomotives imported from France at work and compared them to the two-cylinder Saints, he opted for a four-cylinder simple version instead. And so the prototype was built in this form and, in due course, and after highly successful trials, Churchward decided to modify the design to become a 4-6-0 with a specially designed Walschaerts valve gear. In time the design of these superlative engines would evolve into the GWR's Castle and King Classes. Here the Stars are represented by engine No. 4021 King Edward, pictured on royal duty. (Author's collection)

In 1904 Churchward introduced the first of eleven 4400 Class 2-6-2T light tank engines, with a Standard No. 5 boiler, producing a psi of 165lbs, two-cylinders 16½ x 24in and 4ft 1½in coupled wheels, primarily for use on branch lines where the use of larger, heavier locomotives was restricted. Two years later he developed this theme further, this time with 4ft 7½in diameter wheels, slightly larger cylinders at 17 x 24in and a boiler pressure increased to 180 lb. So successful did the 2-6-2s perform that 306 of the larger engines were built by 1939, some seeing service into the early 1960s, and eleven of the smaller version. Churchward would return to the 2-6-2 theme in 1906 with his 4500/4575 Class with another 175 of these being built by 1929. Here No. 4566 is photographed in preservation, one of four of the class to survive. (DN)

GREAT WESTERN RAILWAY.
4-6-2 EXPRESS LOCOMOTIVE "THE GREAT BEAR," No. 111.
Designed by Mr. G J. CHURCHWARD, Locomotive Superintendent.   Built at Swindon Works.

Coupled Wheels, 6 ft. 8½ in. Diameter.   Cylinders (four), 15 in. Diameter, 26 in. Stroke.
Heating Surface, 3,400·81 sq. ft.   Grate Area, 41·8 sq. ft.   Working Pressure, 225 lbs.   Water Capacity of Tender, 3,500 gallons.
Weight in Working Order: Engine, 97 tons;   Tender, 45 tons 15 cwt.;   Total 142 tons 15 cwt.

Most of Churchward's locomotive development programme conformed to the standardisation plan he began forming when he was Dean's assistant, but in 1907/08 he began constructing an engine that didn't quite fit into this mould. It was, or so it seems, a concept he was urged to follow by his Chairman and General Manager who wished to build the largest passenger engine in Britain, so reaping the benefits of publicity that would surely be attracted to such an enterprise. Whatever the justification for this particular project, Churchward's time was soon committed to designing and building a single four cylinder 4-6-2 locomotive. Using the Star Class as his model and adopting standard features wherever possible, he and his team then designed new frames, a suitable boiler and a trailing truck amongst other things. The picture above captures the engine, No. 111 (named *The Great Bear*) as it appeared in 1908. Teething problems and very restricted route availability, due to weight primarily, limited the engine's use and it was withdrawn in 1924 for rebuilding as a 4-6-0 with no others having been constructed. (Author's collection)

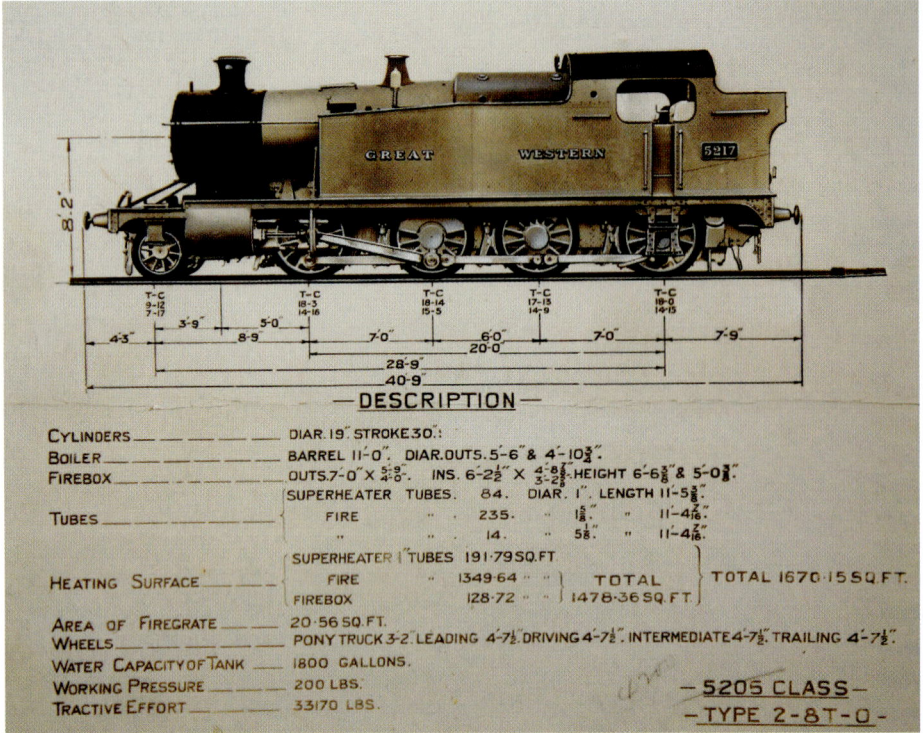

Perhaps of far greater use to the GWR than No. 111 were the 4200 Class two-cylinder 2-8-0T Mineral engines that began appearing in 1910 (top picture). Mineral trains, principally coal, were a staple and very profitable part of the company's business so had to be dealt with in an effective way. The large 2800 Class of 2-8-0 tender engines had proved exceptionally good at this but their number needed to be supplemented by locomotives better suited to short haul work from pithead to port. The 4200s, and later the 5205s, were Churchward's solution, the prototype, No. 4201, appearing in 1910 being joined by another 204 by 1940. During the 1930s some of these engines were rebuilt as 7200 Class 2-8-2Ts (lower picture) so allowing them to carry an additional two-tons of coal and 700 gallons of water so making them better suited to long distance work. The last of the 4200/5205s were withdrawn from traffic in 1965 with five 4200s and three 5205s being preserved. Of the fifty-four 7200s built, three have been preserved. (Author's collection)

Churchward's Life and Work in Colour

Having been involved in Dean's experimental turn of the century 2-6-0 and 4-6-0 designs, resulting in what became known as the Krugers, Churchward returned to the 2-6-0 theme in 1911 with the first of the 4300 Class. This development resulted from the perceived need for an engine to provide motive power for the GWR's secondary services. In due course the Chief Draughtsman was tasked with preparing designs for a two outside cylinder engine with 5ft 8in coupled wheels, a Standard No. 4 boiler and carrying as many standard parts as possible. Twenty of the class were ordered initially and by 1932 342 were in service. Their numbers were greatly enhanced by the coming of war in 1914 in which the class (and later variations) proved themselves to be excellent performers with some, seemingly, serving on the Western Front before being returned to the GWR in 1919. They remained in service until 1964 with two surviving into preservation. (RH)

With the war curtailing most locomotive development work, railway companies suffered a hiatus in new construction unless it could be linked to war. Works across Britain were turned over to armaments production and it wasn't until 1919 that Churchward was able to produce a prototype of his final engine of note, the 4700 Class of 2-8-0 tender engines. This requirement arose from a demand for a locomotive capable of working very heavy, fast vacuum-fitted trains. With the recent success of his 4300 Class 2-6-0 engines in mind he felt that this new requirement could best be met by building an eight-coupled version, but fitted with a larger boiler to provide more power. For this purpose, he chose to fit a Standard No. 1 boiler with lengthened smokebox, producing a pressure of 225lb, to a prototype, marrying this to two 19 x 30in cylinders and 5ft 8in coupled wheels. While this was happening, a new standard boiler (the No. 7) was being designed and built then fitted to all nine of the class all of which entered service in 1923. In this state they survived until 1964 with none being preserved although a new member of the class is, at the time of writing, under construction by the Great Western Society. (Author's collection)

Above left and above right: There is little doubt that the First World War hit the people of all the participating nations very hard, as did the flu epidemic that followed. George Churchward was one of the first to honour those who had sacrificed so much, not least of all from the ranks of those he employed who the statue above, at Paddington, commemorates. For himself, there appears to have been no close family members to grieve, but the war still came at a great cost to him. In peacetime the demands on his time and energy were huge, but in war these multiplied as the GWR turned over many workshops to war production and the wear and tear on locomotives, rolling stock and employees grew each year exponentially. Such huge demands would have broken a lesser man, but Churchward bore the strain with great resolve, though undoubtedly at some cost to his health. (Above right) This picture captures him on the eve of war when in his late 50s, by the end of the conflict he had aged considerably, as photos reveal. Nevertheless, he remained in post until 1921, retiring at 65. (Author's collection/DN)

After retirement Churchward continued to live in his GWR owned home by the Works at Swindon, supported by servants. It was near here that he met his death on 19 December 1933 when he was struck and killed by a Paddington to Fishguard express, pulled by No. 4085 *Berkeley Castle*. His funeral at Christ Church was attended by a huge crowd, including many senior figures from the railway industry, and followed a procession around Swindon watched, according to press reports, by many thousands of people. (Author's collection)

Churchward's Life and Work in Colour 119

In 1922, Churchward was succeeded by Charles Collett who continued with his predecessor's work, including the production of two more significant four-cylinder 4-6-0 classes. First of all came the Castles, which began appearing in 1923, with one, the 1948 built No. 7017, being named *G.J. Churchward* (above) at a ceremony at Paddington on 29 October that year. Then in 1927 the first of thirty-one 4-6-0 Kings rolled out of the works at Swindon (below). (DN/Author's collection)

A common scene from my childhood when on holiday in the West Country – a GWR 4-6-0 Castle Class engine (No. 5057 *Earl Waldegrave*, though up to 1937 given the name *Penrice Castle*) passing through the City of Bath. Although not strictly a Churchward engine it bore all the hallmarks of his work and proved highly successful as a result. (Author)

Chapter 5

Picking Up the Pace

There is little doubt that Churchward hit the floor running when finally succeeding William Dean and his first few years in charge saw many existing and new initiatives being pursued with great vigour. Standardisation was a strategy now becoming a reality, though it still had many years to run before it had truly become established. The 4-6-0s had begun to arrive, admittedly

Churchward's second prototype 4-6-0, No. 98, which was named *Vanguard* in 1907 then *Ernest Cunard* a few months later, stands at Paddington early in her life with a small group of unidentified admirers casting their eyes over her. In the years that followed this engine underwent some modification work, including a new boiler in 1906 that increased its working pressure from 200 to 225psi. Then in 1911 she received a superheated boiler and was renumbered as 2998 a year later. In this guise she enjoyed a fairly long life, being withdrawn from service in 1933. (DN)

as prototypes, but plans were in place to build up their number when Churchward had decided upon the right mechanical combination and which refinements produced the best, most cost effective, results. Then, of course, there were the legacy locomotive projects in which Churchward had played a part as Dean's deputy, still running their course. As we saw in Chapter 3, the 4-4-0 Bulldog, Bird and City Classes were still in production, the last of which wouldn't appear until 1910, and six more 2-6-0 Krugers were built at Swindon in 1903. This work sat alongside a continuous programme of modification to other existing classes as Churchward and his team sought to improve performances and bring in a degree of standardisation.

There was also the 'day job' of simply managing such a huge organisation at Swindon and many other locations as well to contend with. In this, as in many other things, Churchward proved to be an astute and gifted manager and one who seems to have been an excellent judge of character when it came to promoting the right people to fill senior positions in his organisation. The men he chose were, like him, able to fashion an insightful view of the future and how the company's needs might better be met. In addition, they were men with the drive and political acumen to force through change when and where it was deemed necessary. This was nowhere more apparent than in the way the Works at Swindon were developed and expanded in the years post-1902.

Any governing body tasked with managing 'the books' will invariably be cautious when investing in new equipment, buildings or the infrastructure in general. 'Make do and mend' tends to be the mantra that governs the way they prefer to run a business and risk aversion an inevitable consequence. In this the GWR's Chairman, Board and General Manager were no different from any other commercial enterprise, then or now, and needed to be persuaded by strong reasoned arguments if they were to approve anything new. It was here that Churchward and his managers excelled and having identified ways in which the Works could be improved, over a period of time persuaded any doubters of the wisdom of their case and the soundness of the investment. And so one key part of this plan was approved and work began on building a substantial new locomotive erecting shop which opened in 1904. In doing so, the Work's capacity was substantially increased and the growing number of larger engines could be dealt with more effectively than they had been. The new building, which became known as 'A' Shop, also created more space for boiler making and would, in due course, contain an engine testing facility, which Churchward had led in designing.

This Testing Station represented a major step forward and in this guise soon proved its worth. This was especially so when tests were supplemented by mainline trials conducted with a dynamometer car attached to a train to help evaluation. However, this facility appears to have been originally designed simply as a means of 'running in' a locomotive when new or following a period of heavy repair. By doing this it was hoped that the pressure this exerted on the mainline, where this work was conducted, might be significantly reduced. To do this, four test beds were originally planned, each being slightly different in size to meet different wheel configurations. But the concept did not gain much favour because it was found that the first test bed did not produce operating conditions sufficient to exert the right level of external stresses on the wheels or frames as mainline running did. As a result, no more were built in this form with just the one being modified and used for experimental and research purposes, a role it continued to perform well into the 1950s.

The GWR's first dynamometer car was produced, or so it seems, by Daniel Gooch in the middle years of the nineteenth century. By the time Churchward arrived at Swindon, the principles behind their use, although needing refinement, were well established. With his clear analytical mind driving a need to test, experiment and evaluate, the development of more advanced mobile testing cars was growing in importance. And so, when still Dean's deputy, he and his team designed and built the GWR's No. 7 car, at a recorded cost of £895, and had it ready for service in 1901. Sadly, few of the records for this vehicle have survived, so it has been assumed that it was fitted out with all the latest equipment, including a Hallade recorder. This allowed technicians in the coach

Swindon's test facility takes on one of the new 4-4-2 engines, in this case No. 190. The plant consisted of five sets of rollers, three braked, each capable of being moved independently and set up to run engines of different sizes and wheel configurations. The engines were tethered at the rear by a horizontal cross-bar through which pull and total output were measured. Unfortunately, official records for this period are fairly sparce so it is now difficult to assess which engines underwent test. However, with Churchward harbouring ambitious plans for the GWR's locomotive fleet it is likely to have been used very often. (DN)

to monitor speed, steam pressure, fuel and water consumption, tractive effort and much more. It could also monitor the oscillations of the dynamometer car during each journey so providing an indication of the state of the permanent way for the company's civil engineers to act upon. As an aid to this work there was a retractable, flangeless spoked wheel for speed recording, which could be lowered or raised as required. So successful was No. 7 that it remained available for service until 1964 before passing into preservation.

Unfortunately, most of No. 7's early records do not appear to have survived, although it is believed that in April 1901 engine No. 3005 may have been one of the first to use it. This was followed in March 1902 by Churchward's prototype 4-6-0 No. 100, *William Dean*, with a run from Swindon to Taunton, then the second prototype 4-6-0 No. 98 in July 1903 between Bristol and Newton Abbott. Kenneth Cook later recorded, presumably having consulted the records still available to him in 1950, that 'Churchward was a frequent attendee on many runs with No. 7, especially those involving his 4-6-0s. Even after retirement he was known to join trains being pulled by Kings or Castles to see first-hand how they were doing.'

With fixed and mobile test facilities available, Churchward could look forward to a period in which he could analyse many aspects of locomotive design with greater accuracy. By doing

In 1901 Churchward produced a new dynamometer car and gave it the number 7 (Above), which, like the mobile test plant at Swindon, had a very long operational life and remained available for service until the 1960s before entering the preservation movement when purchased by the South Devon Railway Group in 1965. (Below) The car's internal layout and equipment. (DN)

this, he significantly improved his chances of achieving a balanced mix and match solution when developing new engines and when seeking to improve the GWR's existing stock. Armed with such a variety of test equipment, Churchward quickly began to exploit all that was available for the remainder of his time in charge and, in doing so, set an example that others might follow. Nevertheless, there would still be occasions when more was required to make a good engine better or a poor engine rise above the mediocre. In these cases, his and his design team's cleverness, and

This photograph, although showing a King Class 4-6-0 undergoing test with No. 7 dynamometer car (immediately behind the engine), was taken after Churchward had retired. However, it captures the nature of mainline running trials as he would have known them. In this case the front of the engine carries a protective indicator board around its nose which allowed technicians to do a variety of other monitoring tasks in addition to those carried out using measuring equipment contained in the car itself. Together these two methodologies would have provided information on such things as speed, wind resistance, indicated horse-power, steam chest pressure, drawbar pull, vacuum in the smokebox, exhaust steam pressure various temperatures in the smokebox, superheater and much more. (Author's collection)

basic engineering instincts for what was right or wrong, still had a part to play in the production of suitable locomotives.

When it came to his work with carriages and wagons much the same thing applied, although the reliance on test equipment was significantly less. Here, of course, Churchward had had longer to make his mark having been involved in this side of business long before being promoted to senior rank in the locomotive department. In 1882 he had been appointed Assistant Carriage Works Manager and, then three years later, succeeded James Holden as Carriage Works Manager – a post he would hold until 1895. During this time, he focussed on the maintenance of rolling stock and, undoubtedly, played some part in the design and construction of new carriages.

At this stage, carriages with clerestory rooves and skylights, which some thought obsolete, were preferred and their designs up to the mid-1880s, according to Cook, 'reflected a backward rather than a forward view'. This began to change later in the 1880s when the more progressive George Nugent Tyrrell became Superintendent of the Line and James Grierson the new General Manager. Under their leadership, the policy regarding passenger trains soon changed with modern corridor carriages with steam heating, restaurant car services, three classes of accommodation and more becoming the order of the day. With funds to spend, William Dean, aided by Churchward, soon began producing new types of carriages that were deemed to be a major step forward, although remaining true to the classic clerestory outline so well-established within the GWR.

How the transition in carriage design was managed by William Dean then Churchward. (Above) 4-4-2 Engine No. 3067, *Duchess of Teck*, recorded away from GWR territory north of London at Bentley Heath, with a mixed rake of old clerestory carriages. This train reflects the condition of much of the company's stock when Churchward took over. (Below) A somewhat more up to date look but still with clerestory carriages in evidence behind an unidentified member of Churchward's 4-4-2s Scott Class – on an unrecorded date and location. (Bottom) Churchward's modern look of 1905 – a six coach 'Dreadnought' set, as they became known, which was built for the more prestigious services, including the Cornish Riviera Express. In this case, the train is being pulled by a gleaming Churchward Saint Class 4-6-0 (No. 173 *Robin Bolitho*, after the famous Cornish banker who became High Sheriff), which entered service in 1905). (DN/Author's collection)

Churchward's promotion to Superintendent in 1902 re-ignited the debate over the direction in which carriage design should go and heralded in a new standardisation age which some reactionaries thought almost heretical in nature. In this progressive, ambitious programme he was greatly assisted by Frank Marillier. During their joint tenure of these two important posts, they would advance rolling stock design considerably. This was particularly so on the carriage side of business, where their combined efforts would ensure that the company would better meet society's changing demands and produce a fleet to match the new, larger locomotives that soon began appearing in ever greater numbers.

Although the changeover from broad to standard gauge was an expensive and distracting business, which hit the company's finances very hard, it did throw up one unexpected advantage when it came to carriage design. This was an opportunity Churchward was very quick to exploit. Much of the GWR's infrastructure was designed around 7ft ¼in track which, when the changeover occurred, meant there was more space in which the replacement standard gauge locomotives and rolling stock could manoeuvre. As a result, the company were then able to build and operate larger-scale rolling stock over former broad gauge lines including those running from London to the West Country. The first design to make maximum use of the opportunities this offered were the Dreadnought corridor stock – a name derived from a new class of big gun warship then entering service.

The evolution of carriage design under Churchward focussed on producing a standard fleet that could better meet the need of express passenger services, secondary passenger duties and commuter traffic in both town and country. This resulted in a variety of modern designs appearing, including (above) this 70ft long 3rd class corridor carriage, which had two four-wheeled equalized type bolster bogies of a style found in the US, and proved to be a popular design. As this 1913 produced example reveals, it was class of carriage that continued being developed by the GWR for many years. (Below) The 56ft/57ft 'Toplight' stock, here represented by this 1909 built example, first appeared in 1907 for use over secondary cross- country lines and express passenger services where the 70ft carriages could not operate. (RH)

Suddenly, the clerestory form, so faithfully adhered to for so many years, was abandoned and replaced by a 70ft long, 9ft 6in wide colossus which was somewhat bigger than the carriages that went before, the largest of which was a mere 60ft in length. The first into service was a dining car in May 1904, joined by three more later that year, all of which ran with clerestory stock until sufficient Dreadnoughts, of various types – first, second and third class – were available and could be combined into a single rake of carriages for use on the more prestigious express services. And by 1907, sufficient were available to make such a service viable and this very soon attracted great press interest, which helped boost trade.

In shape, the Dreadnoughts had what was described as 'clipper' bodies, with elliptical roofs and recessed end and central doorways. They were fitted with internal compartments that contained sliding doors, large windows with frosted glass top lights, electric lighting, fans in saloons, heating that could be regulated by passengers, high spec furnishings and carpets and much more. All in all, they offered a standard of comfort and modernity that held great appeal for the travelling public, though some thought them externally ugly. In response to this Churchward, possibly stung by the criticism, is reported as saying that 'as far as I am concerned carriages could be finished externally with tar as long as the interiors and quality of ride is to the customers' liking.' Whatever critics thought, the die had been cast and there would be no going back and similar designs soon began to appear. The most noteworthy of these, appeared in 1906 and was a design that soon attracted the nickname 'Concertina', primarily because these 70 footers, narrower at 9ft to give them wider route availability than the Dreadnoughts, had many recessed side doors that gave them a serrated, in and out look.

With production proceeding at a good pace, the company were soon able to form complete sets for express services, particularly those into South Wales where their narrower bodies were unrestricted by the loading gauge. And in this form, they were fitted with bellows type connections between the carriages in an effort to smooth the airflow. In this way Churchward was able to explore some of the issues raised by the developing science of aerodynamics. However, it would still be some years before streamlining of engines and carriages was fully understood or tested. And the everyday use of wind tunnels was still far in the future, although the first in Britain had been built as long ago as 1870 by Francis Wenham, the marine and aeronautical engineer.

Being a man who kept up to date with the latest developments in science across many fields, Churchward would probably have been aware of these highly publicised developments and Wenham's early concept papers on the subject. Membership of the same institutions would also have encouraged an exchange of ideas, at best, or at least a general awareness of them. Did this influence Churchward's work at Swindon in any way? Possibly, but if so, it wasn't something that Kenneth Cook thought worth mentioning in his 1950 paper, so we are left to speculate on the issue.

With Churchward establishing a fleet of new carriages, modifying each design over the years, this side of business was set fair, leaving his work on new engines to take precedence. But one project did in fact cover both spheres of activity and explored a concept that was attracting wide attention in the early years of the twentieth century – steam rail-motors and auto-trailers. Here Churchward was keenly aware of the need to find a practical and economic means of servicing passenger needs on commuter and low density routes. Steam rail-motors seemed to offer a solution to this problem. So, in 1903, trials were undertaken with a Dugald Drummond designed vehicle borrowed from the London, Brighton and South Coast and London, South-West Railways joint East Southsea service. These tests appear to have satisfied Churchward that the concept was sound, and he soon set his team to work designing a similar rail-motor for the GWR. In very quick time their work was complete and in October that same year the first of two units appeared and were assigned to the Stroud Valley Line to run between Chalford and Stonehouse in Gloucestershire.

With the concept firmly established, more rail-motors were soon added to the company's growing fleet and would soon be found operating across the GWR's network where a need for

Paddington Station before the Great War when Churchward was pursuing a standardisation programme for both locomotives and rolling stock. This picture graphically illustrates a railway in transition with a mixture of old and new style carriages and two classic GWR locomotives – in this case both Star Class engines – the 1909 built No. 4023 *King George* to the left and the 1907 built No. 4003 *Lode Star* to the right. (DN)

such a service had been identified. So they soon appeared around London, in Devon, Cornwall, Wiltshire, Berkshire, South Wales and Gloucestershire. In accordance with Churchward's ideas on standardisation, they contained some universal features. For example, all of the fleet were built with four-wheel vertical-boiler powered units and a four-wheel trailing bogie under the carriage. In addition, their driving wheels had diameters ranging from 3ft 5in to 4ft 0in and cylinders ranging from 9x15in to 12x16in, which seemed to offer an ideal combinations in meeting a variety of service needs. Where they didn't prove adequate, or the rail-motor was found to be insufficient for the task, a 'push me – pull you' alternative, with a small tank engine working between two saloon trailer coaches, was used instead.

All in all, ninety-nine vehicles were built between 1903 and 1908, most at Swindon, but lack of capacity probably led to some sub-contracting of this work. So, to complete the number required, fourteen (Nos. 15, 16 and 61 to 72) were produced by Kerr, Stuart and Company, in their California Works at Stoke-on-Trent. Then another eight (Nos. 73 to 80) were turned out by the Gloucester Railway Carriage and Wagon Company, a burgeoning business that would soon be fully committed to constructing rolling stock for London's ever expanding underground network.

So, in Churchward's first year in charge much was happening on the carriage side of his department, but for the design engineers this was probably a side show, albeit a very important one for the business, to the main event – the construction of a new fleet of locomotives and the improvement, where necessary, of the rest. As we have already seen work on the new 4-6-0 and 4-4-2s was moving forward very quickly, but this was only one project amongst many that staff

(Above picture) Two of the steam rail-motor (Nos.40 and 93 photographed at Stourbridge) that Churchward began introducing in 1903 for use in Gloucestershire. This development led to the initiation of a much larger construction, more refined programme that resulted in 99 of these types of units being built by 1908. Such a large fleet allowed the company to begin providing services around parts of West London and Plymouth. Then, in due course, their use spread more widely across the GWR's network. (Below picture) In 1933/34, the first diesel railcars were introduced, but an experiment with an internal combustion engine had preceded this project by more than twenty-years. Having had his interest piqued by work being undertaken by the British-Houston Company, Churchward approved purchase of a single petrol-electric vehicle in 1911. Here a petrol engine produced a current sufficient to power two electric motors mounted on the axle and in this state could run 235 miles on a single tank of petrol and attain speeds of up to 35mph. For some years it worked satisfactorily over the Windsor branch line, but an overheating fault affected performance somewhat. It was finally withdrawn from service in 1919 without any others being purchased or developed. (DN)

Picking Up the Pace 131

(Above picture) This 1905/06 example of the steam rail-motor and auto-trailer, numbered 43 and 53 respectively, was made up of two 70ft cars and took the design of the rail-motors on to a much larger, more sophisticated level. (Below picture) This photo of the interior of trailer coach No. 48, which was built in 1907, shows the sort of internal layout adopted in these vehicles. They were designed to be used by customers over short distances where ease of access and exit were fairly straightforward, but the nature of their work ensured that comfort wasn't high in the list of the designer's priorities. Overall the steam rail-motors were deemed a success with the last remaining in service until 1935, although some underwent conversion. (DN)

in the drawing office were considering at that time, guided by their Superintendent and Chief Draughtsman. Kenneth Cook briefly summarized the direction in which they were going and proposals that lay on the table, with some designs already well advanced by 1904 with four under test as prototypes by then:

The development of the two-cylinder 4-6-0s settled all the relevant standards, and Churchward proceeded to produce six off-shoot classes:

2-8-0 18½in cylinders 225lb pressure 4ft 7½in wheels Tractive Effort 35,380.
4-4-0 18in cylinders 200lb pressure 6ft 8½in wheels Tractive Effort 20,530.

4-4-2T 18in cylinders 195lb pressure 6ft 8½in wheels Tractive Effort 20,010.
2-6-2T 18½in cylinders 200lb pressure 5ft 8in wheels Tractive Effort 25,670.
2-6-0 18½in cylinders 200lb pressure 5ft 8in wheels Tractive Effort 25,670.
2-8-0T 18½in cylinders 200lb pressure 4ft 7½in wheels Tractive Effort 31,450.

All the cylinders had 30 inch stroke and were virtually the same design, differing only in radius of the cast saddle and height of the saddle above the centre line and frame seating. All except the 4-4-2T and the smaller 2-6-2T had the same radius of saddle, standard boiler No. 1 suiting the 4-6-0 and 2-8-0 and the No. 4 the 4-4-0, 2-6-0 and the 2-8-0T, both boilers taking the same smokeboxes. Cylinder ports were identical with the same 10 in piston valves, valve gear differed only in the lengths of extension rods and, in the case of the 2-8-0 mineral engine, in the lengths of the eccentric rods. Therefore, the cylinder characteristics were fully known from the final prototype 4-6-0 engine.

The Stephenson valve gear was designed with large bearing surfaces and has given reliable service with very small degrees of wear and by 1906 Churchward had standardised it with a 6½ inch valve travel. The launch-type links were supported from off-set pins with bearings of 4 7/8 sq inch upper link hanger bearings 8 sq inch and link blocks 12.5 sq inch. Their scheming was pursued until he obtained a diagram giving the free exhaust which he

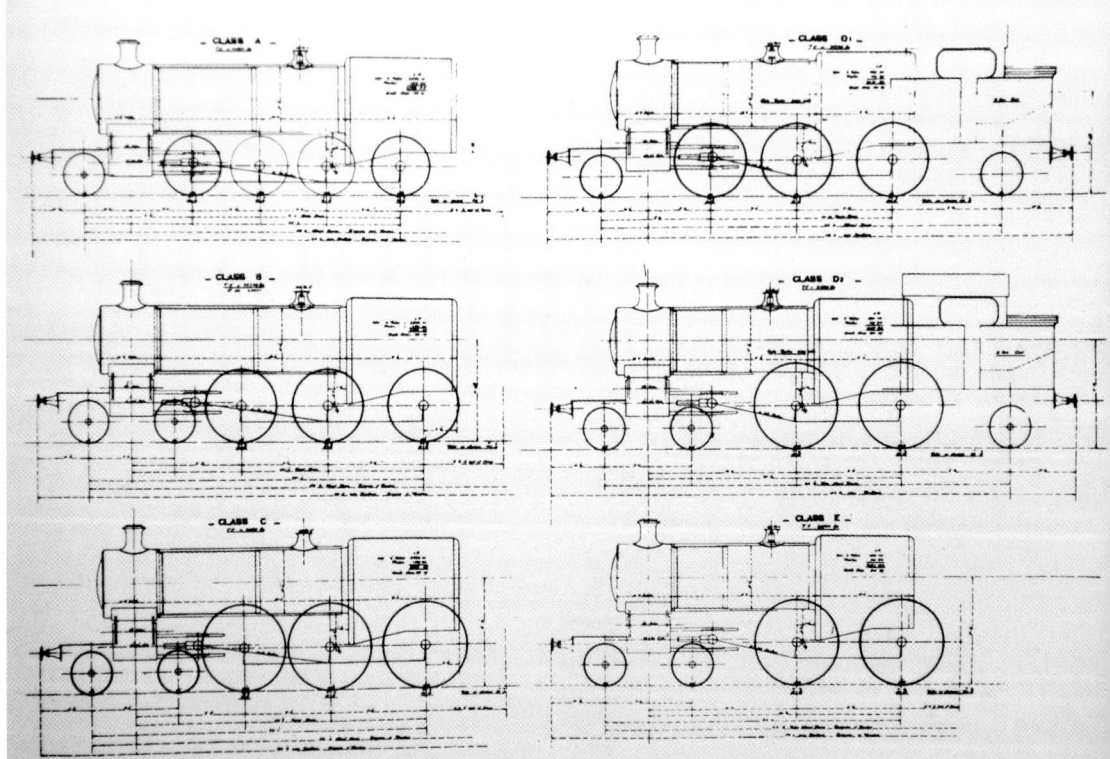

A chart produced in 1901 to accompany a draft paper outlining the shape and type of the first six standardised locomotives designs (and given Class 'A' to 'F' designations) and the types of boiler to be used. Work on these designs appears to have waited, except for the prototype 4-6-0, until Churchward had become Superintendent. At this point, the design work on all six reached a crescendo and one by one they became a reality. The developing familial traits that were a key to this work are easily discernible. (KC)

sought in conjunction with pre-admission compression and cut-off. Valve setting during construction followed with equalised cut-offs and exhaust, which produced the sharp, clear, rhythmic beat which enabled his engines to be recognised from all others.

It is interesting to note how Churchward approached the question of standardisation. There is no strict dogma suggesting only one solution would do, but a measured approach that allowed each design to contain a degree of variation, so that it might better meet the company's needs. So, there is a strong central core slightly softened by some potential variables, thus avoiding the 'one size fits all' solution other less talented engineers or commercial managers might insist upon. The variables did come with some cost implications, when it came to construction and purchasing spares, but far better this way than having locomotives that didn't do the work for which they were intended so incurring a longer term operational cost and penalty.

When describing Churchward's work, Cook's words are a simple statement of fact. As one might expect from an engineer of his standing, the language he uses is unemotional and unembellished by unnecessary detail or conjecture. And yet, he still manages to convey a sense of joy and poetry in his work by expressing the pleasure he felt at hearing the 'sharp, clear, rhythmic beat' of well-constructed steam engines. Engineering is a practical business, but its practitioners seem to see more in it than that. Dedication, I believe, can only be sustained, and perfection sought, when there is a clear attachment to what you are doing. More than this though, there is amongst many design engineers I've known a strong appreciation of aesthetics which they often sum up with the words, 'if it looks right, it is right' when describing a machine.

For a car, aeroplane, ship or locomotive this is easy to understand because good looks are much easier to discern in such things, especially when, as in these cases, the objects are shaped with the needs of hydro and aerodynamic principles in mind. As a result, their form is free flowing which, in the process, creates inherently attractive, harmonious lines. But it is far less so for a loom, a milling machine, a printing press or other engineered device contributing to an industrial process, or so you would think. The truth, I believe, is that men such as Cook see elegance and beauty in any well engineered machine no matter what its purpose and take pleasure in the efficiency of its operation, the sounds it makes and much more.

If this is so, did Churchward show a similar level of aesthetic appreciation or was he immune to such things. Judging by his words when describing carriage design, 'as far as I am concerned carriages could be finished externally with tar etc', one might have thought that he cared little for

By the time Churchward began to plan and then build his first 2-8-0 configured locomotive, the type had been operating successfully in the USA, Australia and Germany for many years. This early example of one of the Pennsylvania Railroad's 2-8-0s shows how far companies in the States had advanced by the time the GWR's prototype, No. 97, appeared in 1903. Unfortunately, I was unable to uncover any performance reports or other information about these engines, so one is left to speculate whether they influenced Churchward in any way. However, as a keen observer of developments in the USA it seems more than likely that he was aware of their existence and through contacts with fellow engineers knew quite a bit about them. (Author's collection)

looks. And yet he still led in producing some of the most handsome, well-balanced locomotives to appear in Britain or anywhere else for that matter, whether they be fast expresses or more mundane freight engines. This, I believe, is no better demonstrated than in the development of his 2-8-0 engines which were designed specifically for the unglamorous task of hauling mineral trains.

In deciding to build a 2-8-0, Churchward would, undoubtedly, have looked to the United States for stimulus, the type being first produced there in the 1860s either by the Pennsylvania Railroad or the Lehigh and Mahonay Railroad. Either way, the type entered service in 1865/66 and by the end of the century many other companies had produced their own versions. So great was their success that when production ended in the mid-twentieth century, more than 23,000 had been built. And it was generally accepted that in service they proved themselves capable of pulling loads twice the size of other types of locomotives and at half the cost. If true, the type was a running manager's, as well as an accountant's, dream. In this situation it was hardly surprising that railway companies in other countries soon adopted the same formula, especially in Australia which began importing American built 2-8-0s from as early as 1879.

Companies in Europe were slower to see the appeal of the 2-8-0s although there is evidence to suggest that examples could be found in Germany quite late in the nineteenth century. By the 1890s, one type in particular, the G7.1 class, had found favour with the Prussian State Railway and in 1893 the first of them appeared from the works of Stettiner Maschinenbau AG Vulcan in Stettin. Once proven in service, the numbers on order increased rapidly and by 1917, when production ended, 1,202 had been built, with other manufacturers being drawn into the programme as demand increased. They were found to be particularly effective when working in Western Germany and Silesia, where the hilly conditions demanded the services of such a strong locomotive, and between 1914 and 1918 they became a mainstay in supporting Germany's war effort.

As numbers increased, so word of their success spread through the engineering world and this would soon have reached and undoubtedly been noted by Churchward. He may not have wished to adopt all elements of its design, but the simple fact that a 2-8-0 was working successfully in a major European country would have been of the greatest interest to him as he considered the GWR's future locomotive needs. And in 1903, the results of his work, the GWR's first 2-8-0, No. 97, made its appearance.

Being much closer to home it seems quite likely that Churchward would have observed the Prussian State Railway's 2-8-0 building programme and the hundreds of these engines – the G7s –that appeared between 1893 and 1917 (1,202 in total). Their sheer number suggests how successful they were and provided an object lesson for others to follow. One wonders whether Churchward ever contemplated buying an example of a G7, as he did for the French SACM 4-4-2s. (Author's collection)

It is clear that the Churchward 2-8-0 and 4-6-0 were developed in parallel, as were two models of his new 2-6-2T (one heavy and one light) and his own version of the 4-4-0. However, construction of the first of all these engines was carefully spread over a twelve-month period. In this way, each prototype could be moulded carefully and then evaluated by engineers as it was put together so giving them time to learn lessons that would inform the development of the next prototype in the programme. This was a methodical and painstaking way of working and probably a slow one too. As a result, the production of these new engines didn't begin in any number until 1905, at which point nineteen 4-6-0s, twenty 2-8-0s, thirty of the two types of 2-6-2Ts and ten 4-4-0s were rolling out of the workshops.

The basic elements of Churchward's first 2-8-0 are set out a little earlier in this chapter alongside the key design features of the six new standard engines, but, of course, there is a great deal more to illustrate when describing these engines. First and foremost it was fitted with a saturated steam boiler which had a total heating surface of 2143.04sqft, made up of a tube heating surface of 1988.65sqft and a firebox heating surface of 154.39sqft. Initially its boiler pressure was set at 200psi to reflect what was happening with the second prototype 4-6-0, No. 98, which had been running operationally for sometime when the 2-8-0 was under construction. However, trial running with the new freight engine soon revealed that this psi could only produce a tractive effort of 29,775lb at 85 per cent cut-off, which engineers quickly concluded was insufficient for their needs. Consequently it was raised to 225lb psi, which allowed the 2-8-0 to produce a

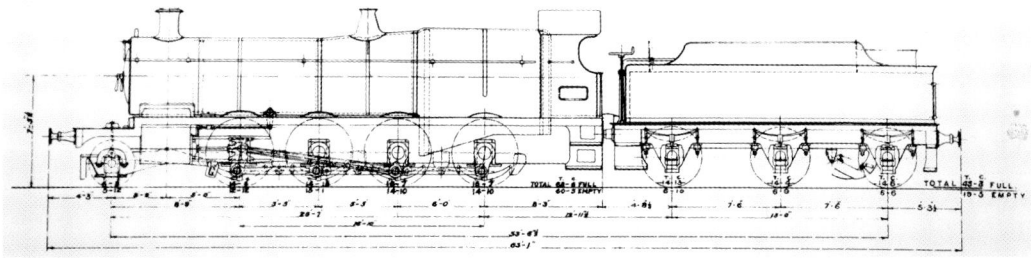

Above and below: Churchward's first 2-8-0. No. 97, as envisioned in the drawing office and as it appeared when constructed in 1903. Although the express passenger services, pulled by the 4-4-0s then the new 4-6-0, attracted most attention and headlines, the company relied more heavily on its freight traffic for profit. With coal production in the South Wales mines reaching an annual total of approximately 60 million tons in the years before the Great War, roughly half of which was exported, the GWR was heavily involved to its movement. The bigger the engines available for this task the better because a higher volume could be moved without recourse to the added expense double heading. So, it is little wonder that Churchward placed such great store in producing his 2-8-0s. (DN)

much healthier 35,380lb of effort, so making it better able to deal with the predicted 1,000 ton coal trains it was scheduled to pull when in service (and revealed in a very public demonstration involving a 1905 built engine, No. 2807, when pulling a vast load of new trucks specifically designed and built for this purpose).

In No. 97's case, the boiler was set at quite a low pitch and, in doing so, sat on the same level as the running plate and splashers. This was considered too restrictive and when the design for the production models was being finalised the boiler was set 8½ inches higher, which, according to Cook, 'allowed easier access to some moving parts and reduced vibrations emanating up through the wheels so making the ride easier for the footplate crew.' In due course, No. 97 would be similarly fitted so conforming to the rest of the class in this and other ways. Of these the boiler pressure was the most noteworthy, then came the cylinder and piston valves, which were increased in size from 18 x 30 in to 18½ x 30 in and 8½in to 10 in diameter respectively, and a tender carrying 3,000 gallons of water replaced one holding 4,000 gallons.

No. 97 became operational in June 1903 and was soon undergoing tests along the mainline beside the prototype 4-6-0s, Nos. 100, 98 and then 171, which soon became a 4-4-2 so that it could be compared to the French built engine No. 102. Sadly, few details of this work appear to have survived and the same can be said of any tests on the rolling road at Swindon carried out later on. However, with such a methodical and astute engineer in charge of the programme, it is probably safe to assume that evaluation and analysis techniques were carefully and rigorously applied. And in this way each breed underwent modification to make them more efficient in performing the tasks for which they were designed. However, this work was in no way hurried and lasted through the remainder of 1903 and into 1904, and only then was approval to build more of each type given.

As the prototype 4-6-0s and 2-8-0 progressed from the drawing board to become living entities, the two new types of 2-6-2 standard tank engine, with different wheel sizes, were also

2800 Class engine No. 2807 built at Swindon in 1905 is photographed pulling a long line of new trucks primarily designed to carry coal. In the notes accompanying this very old print this is described as being 'a train designed to pull up to 1,000 tons of coal with newly designed wagons, 500 of which have just entered service, with another 450 to follow. On this occasion it is heading west to North's Navigation Colliery at Maesteg in an empty state to begin work.' To my mind there can be no better demonstration of the 2800's importance to the GWR and the South Wales mines than this. (DN)

in development. Having reviewed the company's needs, it had become clear to Churchward that engines such as this were needed to service secondary routes where the loading gauge imposed restrictions on larger locomotives. To meet the needs of different weights of train, it was decided to produce heavy and lighter versions, so giving the type the widest possible route availability across the GWR's network.

The first engine developed, in what became known as the 3100, then the 5100 Class, was numbered 99 and appeared in 1903 to begin, as had become usual, a prolonged period of testing before the main batch entered production. Like the prototype 2-8-0 it started out with two 18 x 30in cylinders, which were, in due course, increased in size to 18½ x 30in, and became standard on the remaining members of the class when built. Initially the engine was fitted with a short cone taper boiler that produced 195psi and a tractive effort of 23,690lb at 85 per cent cut-off, a trim cast-iron chimney, straight topped side tanks, 5ft 8in driving wheels and a water tank capable of holding 1380 gallons.

Following tests with No. 99, a Standard No. 2 boiler was fitted which was able to generate 200lb of pressure which allowed the tractive effort to be increased to 24,300lb. In addition,

(Above) The prototype 2-6-2 tank engine, No. 99, as it appeared in 1903. Cook would later write in a letter that he thought this class was 'one of the most elegant, best balanced engines built by Churchward and one he often mentioned when discussing how successfully all the engines produced by Swindon ran. He clearly valued them highly and operationally they proved particularly valuable especially during the Great War where strong engines such as this were worth their weight in gold.' High praise indeed. (Below) A Swindon drawing that shows how the design was modified and, in due course, became the 5100 Class. (DN)

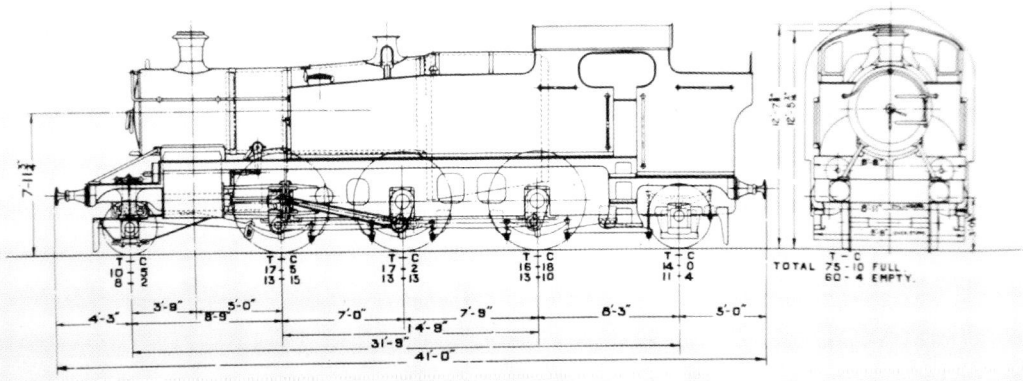

the tanks were made larger and modified with sloping sides, to improve forward visibility from the cab, and were capable of carrying 1,000 gallons each, so allowing an appreciably longer range between refills. Much later on and for the same reason, the bunker was, in the post Great War years, extended so that it could hold an additional 18 cwt of coal. Bearing in mind the increasingly heavy loads these engines were required to pull, during and after the war, this was a simple but effective way of achieving this goal. However, the extra weight of coal and water they now carried could restrict their route availability. As a result, some of the engines ran with a tank capacity deliberately set at 1,600 gallons, which could present the driver and fireman with a small, additional operating problem.

The other new 2-6-2T was a little slower in appearing only making an entrance in 1904 at Swindon. Here again Churchward thought a prototype necessary, although in this case with No. 99 performing so successfully the need was probably not quite so pressing as it might have been. In appearance and concept this engine, soon designated No. 115, was a scaled down version of its bigger sister. It was fitted with a new half-coned taper Standard No. 5 boiler with a heating surface of 1272.6sqft producing a working pressure of 165lb and a tractive effort of 18,514lb at 85 per cent cut-off. Its two outside cylinders were 16½ x 24in and the engine was carried on 4ft 1½in coupled wheels – a solution which gave the 4400 Class, as they became known, a remarkable rate of acceleration. This would prove particularly useful when running over branch lines where frequent halts and challenging gradients were often the order of the day. Here a snappy start and an ability to accelerate up a slope would make these engines an indispensable choice until they were withdrawn in the 1950s.

No. 115 having successfully passed muster and been accepted into service encouraged the GWR to order another ten of the class, all of which were built at the company's Wolverhampton Works in 1905/06. This was itself an interesting outcome because with Swindon expanding rapidly, secondary shops such as Wolverhampton would soon be struggling for new construction work. It says much for Churchward that he was aware of this and sought a means of keeping a

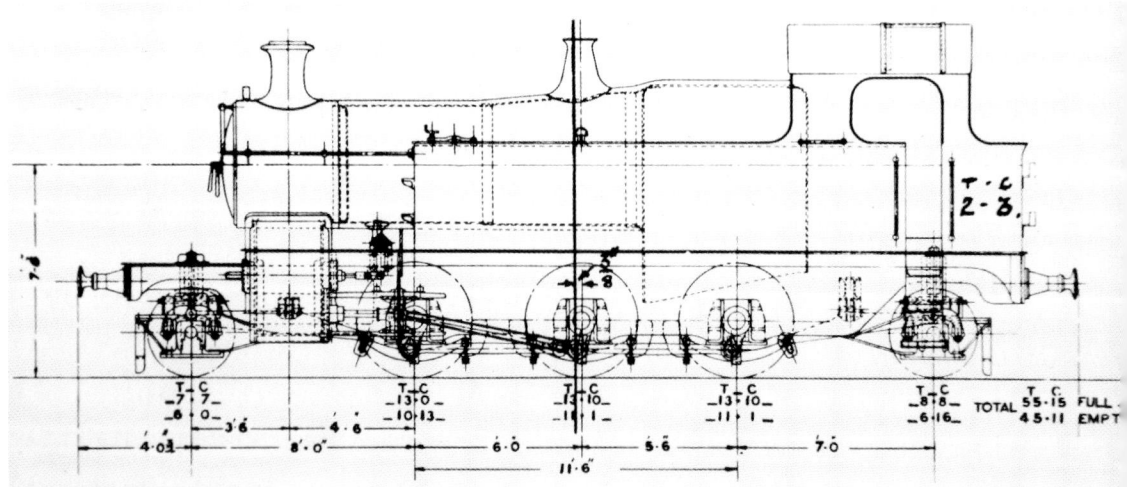

A need was identified for a powerful but fairly small tank engine to service small branch lines where operating conditions could be challenging – steep gradients and sharp curves particularly found in some corners of Devon and Cornwall. The Swindon design team's response was the take the 2-6-2T 3100 Class and scale it down. The result was the prototype 2-6-2 No. 115 which appeared in 1904 and is seen here in drawing form. It successfully underwent trials and by 1906 ten more had been built in the GWR's Stafford Road Works in Gorsebrook to the north of Wolverhampton. (RH)

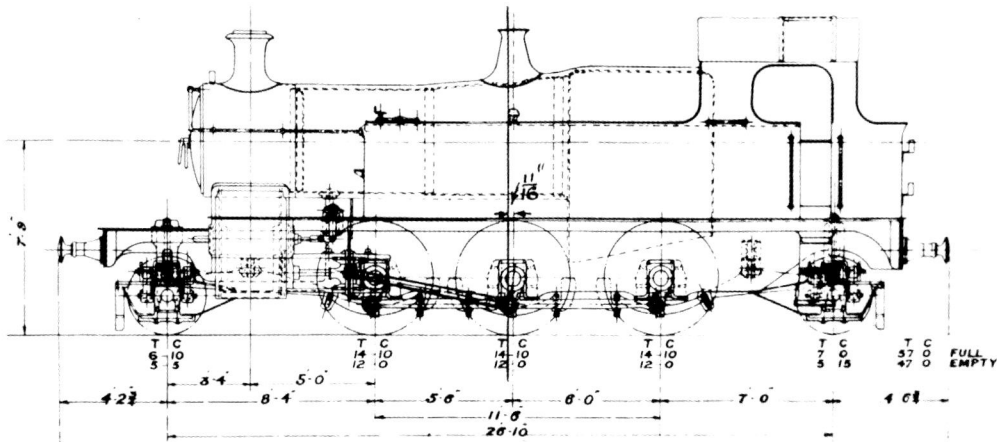

Although the 4400 Class 2-6-2Ts proved to be successful when operating over branch lines, it was soon realised that their number needed to be supplemented by something a little bit more powerful. The 4500 Class was the result, here captured in the design stage (above) and (below) when in service. In this case, the locomotive is No. 2179, one of the first twenty to be built in 1906/08 at the company's Wolverhampton Works. (Author's collection)

well-established workforce as busy as he could for as long as it was possible to do so. However, he was only partially successful in this and in 1908 the Works closed for all but maintenance and repair tasks, which still required quite a large number of employees. But never again did it enjoy the status it had once, perhaps, taken for granted.

In due course, Churchward produced another version of this lighter 2-6-2, the 4500 Class, and again took the opportunity to exploit workshop capacity at Stafford Road to get the first twenty of them built between 1906 and 1908. But they were, it appears, the last engines to be constructed there; the remainder being built at Swindon over a 15 year period beginning in 1909. Later on, a Collett modified version, the 4575, would also be added the first appearing in 1927. By the time this last batch entered service the class had swollen to 175 in total and after long operating lives, lasting in some cases into the 1960s, three 4500s and eleven 4575s were saved from the cutting torch and were preserved.

The reason for designing this new version was simply based on experience gained in running the 4400s. Although they were thought to be good at what they did, it was soon realised that their acceleration might be improved by increasing the size of the driving wheels and, at the same time, alter their wheel spacing. With such a relatively minor change it wasn't thought necessary to build a prototype and so an order was placed on Stafford Road Works to begin construction of the first batch of engines.

In reality, the work was more complex than simply fitting bigger, 4ft 7½in driving wheels and resulted in other modifications. The cylinder sizes were increased to 17x24in from 16½x24in, the boiler pressure went up from 165 to 180psi and the tractive effort from 18,151 to 19,120lbs at 85 per cent cut-off. In the trials that followed it was found that their turn of speed had improved and, if driver reports are correct, they could reach and sustain 60mph. And in this state they entered service at various locations around the network where they seem to have been well liked. In due course their boiler pressure was increased to 200lb, superheaters were fitted and the coal bunkers were enlarged. When the 4575s were built they were fitted with larger water tanks that could carry 1,300 gallons. This made them easily distinguishable from the 4500s because the larger side tanks sloped downwards at the front to try and give the crew a better view forward.

The construction programme for both types of 2-6-2 began in earnest in 1905, as it did for the 4-6-0s and 2-8-0s. By the end of 1906 twenty-nine Saints had been added to the three prototypes, with numbers gradually increasing until seventy-seven were in service by 1913. There might have been more but Churchward had introduced his new four-cylinder 4-6-0 Star 4000 Class in large numbers by then and his 'masterpiece', as some called it, had taken the design of fast express locomotives to a new level. Meanwhile, the number of 2-8-0s had swollen by an additional twenty in 1906 and would continue to rise until the last of 168 appeared in 1942. In the process, they served the South Wales mines, the GWR's other freight requirements and Britain's massive wartime effort in both the 1914/18 and 1939/45 conflicts in a most efficient and effective way.

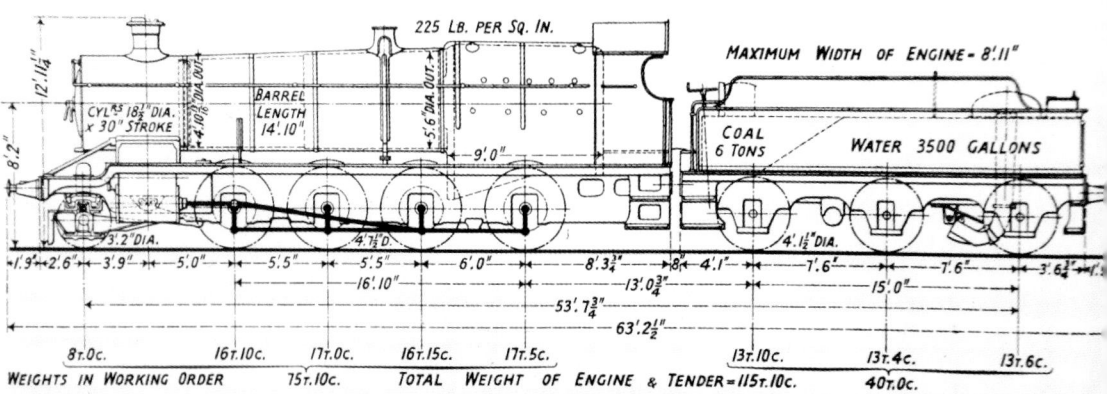

A Swindon diagram showing how the 2-8-0s evolved from prototype No. 97 into a class that eventually reached 168 in number by 1942. There can be no doubt about the success of these engines, in both peace and war, over half a century or more. In due course, Churchward, would add to their number with the 4700 Class, nine of which were built between 1919 and 1923, which were designed to work fast vacuum-fitted freight trains. (DN)

Then there were the eleven 4400 2-6-2s, which did sterling service in many backwaters around the south-west and South Wales. As they tackled these duties their bigger 3100 Class sisters increased in number to forty-one in 1906, with the last of this group then being treated as a prototype, being fitted with a Standard No. 4 boiler. This increased the engine's size and power quite considerably and so led to the creation of the more potent 3150 Class, which grew in numbers until 40 were in service by 1908.

The 3150s did in fact differ slightly to the prototype in having 18½ x 30in cylinders and a higher tractive effort – 25,670lb as compared to 24,300lb. Other than this they were virtually the same and in this form found active service as banking engines, a role which they appear to have undertaken fairly well, on piloting duties through the Severn Tunnel and on more general passenger and freight turns when required. However, it is thought that banking heavy trains up steep gradients exerted too much pressure through the leading pony truck to be safely absorbed by their front-end frames. As a result, they suffered some stress fractures that required occasional repair. To correct this defect, it was found necessary to fit strengthening struts, which, after careful monitoring and evaluation, became a standard feature on other engines with this leading truck arrangement.

Sandwiched amongst all this new work were other projects, some purely theoretical in nature to explore different concepts, others with a more practical end in mind. This second group would, in time, go beyond the drawing board to be constructed, while the others remained abstract in

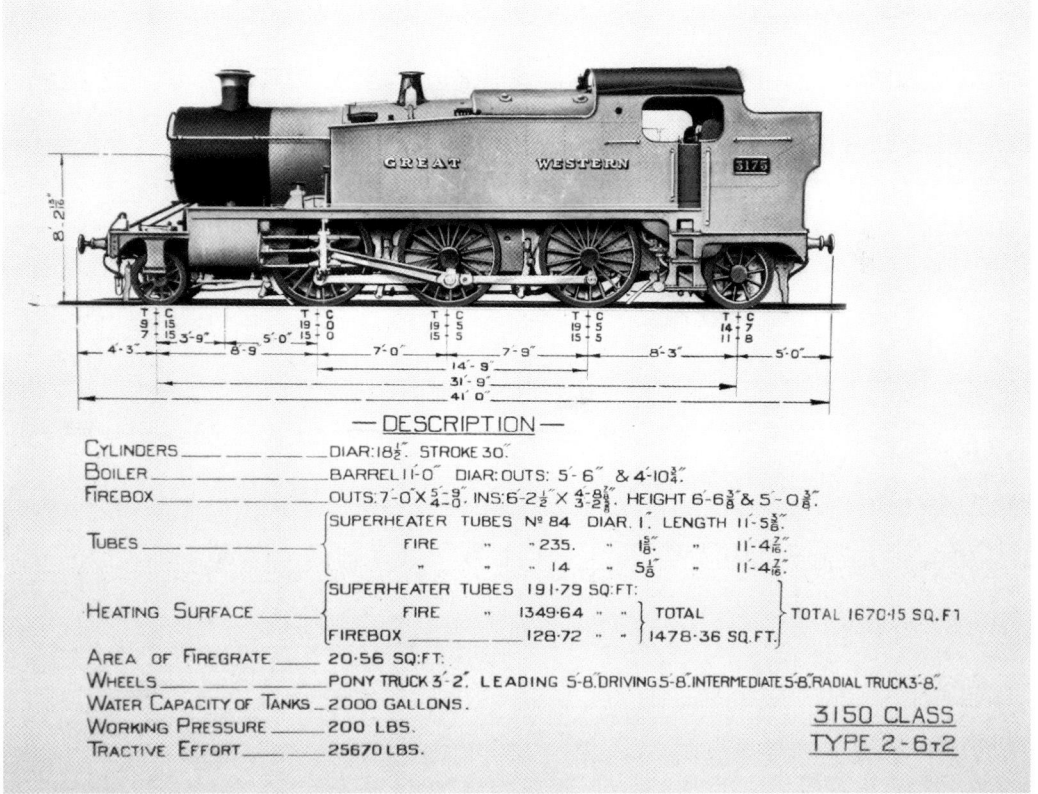

The Swindon diagram for the 3150 Class of 2-6-2T which evolved from the 3100 Class, the last of which was built as a prototype to carry a Standard No. 4 boiler with a higher working pressure, a bigger heating surface and greater tractive effort. (Author's collection)

nature – interesting to view, but unlikely to progress further. To consider what might have been is always an interesting path to follow, though, inevitably, a fruitless one when based on speculation and guesswork. The importance of such flights of fancy really rests on the way any leader is prepared to be broad and expansive in the way they consider all options and not be limited by lack of imagination, and in doing so encourage their followers to be equally as inventive.

To be a true scientist is to be constantly curious and driven to explore all aspects of need and how it might be best met. Churchward did this naturally and his team gladly followed their inspired leader. In this he truly excelled, but he did so with a profound understanding of his business and the best way of balancing, what could at times be conflicting demands. By 1905/06 he had reached the pinnacle of his career and was able to serve these scientific and commercial needs with a master's touch. As a result, he and his team were open in their exploration and although many records of their work no longer exist sufficient remains to allow us to view some of his more speculative ventures. Two in particular are noteworthy, both tank engines, neither of which seems to have appeared in his standardisation plans, though undoubtedly contained some standard features.

The first of these was a 0-8-0 tank engine. This locomotive, which was designed to fulfil a variety of shunting duties, was to be fitted with a Swindon No. 5 boiler, 4ft 1½in coupled wheels, two standard type outside 16½x24in cylinders and 8in valves. In the event the idea was dropped when it was decided that existing engines, plus other new standard classes then entering service could cope with these tasks just as well. Nevertheless, it was hardly wasted effort because it allowed designers to evaluate the requirement logically and in some detail.

The same might be said of a separate experiment with a 4-4-4 passenger tank engine considered at the same time which built upon work being undertaken on a 4-4-2 tank locomotives, which entered service in 1905. The 4-4-4 engine would have carried a Standard Boiler No. 4 producing 195psi and be fitted with 6ft 8½in coupled wheels. In addition, it would have carried some of the other standard features found on the new 4-4-2, including cylinders and valves, a similar leading truck and grate area plus water and coal carrying capacity. Here, once again, the design was destined to remain a paper exercise only, to be filed when it was discovered that good alternatives already existed.

Although some of this speculative development work may have seemed to be so much wasted effort it still added much to the sum total of the designer's knowledge. And sometimes, years later, an idea once explored in detail and then put on hold was resurrected to become a reality. Here it was usually a case that business or operational conditions had changed for some reason and an idea once rejected in principle quickly gained ground. As we shall see, these included a 4-6-0 with 5ft 8in coupled wheels, a second 4-6-0 with a Standard No. 7 boiler with 6ft 8½in wheels and a 2-8-2T which was eventually built as a 2-8-0T instead.

In the meantime, Churchward pressed on with two other new standard locomotives for which a clear need had been recognised – a new 4-4-0 and, as mentioned earlier, a 4-4-2T. In due course, these engines became known as the 3800 County Class and the 2221 Country Tank Class, respectively.

The first ten of the two-cylinder 3800s entered service in 1904. Having been so closely involved in Dean's 4-4-0 programme, the last of which were still being built well into Churchward's reign as Superintendent, it isn't surprising that he should seek to continue with such a successful programme and include it in his standardisation plans. And here, once again, he produced a prototype, No. 3473, to test his ideas, though in this case the test and evaluation schedule was much shorter for reasons that aren't entirely clear. However, it may simply have been a case that the engine's constituent parts had been so extensively tested by then that anything more detailed was thought unnecessary. So, the engine quickly proved itself, where it mattered, on the mainline, and within the year nine more had been added to the fleet, with another thirty, built in two batches in 1906 and 1911/12, added later.

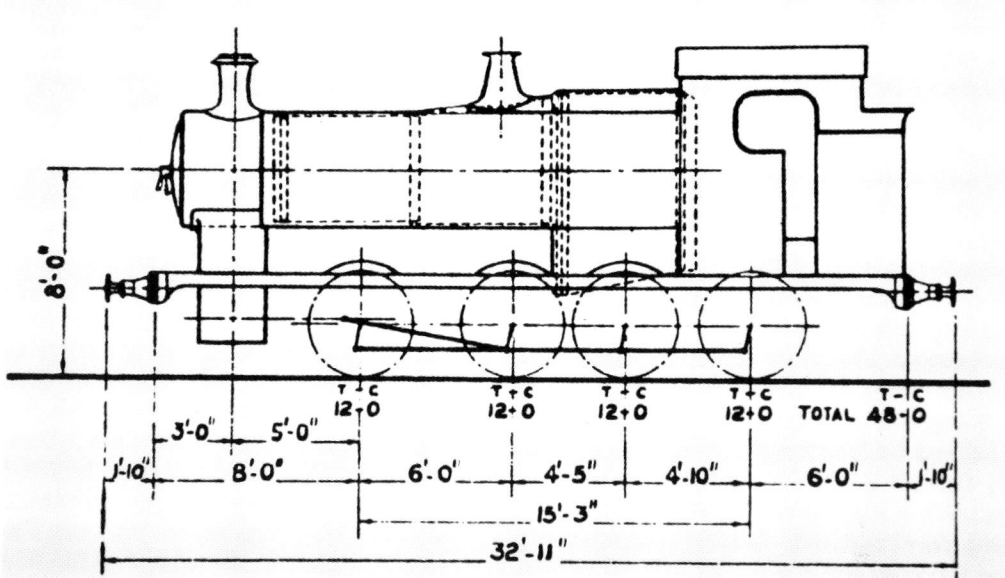

Theoretical speculation and exploration are essential skills for scientists and design engineers to possess and then exploit in their drive to invent new, hopefully better solutions. Churchward and his team remained open minded when developing new types of locomotive. Some of their ideas came to fruition while others remained on the drawing board. (Above) One of these was an 0-8-0T for shunting duties and (below) the other a 4-4-4T, presumably designed as a mixed traffic engine. Neither came to fruition, other engines, both old and new, being thought sufficiently effective for the GWR's needs. (DN)

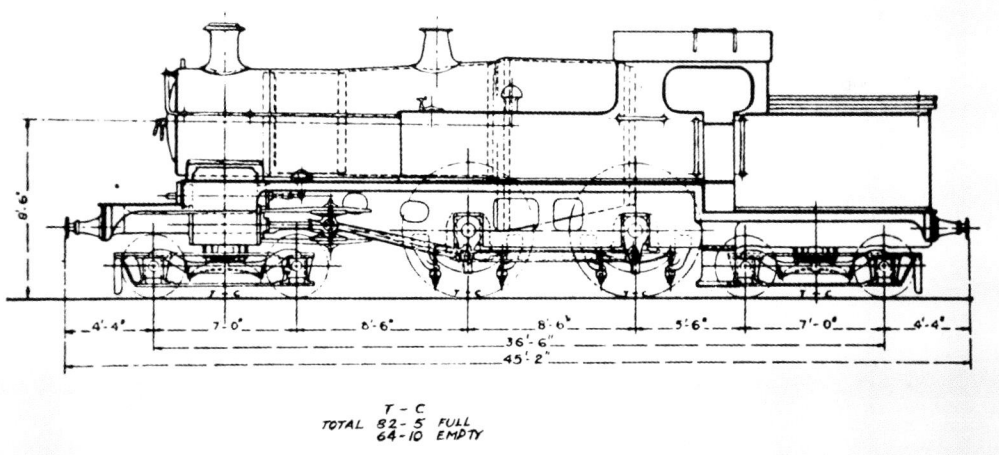

In concept the first of this new class has been quoted as being a shortened version of Churchward's 4-6-0 prototype No. 98. As such it had two outside cylinders measuring 18 x 30in, 6ft 8½in coupled wheels and more. For power it relied upon a non-superheated Standard Type 4 boiler, which had proved so successful on the City Class. With a total heating surface of 1818.12sqft and a grate area of 20.56sqft, it could produce a working pressure of 200psi and a tractive effort of 20,530lb at 85 per cent cut-off.

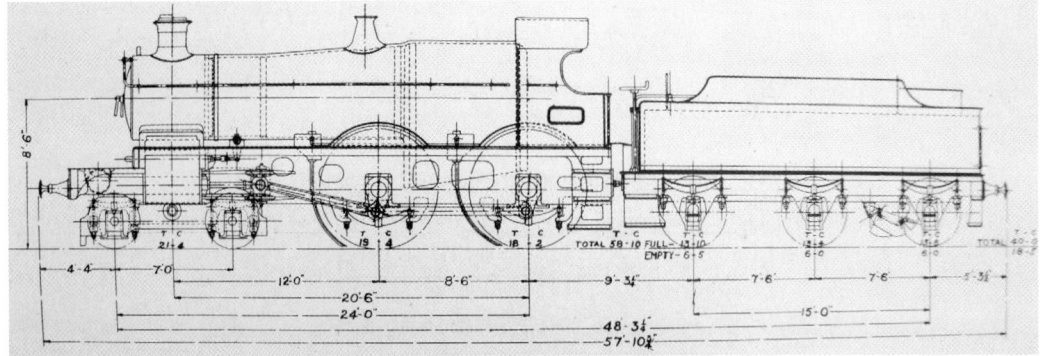

Above and below: Churchward's prototype 3800 Class 4-4-0 No. 3473, *County of Middlesex*, as drawn and when constructed at Swindon. Unlike the City Class 4-4-0s, which were built a year before 3473 and nine sisters appeared, the new 4-4-0 had an overstretched slightly unbalanced look. This was caused by the wide gap between the coupled wheels and the leading truck which had been created to provide adequate space in which the two large cylinders and motion could operate. In service the class gained a reputation for rough riding. All were withdrawn from traffic by 1933. (DN/Author's collection)

When these engines entered service in May 1904 they soon gained a reputation for 'rough riding', when compared to the inside cylinder 4-4-0s, with a very noticeable habit of rolling badly. This was thought to be a result of such large cylinders being matched to 6ft 8½in wheels on a short coupled wheelbase. True or not, it is said that they soon gained the slightly unwelcome soubriquet 'Churchward's Rough Riders', a name Cook thought, when recording some background notes for his 1950 presentation, to be 'Thoroughly deserved and one they couldn't shake off even when undergoing periodic adjustment and modification. They were not thought to be one of Churchward's better engines, though some still survived in service until 1933.'

The remainder of the class appeared in two batches – one in 1906 and the other in 1911/12 – bringing the total number of locomotives up to forty. In the meantime, they were being modified with vacuum cylinder brakes rather than a steam operated version, superheaters, lengthened smokeboxes, larger chimney's and one, No. 3805, was fitted with a Standard Type 2 boiler carried by members of the Bulldog Class as an experiment. In this state plus the addition of a plate frame bogie, it ran for two years or so, presumably so that the two types might be compared. If so, it doesn't seem as though any comparability data has survived, so we are left to speculate why this work was undertaken.

The design of the 2221 Class, with 6ft 8½in coupled wheels, tended to mirror the work being undertaken on the 3800s, though in this case a Standard No. 2 boiler was used instead. However, Churchward decided that no prototype was needed, so allowed production of the first

This undated photo, though thought to be taken in the 1920s, shows an unidentified 3800 Class engine dropping down towards Totnes, its crew enjoying a brief rest during a run back and forth on the challenging Exeter to Plymouth line. It is interesting to note the mixed type of carriages in use and the exposed nature of the cabs particularly on passenger locomotives. The crew only had minimal protection and must have suffered considerably in Britain's challenging climate. Records show that short and long term illnesses ran at a high level due to these poor working conditions. Lung diseases and skin conditions, such as cancers and dermatitis, were the most common complaints, but there were many other work related illnesses too. You had to be made of very stern stuff to survive on the footplate. (DN)

ten locomotives to proceed in one go. By this stage, other prototypes and sufficient numbers of production models had been tested to show which elements of the standard class designs were successful, and this tended to render another test programme of limited value. In addition, any potential faults in the specific engine from which it was derived had been considered too minor to cause a problem or, if more severe, had been overcome by applying modifications or adjustments in the workshops. The principal concern over the 3800's ride quality is not reported as having been a problem with these smaller engines. Although with the same cylinders and short coupled wheelbase such a problem might have been unavoidable, but far less noticeable than on the bigger engines which probably ran at much higher speeds when pulling fast passenger services.

In terms of its design, the 2221s were following a well-worn path through the Drawing Office and workshops, in the process relying on many already tried and tested standard features. The boiler had a total heating surface of 1517.89sqft and a grate area of 20.35sqft which produced 195lb of pressure and generated a tractive effort of 20,010lb. In addition, the engine could carry a maximum of 3 tons of coal and 2,000 gallons of water in side tanks which, like some of the 3100 Class and all of the 3150 Class, sloped downwards at the front. This was done for the good practical reason of improving visibility, but, nonetheless, seemed to improve the lines of an already

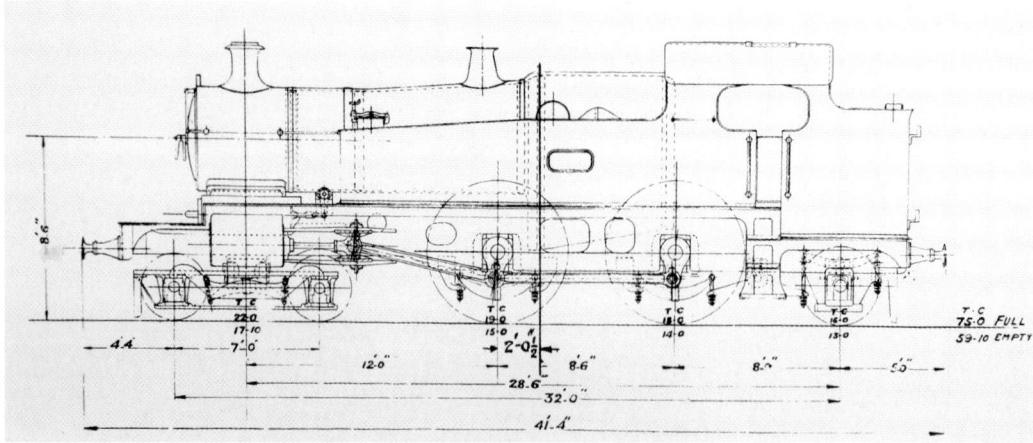

(Above) The first of Churchward's 2221 Class 4-4-2 tank engines appeared in December 1905 and adopted many of the features used on the 3800 Class. It also copied its slightly overstretched look, a result of the spacing of the front bogie in relation to the coupled wheels. Twenty more would be built in two batches in 1908/09 and 1912, with some surviving in service well into the 1930s. During their operating lives they appear to have been mostly employed around London on semi-fast suburban passenger duties and seem to have undertaken this work fairly effectively. (Below) Engine No. 2223, which first appeared in 1906, is photographed at Didcot. This locomotive survived in service until 1932 (DN/Author's collection)

elegant engine. Those built later also had curved drop ends fitted at the front, a modification also applied to the 3800s so improving, even further, the looks of both engines.

In due course, other modifications were carried out including the fitting of superheaters, top-feed and lengthened smokeboxes. With this work completed, the combined heating surface had reduced to 1316.14sqft, with the superheater contributing 184.75sqft to this total. All this had the effect of raising their tractive effort by 520lb to 20,530lb so equalling that of the 3800 Class. This power to weight ratio and tractive effort probably made them ideally suited for the role for which they were intended – pulling semi-fast outer suburban services particularly in the London area. At this they appear to have been successful for nearly 30 years, but ever changing needs often requires new solutions. So, in the 1930s Collett and his team began introducing the

The changing face of the GWR in Churchward's hands. County Class 4-4-0 No. 3816, *County of Leicester*, was discovered by the photographer idling in a siding at Weymouth in about 1906. Her bulk easily casts a shadow over the diminutive and quaintly old-fashioned 0-6-0 saddle tank No. 1978, which was built at the Stafford Road Works in 1890/91 as a member of the 120 strong 1901 Class. Only sixteen years separated the construction of these two engines but in shape and form they seem to come from different ages. However, many of the 1901s were later rebuilt as pannier tank engines with some surviving into British Railway's service long after all of the County Class 4-4-0s had been scrapped. (Author's collection)

first of seventy updated 2-6-2T, the 6100 Class, and these more advanced, powerful models soon began to supersede the 2221s. Some lingered for a while, but by 1935 they were all gone with none of them finding their way into preservation.

With so much achieved in the three years since taking office, Churchward must have looked to the future with a degree of optimism. However, he must also have realised that there was still a mountain to climb if he was to ensure the GWR had the right locomotives, carriages and waggons to meet all their developing needs. So far, the Chairman and Board's choice in promoting him to be Superintendent had proved sound, but only time would tell if he could cement his growing reputation in the industry and continue taking the company forward.

Chapter 6
Changing Times and Competing Expectations

Britain by 1906 was a country undergoing a period of rapid social change, undoubtedly spurred on by many reforming voices raised in protest on issues such as workers' rights and women's suffrage. For a man such as Churchward, who grew to maturity as a member of a privileged class in the mid-years of Queen Victoria's reign, where stifling conformity and unquestioning obedience were expected by a small ruling elite, the spread of such non-conformist views may well have

It is very difficult to convey in photographs the challenging conditions faced each day by workers in heavy industry. This was none more so than on the railways, with this picture, taken at Swindon in 1908, mistakenly suggesting a world of order and calm. In reality, life in the factories meant hard physical graft, in the poorest possible working conditions and long working days submerged by excessive levels of noise, and surrounded by noxious substances, fumes and the dirt generated by heavy and light machinery alike. The result for all was a very hard physical life that brought with it many work related illnesses and frequent accidents, both fatal and crippling, all for a poor level of pay and few, if any, benefits. It was this world that Churchward managed with an iron hand, though, it seems, not always inside a velvet glove. (DN)

been troubling. But the Industrial Revolution, the growing power of trades unions and the slow spread of socialism in the late nineteenth century, had created a desire for something more than a continuation of old acquiescent attitudes and a poverty of expectations.

It was a slow spreading movement punctuated by conflict and containment and yet the need for better lives and a fairer share for all became a rallying call that couldn't be stifled forever. This clamour for change began to reach a peak in Edwardian Britain and very soon sustained a level of protest that many leaders in society, politics and industry found hard to accept or deal with satisfactorily. Some adapted, when faced with an inevitable impasse, but others simply refused to change until forced to do so and then only grudgingly. It remained to be seen which of these paths Churchward, as a leader in industry and local politics, would follow.

Kenneth Cook, who was able to observe him closely, and was an undoubted admirer, believed that Churchward may have been more a conservative than liberal when it came to dealing with these changes in society. In a letter written in 1965 he recorded that:

> He was not a cruel, vindictive or unsympathetic man, in fact he displayed a general warmth and generosity to those around him, especially at work, provided they laboured hard and earnestly and did not question what he did or his decisions. He had little time for 'shirkers' or 'layabouts', as he called them, and dealt with them severely and ruthlessly whenever necessary. For him the success of the business and his engineering projects were all that seemed to matter and the conditions under which people lived and worked was of secondary importance to that. This inevitably put him on a path of conflict with the reformers in a battle in which he was seen to favour capital over labour.
>
> It is probably true to say that he found it particularly difficult dealing with trades unions at times, which were growing in strength even before the Great War changed society in so many ways. He saw them as an unnecessary evil so could and would continue to be very dismissive of their efforts to improve pay and working conditions. Younger managers such as Collett and Stanier were prepared to move with the times (though both could be intransigent and ruthless when the need arose), not so the 'old man'. But he genuinely believed that he was a generous employer and manager and one who had the workers' welfare at heart. As a result, he didn't see any need for any union committee to come between him and the people for whom he ultimately bore responsibility. And, in truth, he was keenly aware of this responsibility and strove to be as generous and accommodating as he could within the strictures of what the company could afford and the law as it stood then, which greatly favoured the employer and did so until the 1930s and '40s.

If this is so, then he reflected the attitude of many leaders at that time, who saw industry as a one-way process in which an unsympathetic take it or leave it approach flourished. If this way of working applied at Swindon, Churchward did, at least, try to temper it with some understanding of what his workforce faced and earnt some respect in the process. However, whether this respect was based on fear of what he could do with all the powers vested in him when crossed or arose from a genuine admiration for the man himself is unclear. Either way, the shops he ruled over were not places for the faint hearted, as Alfred Williams, in his 1915 autobiography *Life in a Railway Factory* makes very clear. In this classic, painfully honest book he describes in a very revealing way the poor quality of life in the workshops at Swindon in Churchward's time in charge. In doing this he could fall back on many years of experience having begun work there when aged 14 in 1891 as a rivet hotter and then spent much of his career as a skilled craftsman operating steam hammers, 'forging and smithing besides lines of furnaces (fifteen in all)' as he described it:

> Southward the shed faces a yard of about 10 acres in extent. This is bounded on every side by other workshops and premises, all built of the same dingy materials blackened with

Scenes inside the workshops in the early years of the twentieth century. (Above) A typical group of GWR industrial workers whose only protective clothing seems to be stout boots and an array of hats, mostly of the flat cap variety, yet all seem to wear shirts and jackets. The two men wearing bowler hats are probably supervisory staff. (Below) Gradually the age at which children could be employed in factories, mines and so on had gone up from having no limit to ten years of age and by 1902 fourteen was the norm, although with few inspectors to audit the way companies worked this was a law not always observed. This picture of a young boy, who looks no older than ten or eleven, employed to chop wood to feed fires and furnaces captures the nature of the hard, repetitive work and Dickensian conditions inflicted on young minds and bodies. (DN/RH)

smoke, dust and steam, surmounted with tall chimneys, innumerable ventilators, and poles for telephone wires, which effectually block out all perspective. To view it from the interior is like looking around the inner walls of a fortress...It is ugly; and the sense of confinement within the prison-like walls of the factory renders it still more dismal.... There is no escape, he accepts the conditions and is swallowed up by his environment.

A great alteration, physically and morally, usually takes place in the man or boy newly arrived from the country into the workshop. His fresh complexion and generally healthy appearance soon disappears.....In a few weeks' time he becomes thin and pale, or blue and hollow-eyed. His appetite fails; he is always tired and weary.

When Alfred Williams first entered the works in 1891 as a child he was employed as a rivet hotter for craftsmen who then beat or machined the rivets into place. (Above left) Here two boys stand over a fire preparing rivets to be fitted to what looks like a wagon under construction. (Above right) The Carriage and Wagon Stamping Shop containing a line of steam drop hammers. (Below) A group of industrial workers and their supervisory staff again revealing an absence of any protective clothing. On this occasion it is boilermakers, though what they are wearing has a strangely uniform quality about it. (DN/RH)

The change in character and morals is often pronounced as is the physical transformation: the newcomer, especially if he is a juvenile, is speedily initiated into the vices prevalent in the factory.....Some of the workmen are greatly to blame in respect of this, and are guilty of almost criminal behavior in their dealings with young boys.

While the men are inside the walls of the factory, they are under the most severe laws and restrictions, many of which are utterly ridiculous and out of all reason considering the general circumstances of the toil and conditions in vogue; they are indeed prisoners in every sense of the term.....There is little or no thought taken for the future, no knowledge of the value of life and not much desire to know, either. The workmen do not think for themselves and if you should be at pains of pointing out anything for their benefit they will tell you that you are mad, or curse you for a socialist. Anyone at the works who holds a view different from that expressed by the crowd is called a Socialist, rightly or wrongly; it would need an earthquake to rouse many men out of their apathy and indifference.

Thus, the workman's sphere is very narrow and limited. There is no freedom, nothing but the same coming and going, the still monotonous journey to and fro and the old hours, month after month, year after year. It is no wonder that the factory workmen come to lead a dull existence and to lose interest in all life beyond their own smoky walls and dwellings.

As soon as it becomes known that it is intended to discharge a number of hands (usually during periods when there is less work to do) considerable anxiety is evidenced in the rank and file, and especially by the unskilled of the shed....It is usually men of their class who are chosen to go, together with any who are old and feeble, those who are subject to periodical attacks of illness or have met with an accident at some time and those who are clumsy, and those to whom the foreman owes a grudge.

I remember once, when the work was slack in the shed, the day overseer left orders for the night boss to send the men outside in the yard and keep them there for two or three hours shifting scrap iron, in order that they might 'catch cold and stop at home and give the others a chance'. After the last great discharge at the factory, in the year 1909, when a thousand men were dismissed, in order to 'reduce expenses', it was reported that every manager at the works was granted a substantial increase in salary

Sometimes as many as a hundred men of the same shed have received their notices of dismissal on one day... they are quickly removed after a day's notice and are presently forgotten....For those who are subject to illness, contracted on the premises, or are getting

For most of his career Williams worked as a skilled craftsman operating steam hammers, 'forging and smithing besides lines of furnaces (fifteen in all)' as he later recalled. This picture captures one of the hammers he worked and some of his fellow labourers. It was hard, hot, dirty work which his doctor came to believe had 'destroyed the whole of his digestive system'. True or not such work was, like many others tasks undertaken at Swindon, extremely damaging to the health of employees. (DN)

on in life it is little less than a tragedy....Some find their way into the workhouse to end their days there and others develop into permanent loafers and outcasts and beg their food from door to door.

A principal cause of trouble everywhere between employer and the employed is the lack of recognition of the worker. I do not mean merely that great and powerful combinations do not want to recognize Trades Unions. We all know that. It is part of their policy and is dictated by pride and the spirit of intolerance. But they make a more serious and fatal mistake. They refuse to recognize a man. All kinds of employer are guilty of this. The mine owner, the trading syndicate, the railway or steamship company. Municipal authorities and more. If they would recognize the man, they might be led to a consideration of his legitimate needs.

[To do this] they must first admit him to be equally a member of the human family and then recognize that, as such, he has claims as righteous and sacred as their own. This is where the representative of capital invariably fails. He will not admit that the one under his authority has any rights of his own. To him the worker is as much a slave as ever he was.... As he flouts the individual so he condemns the collective organizations of the men. He is determined not to recognize them. He considers this to be proof of his strength. In reality it is a badge of weakness. Sooner or later it will prove to be his undoing."

Williams was a clever, perceptive and articulate man who through self-education gradually found a cause to pursue with great passion. He then felt able to voice his concerns and describe in very vivid terms the injustices he saw around him in Swindon. As a result, he pulled few punches in his criticisms and one is left to wonder whether he had been thought of as a radical and a troublemaker even before publication? Certainly an unnamed reviewer of the book, working

During Churchward's time in charge at Swindon there were undoubted improvements made to many workshops in an effort to increase their productivity, but also, one hopes, to improve working conditions. This picture, which shows a clear, wide walkway running the length of the shop and defined space around each item of plant and machinery, demonstrates a growing awareness of industrial ergonomics. However, in what was clearly a noisy shop with belt drive constantly running and machinery clattering and banging away, plus all the other unpleasant features of factory life to contend with, the absence of any protection for the workers is only too clear, except the traditional caps, of course. (Author's collection)

Above and below: Seeing Swindon today it is hard to imagine what it looked and felt like before the Great War. It was a world where a class system was rigidly applied, most lived in poverty, as we judge it today, no health service existed, only the most rudimentary education was available to the vast majority and illnesses such as cholera, typhoid and smallpox were still some of the greatest killers in society. The temptation is to see the Edwardian Era as some sort of golden age, which it was for the wealthy and titled. However, these years saw an upsurge in protest and a growing desire for a society that better shared its riches. It was a changing world which was beginning to show the first signs of a fairer welfare state being created and which we now have and take for granted. These two pictures capture Swindon as it was then – the style of living, the drabness and a hint of the aspirations for better lives reflected in the clothes and hats on view. (DN/Author's collection)

for the GWR in-house magazine, took issue with his claims, many of which he repudiated in a very long quite bitter, even scurrilous article. In so doing, the writer pulled few punches when criticizing the author and his work, suggesting that Williams was indeed thought of as an agitator and so his words could not be thought fair or his claims trusted. The reaction and condemnation was, in fact, so strong that the hand of someone very senior in the organization, at Swindon or Paddington, was probably behind such a response. After all, reputations were at stake and the wider world was watching even though much of the press which then ran the story and reported on it were of a distinctive pro-establishment hue.

As the book only appeared after Williams had left the Works, he had probably kept his protests in check when still a GWR employee, so avoiding condemnation, censure or the sack. With a wife to protect, anything else would have been unthinkable because it could have ended up with summary dismissal, without a reference, and then a struggle to find alternative employment. In fact, it seems to have been the poor working conditions in which he laboured that led to his 'retirement' on 3 September 1914 when only 37.

Bearing in mind his description of men being regularly dismissed due to 'periodical attacks of illness', this may have been a fate that befell him too, though he makes no claim for this himself. Yet despite a doctor's diagnosis suggesting that from the furnaces destroyed the whole of his digestive system' he still managed to join the Army in 1916 and served with the Royal Horse Artillery in Ireland then India until discharged in 1919. Sadly, though his health didn't improve greatly and following his wife's death from cancer in 1930 he also succumbed to illness.

So where might the truth lie in judging whether Churchward was a good or bad leader of such a large, diverse workforce? Did he value them in a social as well as an economic way, or did he see them simply as just another commodity to be used and exploited in the name of his industry? To be balanced in reaching any conclusions is it fair and reasonable to judge him by today's standards or should we, instead, judge him by the values of his age? For myself, I think this second approach should apply, especially as he led during a dynamic period in Britain's industrial, social and political history, where rapid change and progress were driven through despite the protests and resistance of the old order. This was a juggernaut that took a long time to get going and made slow progress for many years in the nineteenth century, but once momentum had built up it became an almost unstoppable mass. In such a situation a good leader had to be clear on what was needed, and flexible and magnanimous in their response.

The first thing to recognize, when assessing the way Churchward managed his workers, is that he did so at a time when there was little statutory law to guide him, in terms of employment rights or health and safety legislation. During his time in charge, this position changed radically and rapidly, so he was managing, learning and having to adapt to ever changing conditions all at the same time, which, when bearing in mind the extent of his duties, would test even the ablest, most conscientious manager. This was especially so in such a competitive industry where profit and loss were the principal considerations and woe betide any manager who allowed staff and welfare costs to increase to an unsustainable level, as viewed by chairmen and board members. In this situation, men such as Churchward had to achieve a difficult balancing act, juggling many competing claims to ensure the company remained solvent and shareholders and investors were paid the bonuses they had come to expect.

When Churchward reached senior rank at Swindon in the 1890s, any laws that governed employment and welfare in heavy industry were fairly shallow in depth and content. Nevertheless, some progress had been made since the Factory Act of 1833 which, amongst other things set up an independent inspection service with limited powers to scrutinize businesses where unacceptable practices were in evidence. But without more legislation, their powers to enforce change were muted. It would take more new laws in the 1860s and 70s, including two revised Factory and Workshop Acts (1874 and 1878) to truly begin the march towards even slightly better working conditions. These, for example, decriminalized trades union activities and gave them a clearer bargaining role, produced guidelines for managing workshops, introduced clearer rules on working hours and raised the employment age of children to ten.

As always when trying to make progress on complex issues where the law is involved, producing new legislation tends to be a slow and ponderous business. But soon after Churchward became Dean's second in command, the Factory and Workshop Acts of 1891 and 1895 were in place forcing employers, amongst other things to:

> Render administration of the law relating to workshops more efficient, particularly as regards sanitation....Provide for greater security against accidents and more efficient fencing of machinery in factories....Extend the method of regulation of unhealthy or dangerous occupations by application of special rules and requirements to any incident of employment certified by the secretary of state to be dangerous or injurious to health or dangerous to life or limb.

It would be a further six years before these two pieces of legislation were reviewed in any depth, but in 1901 the next Factory and Workshop Act was passed into law and with it the control of working conditions and Trades Union activities became more clearly defined. All this was just in time for Churchward's promotion to LCWS and greatly increased the level of scrutiny on him and the way he ran the workshops under his control.

To understand more clearly what all this meant we have a very important report produced in 1910 by Sidney Webb, a leading economist and reformer of the time who rose to become President of the Board of Trade, to help guide us. In summary he wrote that:

> The system of regulation which began with the protection of the tiny class of pauper apprentices in textile mills now includes within its scope every manual worker in every manufacturing industry. From the hours of labour and sanitation, the law has extended to the age of commencing work, protection against accidents, mealtimes and holidays, the

In the days before paid leave few if any industrial workers could afford the luxury of a holiday. Perhaps recognising that their workers might benefit from a day at the seaside, special excursions were arranged to such places as Weston-super-Mare and Weymouth and became an annual event in July when the works were closed. In 1905, for example, more than 24,000 took advantage of this service, which was provided free of charge, so offering some small compensation for the loss of pay incurred by their day-trip and the closure of the Works for a week in the summer. (DN)

methods of remuneration, and the rate of wages itself. The range of Factory Legislation has, in fact, become co-extensive with the conditions of industrial employment. No class of manual-working wage-earners, no item in the wage-contract, no age, no sex, no trade or occupation, is now beyond its scope.

The only trouble with this evaluation is that, although marking an important advance, it was based on a system where the bar had been set very low. This is nowhere better demonstrated than in accident statistics of the early twentieth century, which highlighted the colossal number of deaths and mutilations each year in the railway industry caused by burns, scaldings, severe cuts and lacerations, crush wounds, explosions, chemical spills and much more. Then there is the low average lifespan of those employed in industry caused by the unhealthy and dangerous working environments (48 years for men 54 for women in 1900, figures compounded by poor diets and living conditions). Here respiratory diseases, including tuberculosis, pneumonia, emphysema and pneumoconiosis were quite common as were such things as cancers, chronic stomach and liver ailments, renal illnesses, rheumatic conditions, both short and long term, eczema, dermatitis and so on. All this was probably ignored in an earlier age when life was valued quite cheaply, but by 1901, as medical science advanced, more was expected from employers in terms of health and safety, to help alleviate the problems. Sadly, the GWR's response appears to have been tardy and would remain so, as it did in most industries until well into the 1930s. In this, if nowhere else, Alfred Williams' book was remarkably sentient.

So how did Churchward, and the wider GWR management, rise to the challenge imposed by this ever growing and lawfully monitored legislation and did they take steps to improve conditions before the government imposed higher standards on them? In truth, Churchward inherited a number of progressive measures introduced decades earlier by the company. This suggests that its senior managers were aware of the reformers' work then slowly passing into law and the changes this wrought. However, there may also have been another motive at work here – a healthier, better educated workforce probably worked harder and, in so doing, increased production. Either way, some measures were taken to improve the lives of their workers from very early in the life of the GWR, albeit improvements which were probably hard to detect at times being so slight.

In terms of Swindon, one development that stands out was the gradual evolution of the Mechanics Institute, which from small beginnings as a library in the Works flourished into a centre 'for the purpose of disseminating useful knowledge and encouraging rational amusement'. In time its role became so important that it was decided to construct a large, two-storey purpose built facility close to the workshops. This was funded by subscriptions collected from GWR staff at Swindon and in 1855 it opened to great acclaim and was soon fulfilling an important role in the life of the Works, albeit one still in an early stage of development. Very quickly it became more than a library and soon became a place offering a most basic level of health service to workers, both non-industrial and craft and non-craft industrial employees. And here it is important to distinguish between the two because each had different expectations and quality of working conditions and life.

Often what differentiated the two was the standard of education they received and any benefit derived in coming from a family enjoying a higher standard of living, such as Churchward did himself. Birth right in this class ridden age was all that often mattered and those who were poor would often carry this disadvantage to the end of their days. So the deprived tended to end up as industrial, shop floor workers who, if they were lucky, would aspire to an apprenticeship and learning a trade. Some might reach junior management positions, but most didn't and remained rooted to the ethos of manual work. Meanwhile, those from 'better' backgrounds received a superior education by the standard of the age and this opened many more doors. In the railway industry this could mean becoming office workers and premium apprentices, for example, and enjoy more career opportunities and a healthier cleaner, less demanding working environment than that to which industrial workers faced each day. It was here that the Mechanics Institute,

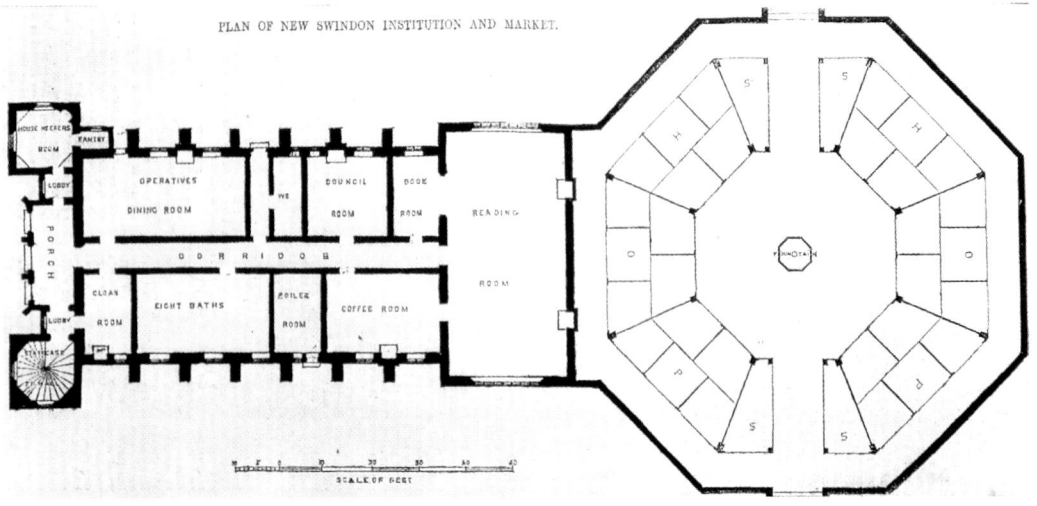

PLAN OF NEW SWINDON INSTITUTION AND MARKET.

In a world where little was done to ease the lot of industrial workers, who for the most part suffered in silence and had no adequate representation, it was often left to the men themselves to set up self-help services. Inevitably any advances were small ones, even with the support of managers. In the early days of the GWR at Swindon, some workers took the decision to set up a small library in a spare room within the workshops. This was an idea that soon grew into a strong social movement and, through subscriptions levied on workers, the Mechanics Institute was conceived (top shows one of its preliminary designs) and opened in 1855. This proved so successful as a place of learning and other community activities, that it continued to expand and was extended in 1892 (above). In the photo opposite above we see the Institute's beautifully laid out Reading Room, which was eventually opened, with its extensive library, to all employees, their families and Swindon residents unconnected with the Works. Opposite middle shows the Institute's substantial theatre. In opposite bottom a formal dinner is being held in one of the Institute's larger rooms in July 1908, with George Churchward himself in the centre of the top table. Indeed, he would play an active role in the educational side of the Institute's work and actively encouraged his staff to pursue technical course run within its walls to help improve their skills and, hopefully, their employability. (DN/Author's collection)

and its later additions, provided some balance between the two groups and began to introduce the concept of industrial democracy.

As the role of the Institute grew, so it gradually became more important to the citizens of Swindon's new town, as opposed to the old town which sat on a hill nearby. This was particularly so of the medical service it offered, which was sponsored by the Workers' Medical Fund Society, and were soon flooded with more patients than they could deal with satisfactorily. This was despite the provision of a slightly larger facility, which included a five bed ward to cope with

In a society grown used to the huge benefits given virtually free of charge by the NHS it is hard to comprehend what life was like before it was established in 1948. To say it was difficult would be an understatement so when the Mechanics Institute set aside space for a medical centre of sorts, it was a major step forward. With few able to afford even the most basic level of medical attention, this facility flourished and demand soon outstripped its ability to cope. So, in 1871 plans to open a larger, permanent accident hospital came to fruition when the Wiltshire Volunteer Rifle Corps armoury was converted (top). (Above) Thought to be a photograph of the five bed ward set up within this modified building. (Opposite above) The GWR's new cottage hospital that opened in 1892 and two scenes that came to typify its work. (Opposite middle and bottom) Two railway employees recuperating after treatment, presumably following accidents, and the hospitals large and extensive dispensary. (DN/GWR)

accident cases, which opened in December 1871. This was accomplished by converting the Xl Wiltshire Volunteer Rifle Corps armoury and drill hall, which itself had only been established in 1862. To pay for this conversion it is believed that Joseph Armstrong decided that the GWR pay the building costs of £130, while workers' subscriptions were used to buy all furniture and internal fittings.

Further improvements to the medical facilities were slow in coming despite the growing demand. Then, in 1888, shortly after the first dental clinic had been opened, the GWR's Medical Fund Society managers, in co-operation with Dr G.M. Swinhoe, the Medical Superintendent, took the decision to gather together many health related activities, spread over several sites, into one new building. So, in 1892, with Churchward now firmly established as Dean's Carriage Works Manager, the new facility, containing consulting rooms, a large dispensary and a swimming pool, opened on a site adjacent to the cottage hospital.

To raise the substantial amount of money needed to complete such an ambitious project, the Medical Fund's contribution had to be boosted by the GWR, in the form of a £2,000 grant and a £4,500 loan set at 2 per cent interest. Such a move, though seemingly quite obliging in nature, was nevertheless a mean spirited act when considering that the GWR would be one of the main beneficiaries of the medical centre. The company would, in effect, have a fitter workforce, an active occupational health centre and lose less time to sick absences. But this wasn't the nature of industry then and with no statutory right to 'sick pay' employers could simply write-off that person and recruit another from the long lines of those eager for work.

While the new hospital was being built, the Mechanics Institute, which was described at the time as 'bursting at the seams' it was so busy, was in the middle of a major refurbishment. This work involved the demolition of a market attached to the building when originally built and a substantial extension put up in its place. Work proceeded quickly and the new Institute was officially opened by the GWR's deputy chairman, Viscount Emlyn, on 1 March 1893. In the days that followed, the company was quick to advertise all that was on offer and gain kudos for doing so, even though much of the work was paid for by subscriptions. Once again they were the main recipients, in terms of specialist technical training, a generally better educated and healthier workforce. Sadly, though, the source of so much ill-health – the Works itself – remained a dangerous place to be. If productivity was indeed being improved by new ergonomically sound workshops, the level of health and safety applied to the workers in these facilities did not equal these advances. This was an issue Alfred Williams was quick to point out in his book and was something identified, with some concern, by newly forming trades unions.

For unregulated or even poorly regulated industries, unions were soon seen as enemies. As a result, many remained unrecognised even when legislation was put in place establishing their status in law. This was especially so with the Trades Union Act of 1871 which was preceded by the formation of the Trades Union Council in 1868. However, it wasn't until the 1890s that they became truly effective in the railway industry. Before that, craftsmen had achieved a degree of representation through the good offices of the Amalgamated Society of Engineers, Machinists, Millwrights, Smiths and Patternmakers which had been formed in 1826. As it continued to grow, a Swindon Branch was set up but only attracted a small number of workers, possibly no more than 300. But to this number could be added several other Societies formed at the time that covered other trades – boilermakers, carpenters, joiners and other.

It was a slow spreading movement that really didn't gather a significant amount of pace or influence until the Swindon and District Trades Council was set up in January 1891. This new group brought together a number of interested groups which would later form part of the National Union of Railwaymen. Yet despite the progress being made their activities nearly foundered on the slow rate at which members could be signed up. Whether they were actively discouraged to do by their managers is unclear, but Churchward as we have seen, saw the unions as 'an unnecessary evil so could and would continue to be very dismissive of their efforts to

Changing Times and Competing Expectations 163

In such illiberal, unequal times where workers' rights were rarely recognised, any move to improve the quality of their lives, in the Works and at home, was siezed upon as evidence of good intentions. But sadly these were rarely more than sticking plaster remedies for such a immense workforce and resolving the extreme problems they faced at home and work. Even the gradual evolution of the Mechanics Institute, medical facilities and such like, didn't ultimately produce significant changes or improvements. Other fairly minor measures were tried, as these two pictures reveal. (Top) In the 1840s, the GWR purchased some land adjacent to the Works for use as a playing field with cricket, as this pavilion reveals, being one of the chosen sports. It is said that this facility was thought necessary 'for the well being of workers living in GWR houses nearby'. Other less charitable souls saw it as as acquiring land on which the Works might be developed at some point in the future. This didn't happen and in 1871 the fields were landscaped as a 'Pleasure Garden' and, as such, is still enjoyed to this day. (Above) Each year from 1843 the Mechanics' Institute held an annual soiree for all workers and their families, this in 1866 became the 'Juvenile Fete' held in the summer. All children under the age of 14 were admitted free of charge and given tea and a slab of cake plus one free ride (others had to be paid for) As this photo reveals it proved to be a popular event, though whether it helped improve workers' morale is open to debate. (DN)

improve pay and working conditions', or so Kenneth Cook believed. In the light of this he seems to have remained a fairly strong opponent of the union movement and remained so until he retired, which may have unnecessarily and seriously damaged relationship between capital and labour. As his workers began to acquire a voice of protest, especially in his later years, a more accommodating attitude could have paid many dividends. But it wasn't to be and the encounters between manager and workers over the twenty years of his tenure proved to be bruising ones for he and his staff at times, as we shall see.

One of the other ways in which many companies were beginning to explore as a means of improving the lives of workers concerned housing. This was doubly important in Swindon because the rapid expansion in employee numbers could not be met by the town itself. So workers had to be recruited from far afield to fill the many vacancies that arose, but when they arrived there was insufficient housing, even of the most basic kind, to meet their needs. So, from very early in the life of the GWR at Swindon it was decided to construct a purpose built estate of commercially viable cottages within walking distance of the Works to ease the problem. By 1842 outline plans for 300 cottages had been drawn up and approved, but to save the company having to invest in the scheme itself the construction was funded by the builder, Messrs. J. & C. Rigby of London who were chosen to undertake the work. In due course, and to turn a profit, their costs were offset by receiving the tenants' rents directly and, as a sweetener, they were also awarded the profits made by mainline station's refreshment room for 99 years. As a result, a ten-minute

In the early days of the GWR's existence Brunel saw a need to provide housing for employees at Swindon. With such a small town as its hinterland providing a trained and ever growing workforce drove the GWR to look elsewhere for these men, but to help attract them more local accommodation was needed. Plans were laid for an estate of 300 cottages adjacent to the Works, built around the Mechanics Institute, and construction began in 1842 and ran on to 1855. Soon demand outstripped resources and the cottages became exceedingly overcrowded and developed slum like conditions similar to those found in other workers' accommodation around Swindon and the surrounding countryside. Sadly, the GWR neither built more houses nor sought to improve what was already available, so helping create a problem as huge as that caused by very poor working condition in the factories themselves. The photo shows one of the streets within the 'GWR village' in later years by which time some remedial work had been carried out and street lights had been fitted. (DN/Author's collection)

stop at Swindon became compulsory until 1895, by which time Rigby's had turned in a very handsome profit, which in truth might have been better invested in housing for Work's staff and their families.

The rate of progress in building the 300 cottages was extremely slow and it took until 1855 for the work to be completed, having begun in 1842, so could hardly be thought an adequate response to a problem growing ever larger each year. It was also an experiment that the company didn't repeat and in doing nothing else, beyond some investment in the Mechanic's Institute, medical facilities and the park it left employees to muddle through as best they could with what was available locally.

So when additional accommodation was needed it was mostly left to speculators to provide, a programme in which the GWR appear not to have taken any direct part as the population of the town grew in size from nearly 5,000 in 1851 to 45,006 people by 1900; with the majority of these people having direct links with the GWR. After a good beginning in the 1840s, which was heavily funded by subscriptions from workers, the non-interventionist attitude displayed by the GWR towards their employees when in the Works, seems to have spread over into in their domestic lives as well, and this remained the case until well into the twentieth century.

Very soon, as the number of staff employed in the factories increased from 423 in 1843, 1800 in 1848 and ever upwards to 12,000 or so, the lack of good accommodation become

The ever expanding Swindon Works as it appeared in the early years of the twentieth century. Despite having been in existence since the 1840s and grown so large and modern in output the working and living conditions of the majority of its staff had not kept pace with these advances and condemned many of them to live in barely relieved poverty where illnesses and early deaths were common.. For William Dean and then George Churchward and their managers, the living was much, much better, as Newburn House, the Superintendent's accommodation, in the foreground bears witness. Here Churchward would live alone and in some comfort from 1902 to the end of his life, supported by three or four servants. When he died in 1933 his estate totalled something in the region of £62k, which today would have a purchasing power of more than £3.5m according to the Bank of England's Inflation Calculator. The vast difference in living standards and wages had barely begun to narrow during his lifetime, with change often being vehemently challenged by many leaders. In 1905, for example, it is estimated that the total wage bill for the Works was in the region of £600k. This, in simple terms, produced an average income of £52 per person per year (estimated at £5,300 in 2024) with little or no sign of greater remuneration as living costs increased. (RH/Author)

an uncomfortable reality. This was especially so in the GWR built houses which soon became overcrowded, with one report suggesting that these 'tiny houses often contained between 7 and 12 occupants'. With only the most basic sanitation installed these properties soon failed to cope which such large numbers. All of this quickly resulted in squalid, slum like living conditions which inevitably led to a rise in poverty related illnesses.

However, it was little better elsewhere in the town where men, women and children were also packed into similarly cramped, foetid homes and this unchanging state remained the case as the years slowly passed. However, the local council, prompted by outbreaks of cholera, did undertake work on water and sewer systems to help ward off such appalling illnesses. So, all was not lost, though these improvements hardly eased the level of poverty that existed, a problem made worse when GWR employees were temporarily laid off, without pay, when the workshops had insufficient tasks for them to undertake. Churchward, one assumes being part of senior management, would surely have been aware of this and sought, whenever he could, to alleviate the problems. There is little or no evidence that he did so to any great extent, even when promoted to replace Dean in 1902. Nevertheless, his increasing involvement in civic duties did place him in a unique position as new legislation was gradually enacted requiring more action by local authorities to improve living conditions. And so, by chance he found himself at the apex of a system profoundly affected by rapidly changing industrial and social law. It remained to be seen whether he had the skills or desire to make the changes necessary and so improve the lot of those dependent on him – at work or in their homes.

Building wonderful new locomotives and carriages, with the aim of achieving engineering perfection, a good production flow, while increasing company profits at the same time, was one thing. Achieving social justice for the men and women who looked to him for help and guidance was quite another. This would be a much harder nut to crack than the comparatively solvable problems generated by engineering and commercial issues. And so, he found himself, by accident or design, in a position where he could, if he chose to, make a long-lasting and meaningful contribution

The glory of steam here personified by a gleaming No. 3801 *County Carlow*, built at Swindon in 1906. Engines such as this were the product of almost slave labour conditions, if Alfred Williams is to believed, but were not seen this way, or so it seems, by the company's senior managers who seemed unable to offer any significant improvements. It would take a great deal of protest, two world wars and the creation of the Welfare State to finally bring the legislation and radical change needed to finally beget a much better quality of life for industrial workers such as those at Swindon. (TC)

to the community that had served him so well. Only time would tell if he did indeed have a social conscience and whether he could act on it or simply sit back and allow the perceived injustices to continue and keep accruing. Or, in other words, would he adopt more than a sticking plaster approach to the problems and use the immense powers vested in him to pursue significant changes?

His opportunity to increase his influence over life in Swindon and, by association the Works, came in 1900. After a period of lobbying for change in Swindon's status, the government was persuaded to combine old and new towns into one and give the new authority municipal status. Their bid was accepted and Queen Victoria, in the last year of her life, duly signed the charter. In 1901 it came into full effect and Churchward, who undoubtedly had used his influence to bring this change about, was elected this new body's first Mayor. However, he had been active in local politics for some years by then, having become a town councillor for the urban authority in 1894, and become its chairman three years later as well as the first Chairman of the Technical Education Committee. He also became a local Justice of the Peace, in which capacity he sat in the local magistrate's courts where he may have had to be in judgement on his own workers from time to time.

As a leading figure in this Wiltshire community, and holding a very senior position in both business and civic lives, Churchward was able to play a leading role in the development of such things as the construction of an electricity power station, improvements to both water and sewage systems, bringing a tram network to the town and much more besides. All of this would undoubtedly have improved life in the town and helped build on the accomplishments of the GWR over the previous 60 years or so. But this intervention doesn't seem to gone more deeply into resolving the many problems created by slum housing or poor working conditions in the Works.

In 1900 Queen Victoria signed a charter that awarded Swindon municipal status, in the process bringing the old and new towns together under one authority. This took effect when Churchward, who had been active in local politics for some time by then, became new borough's first Mayor. It was a post he held until 1902 when succeeded by Frederick Wright, who would become Churchward's Chief Assistant in 1903. As a sign of growing civic pride and influence an impressive town hall (above) was created. It was undoubtedly the case that the GWR and Churchward were a dominating force in the work of the council. (Author's collection)

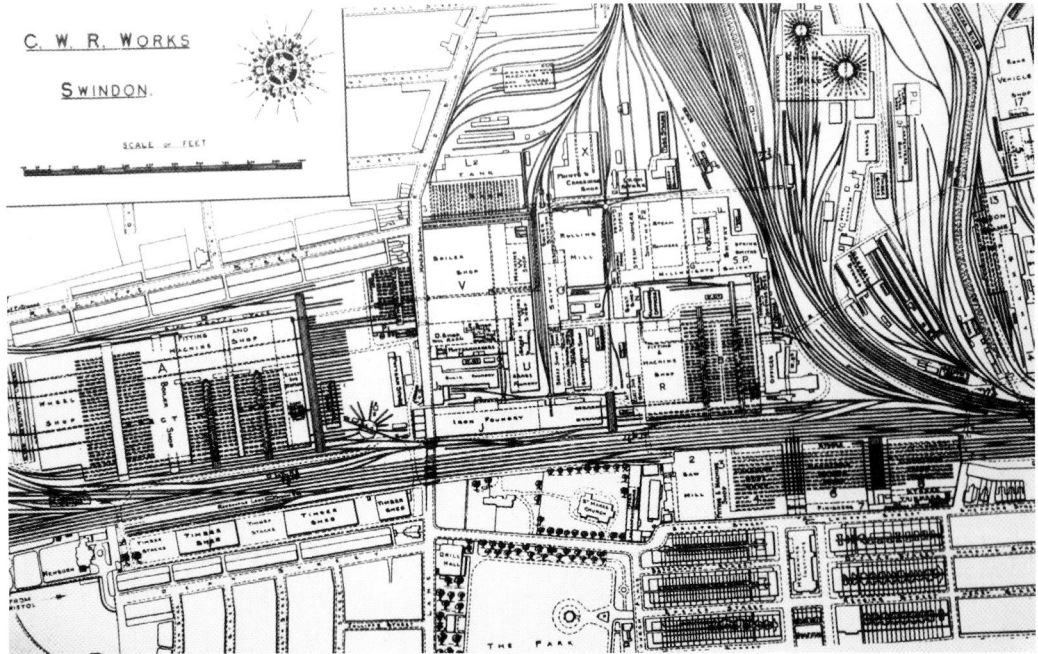

During Churchward's time in charge, the Swindon Works continued to grow as this drawing shows. By any standards it was a major industrial concern in which 12,000 people laboured in conditions with varying degrees of hardship or comfort, depending on their status as non-industrial or industrial workers. This drawing also captures, in the bottom right hand corner, the extent of social developments to support the GWR's employees – housing, park, Mechanics Institute and the rest. However, a simple drawing such as this cannot convey or describe the conditions that existed and the desperate need for improvements and reform. (DN)

With the passage of time the GWR had taken a number of small steps to improve the lot of its workers at Swindon, and the future seemed to hold more of the same with Churchward in charge. And it would remain this way until a seismic shock of unimaginable proportions shook politicians and industry leaders out of their apathy and forced them to make changes. But in 1906, with Churchward about to embark on the next stage of his development's plans, the Great War, with all its tumultuous social and economic consequences, was still far in the future.

So, this is the situation faced by Churchward as an employer and civic leader as the clock clicked down to this world conflict. As it did so, his workforce, which had for so long lacked representation of any sort, was developing a protesting voice that would gradually and irrevocably, lead to industrial action and conflict. It would be a difficult, frustrating time to be a senior manager and slowly but surely test Churchward's patience and negotiating skills to the limit. For the moment, though, press ahead with his Star class 4-6-0 locomotive.

The importance of this engine may be measured by the time given to it by Kenneth Cook in his 1950 paper and the additional notes he wrote at the time in preparation:

> With the arrival of two larger De Glehn/Bousquet four-cylinder compound locomotives – Nos. 103, *President*, and 104, *Alliance*, Churchward pressed ahead with more extensive comparability trials. At the same time, he could study in much greater depth their use of four-cylinders, although he soon rejected the idea of compounding, believing it added little

Churchward's Saint Class programme ran on until 1913 when the seventy-seventh appeared – the last twenty-five being built with superheaters, top-feed and extended smokeboxes. Here one of the Saints, in this case No. 2935 *Caynham Court*, is seen being attended to by one of its crew. Following Churchward's retirement this engine and No. 2925, *St Martin*, underwent extensive modification. In No. 2935's case the work will include fitting rotary cam poppet valve gear and new cylinders. No. 2925 will, in due course, be rebuilt and became the model for the new Hall Class of 4-6-0. (Author's collection)

or nothing to the development work he and his draughtsmen were then conducting. In this he took the view that it was overly complex for what he wanted. As a result, he then set out to design his own four-cylinder engine and in April 1906 *North Star*, No. 40, was completed – a worthy successor to a previously celebrated prototype. This, like the French engines, initially employed a 4-4-2 wheel configuration so that the two types might be fairly compared. In doing this he repeated a similar experiment conducted with the Saint Class. Later No. 40 was converted into a 4-6-0.

This engine combined the general external layout similar to the recently developed two-cylinder engine, with cylinder arrangement of the French engines, except that it was simple expansion. It took the Standard No. 1 boiler (one of which was also fitted to No. 103 *President*) at that time developed with 225lbs working pressure and had four-cylinders 14½ inch by 26 inch, the two inside cylinders combining in their casting a saddle upon which part of the smokebox rested and drove the leading coupled crank-axle. The outside cylinders were fitted further towards the rear of the engine and drove the trailing coupled wheels.

The valve movement, which was referred to locally as the 'Scissors gear' was derived from a compound motion from the two inside crossheads, the left crosshead driving an extension of the right-hand quadrant and obtaining also a combining motion from the right-hand crosshead and vice versa. This gear operated both the inside valves direct and through a rocking lever to the outside valves on the same side of the engine. The piston valves were 8in diameter, had 7in travel with a constant lead ⅛in, and the rated tractive effort was 25,090lb. The inside crank was set at 180 degrees from the outside crank on the same side and the right-hand side led the left-hand by 90 degrees

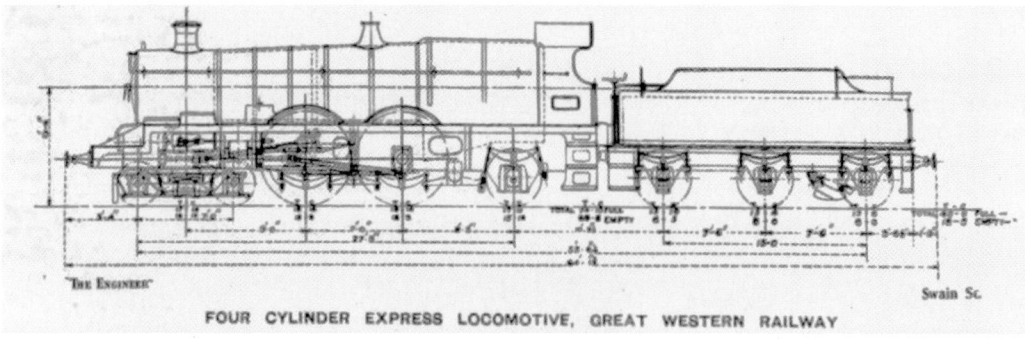

FOUR CYLINDER EXPRESS LOCOMOTIVE, GREAT WESTERN RAILWAY

Churchward's four-cylinder 4-6-0 Star 4000 Class engines are considered to be his master work and in service they were thought to have been excellent performers. But as with any mechanically engineered device it had to go through a trial and error process as it evolved when there was little evidence to suggest that four cylinders would be better than two. For this reason, it is interesting to observe how the Stars went from the drawing board to the mainline, gradually developing into such fine, good-looking engines. (Top) A drawing that was released for publication to the editor of the influential Engineer journal when the engine was still being designed. (Middle) No. 40, soon to be named *North Star*, in commemoration of Gooch's famous locomotive of the same name, waits outside the Works at Swindon ready to begin a period of trial running. (Above) No. 40 photographed when thought to be running in regular service. She remained with the 4-4-2 wheel configuration until rebuilt as a 4-6-0 in late 1909, by which time ten new Stars (Nos. 4001 to 4010) had been built. By 1923 seventy-three will be in service. (Opposite above) Two drawings also released to the Engineer for publication in 1907 when the main production batch was in planning, but now much more detail, than the simple diagram that preceded the launch of No. 40 in 1906, has been added. It is probably safe to assume that Churchward and the GWR's senior managers were very aware of the value of good publicity and regularly sanctioned the release of this material to the press. And when running the Stars soon attracted even more attention. (Opposite middle) A diagram of a Star produced as a simple guide to their dimensions and capacities. (Opposite bottom) No. 40 now in her 4-6-0 form and soon to be renumbered 4000. This famous engine will not see out her life in this form and will be one of five converted to become members of the Castle Class between 1925 and '29, then being joined by ten more between 1937 and '40. Only one Star survived into preservation – No. 4003 *Lode Star*. (DN/RH/Author's collection)

Changing Times and Competing Expectations 171

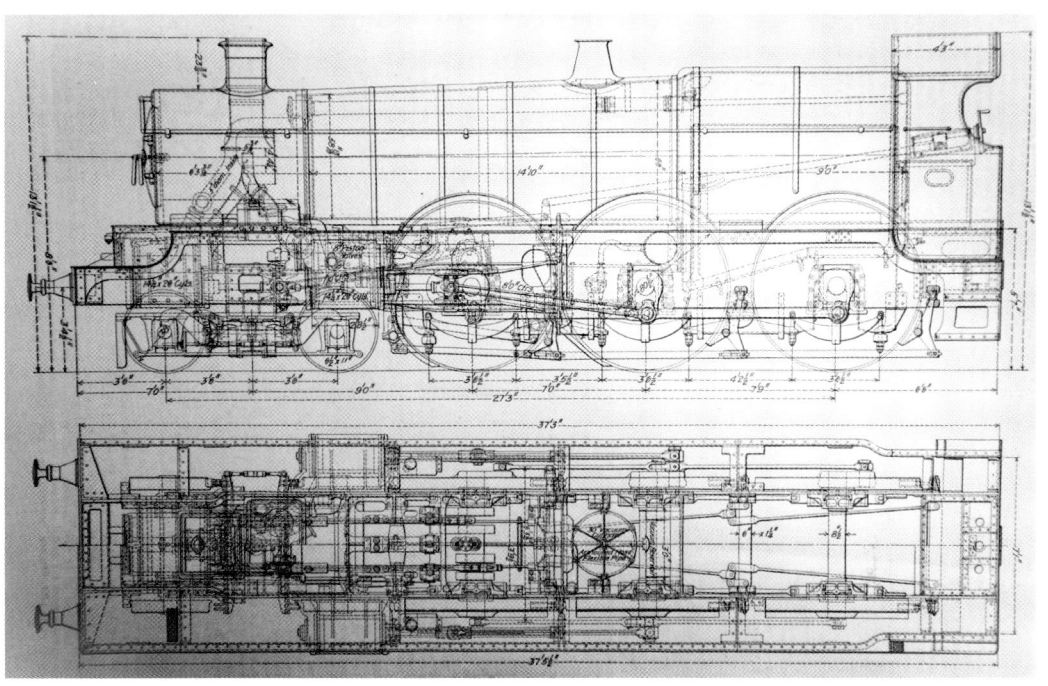

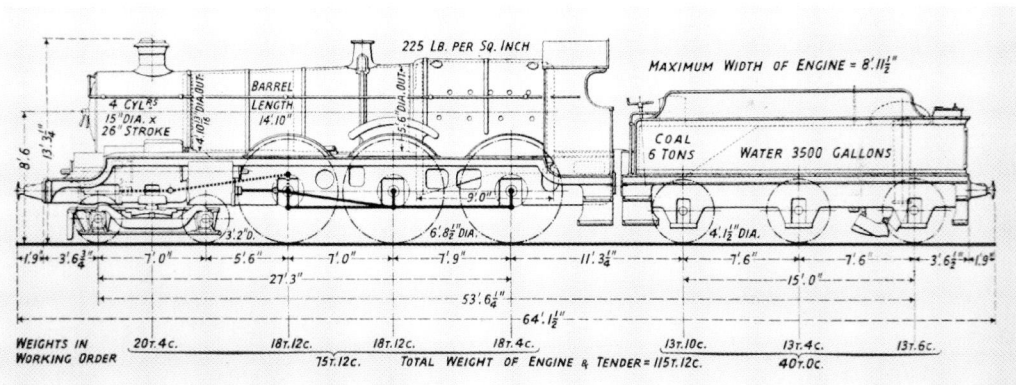

This engine was extremely successful, and the Churchward design as a simple expansion engine was shown to be a very much freer engine when working heavily, this was particularly important when the engine was later converted to the 4-6-0 wheel arrangement. Shortly after the conclusion of the trials between the de Glehn Nos 102, 103 and 104, and No. 171, the third Churchward 4-6-0 when running as a 4-4-2 engine, and No. 40, a further number of the Churchward design were built. But in standardizing the valve motion he adopted a modified Walschaerts gear which derived its motion from one eccentric on the middle axle in combination with a link from the inside crosshead. This then operated both the inside valve of that side direct and the outside valves through a rocking lever. Whilst this may have complicated the layout between the frames, it produced a graceful engine with clear-cut externals.

In essence, in building the Stars, Churchward was doing what he did best. In a well-founded, well-rehearsed model he established the commercial need, analyzed what had already been achieved in design, consider any new developments or alternatives at home or abroad, especially where evidence of success existed. He then added ideas conceived at Swindon to produce a prototype which could be compared to other engines of a similar type. It was a formula that had served him well and in the Star Class it might be thought that he reached the pinnacle of his powers and built a well-balanced, well-constructed class of engine that met the company's needs to perfection.

Clearly the French engines, as well as his own well-honed ideas, influenced the way the new class was developed, but in this case it had the added refinement of superheating, the value of which was only just beginning to be appreciated by engineers. In simple terms, it is a process where saturated 'wet' steam is converted into superheated 'dry' steam and in this state increases thermal efficiency whilst reducing the possibility of steam condensing inside the engine with

The Stars arrive and become a dominating presence on the mainline pulling fast express services to and from the West Country. In this case the engine appears to be the 1909 built No. 4021, *King Edward* (although the last number is hidden by the buffer) and is captured leaving Paddington on 17 December 1910 with the Blue Funnel Special taking a party on a day trip to Southampton where they will enjoy a brief voyage around the Isle of White and along the coast. (DN)

damaging effects. From early in its development, it was predicted that superheating could increase an engines output by up to 25 per cent and reduce coal and water consumption appreciably. For companies eager to achieve greater efficiency and economy, these were very desirable goals

In assessing the value of this invention, Churchward had two examples to observe in practice. The most important was in Germany where Wilhelm Schmidt produced the first practical superheater in the last two decades of the nineteenth century. In due course, engineers working for the Prussian State Railway built their S4 class 4-4-0 locomotive with a superheater of Schmidt's design. The first of the class appeared in 1898 but teething problems meant that the main production programme didn't get underway until 1902. By 1909, another 103 had been added and, in service, they appear to have been a success with some remaining operational until 1927.

Meanwhile in Britain, John Aspinall, CME of the Lancashire and Yorkshire Railway, undoubtedly aware of Schmidt's work, decided to fit an experimental low heat superheater to a Class 7 4-4-2 two inside cylinder engine, in this case No. 737. Aspinall's model, which was set within a 3ft 6in long cylindrical drum fitted into the smokebox in a space created by recessing the front tubeplate. However, this was found to produce a level of superheat only slightly above the normal steam temperatures. Heat dissipation quickly reduced this gap still further so making any advantage gained by superheating of limited value. Nevertheless, the trials continued with five other engines being similarly fitted in 1902. But despite the poor results, these engines kept their superheaters until 1917 when they were all removed and the locomotives reverted to the standard design of the other 34 members of the class.

It is unclear whether Churchward knew of Aspinall's work, though being in the same profession and both being members of the Institution of Mechanical Enginers, it is more than likely that he was aware of what was happening in the L&YR's offices. In which case he probably realised that Aspinall's direction of travel was not one worth following and Schmidt and the Prussian State Railway's version was. However, being such an ingenious designer he saw from the outset that the German invention might be bettered. In so doing he took the concept on to another stage as he attempted to find a solution that might better suit his newly developing locomotives and suitable members of his existing fleet. So, at some point early in Churchward's time as Superintendent, a Schmidt superheater was procured and work began on adapting it for GWR use. This was then fitted for test purposes into Saint Class engine No. 2901, *Lady Superior*, in 1906 when it was under construction at Swindon.

A photo that shows the classic lines of a Star to perfection, in this case the 1908 built engine No. 4020, *Knight Commander*. Unlike some of her sisters, which were converted into Castle Class Locomotives, this engine remained a Star until withdrawn from service in March 1951. (Author's collection)

By this stage another version had also appeared in the USA developed by the American Locomotive Company in partnership with Purdue University. The mechanism they created was given the name Schenectady or Cole Superheater and in this form was installed in an experimental locomotive designed by staff at the university (which later became known as the Schenectady No. 2, then No. 3 when refined further). Trials soon revealed that this model worked well enough for production to begin with at least one unit being procured by the GWR in 1907 for evaluation.

Armed with two tried and tested versions of superheater, and perhaps encouraged by Aspinall's work, Churchward and his team pressed ahead with development and evaluation of the alternatives on offer. From this, it was hoped, they might find a way to adapt or improve what was on offer to suit GWR needs, as Cook later recalled:

> Churchward did not favour a high degree of superheat, and decided that this requirement could best be met by having a low degree of superheat. This, he believed, was sufficient to ensure the absence of condensation in the cylinders but still ensured the boost to performance that superheating gave. It was all a matter of balance and compromise in order

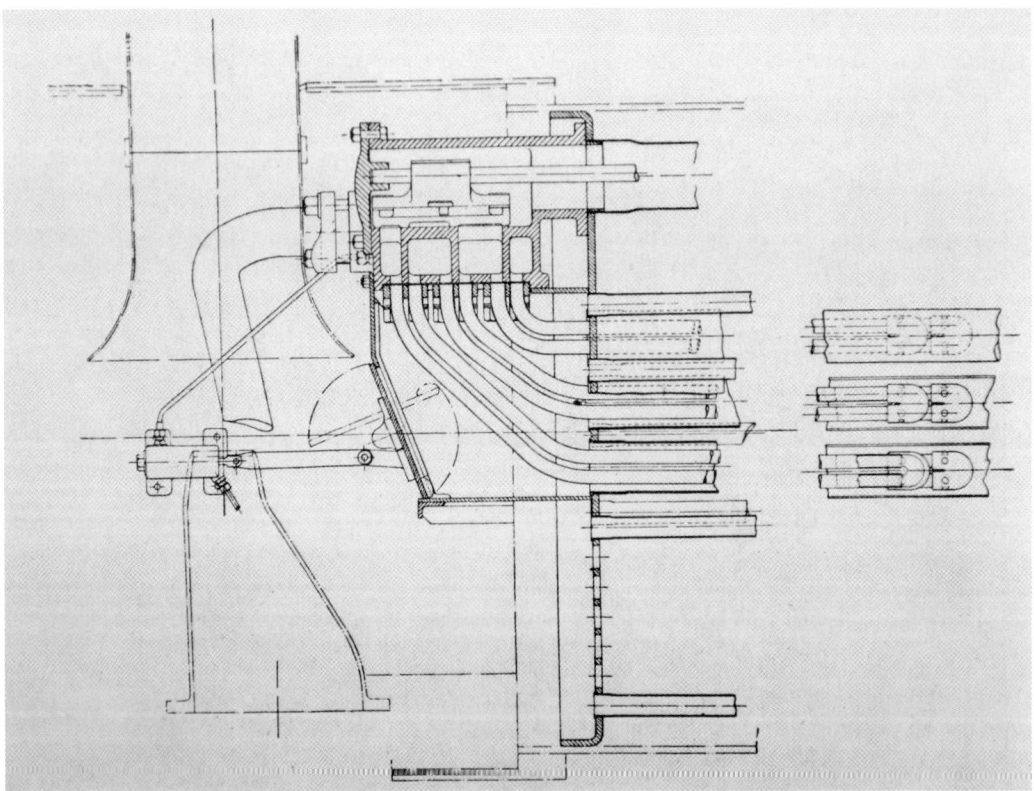

The evolution of superheaters at Swindon began as a theoretical exercise and undoubtedly progressed as a result of observing the work of Wilhelm Schmidt in Germany and the American Locomotive Company in partnership with Purdue University. Churchward may also have been aware of similar work being undertaken by John Aspinall on the Lancashire and Yorkshire Railway. (Above) By 1906 the GWR had acquired a Schmidt superheater which was then fitted to engine No. 2901, *Lady Superior*. (Opposite above) A little later a Cole superheater was acquired from the USA and installed in the brand new engine No. 4010, *Western Star*. (Opposite below) In developing a Swindon solution Churchward and his team came up with three alternatives with this one being selected for production as the standard model. (KC/ILocoE)

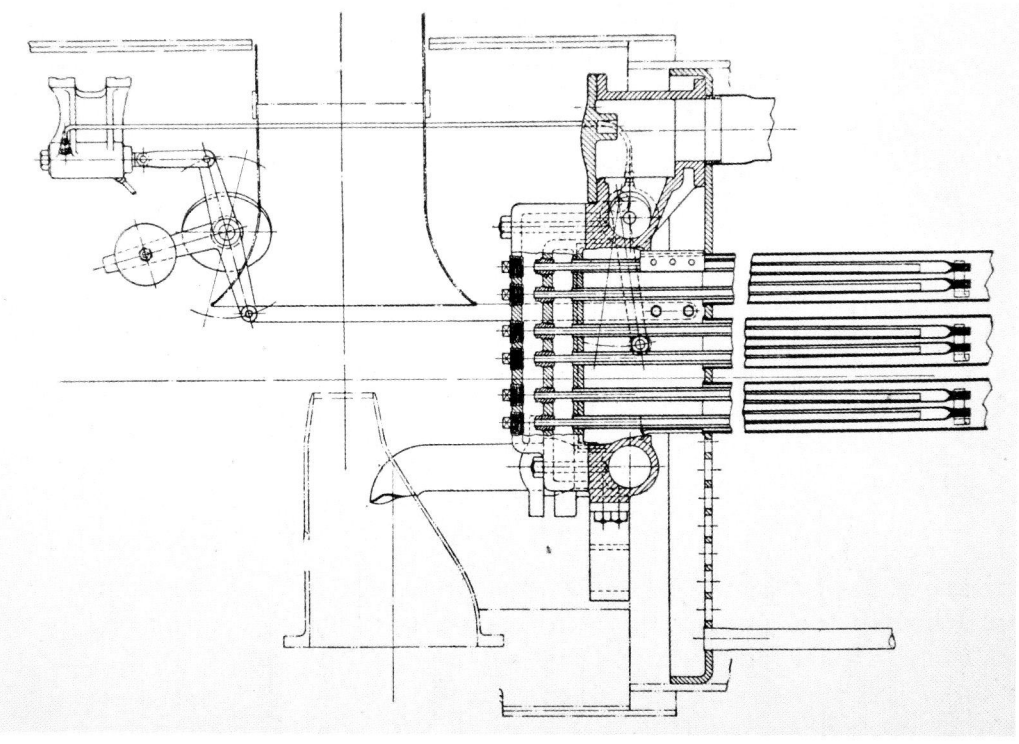

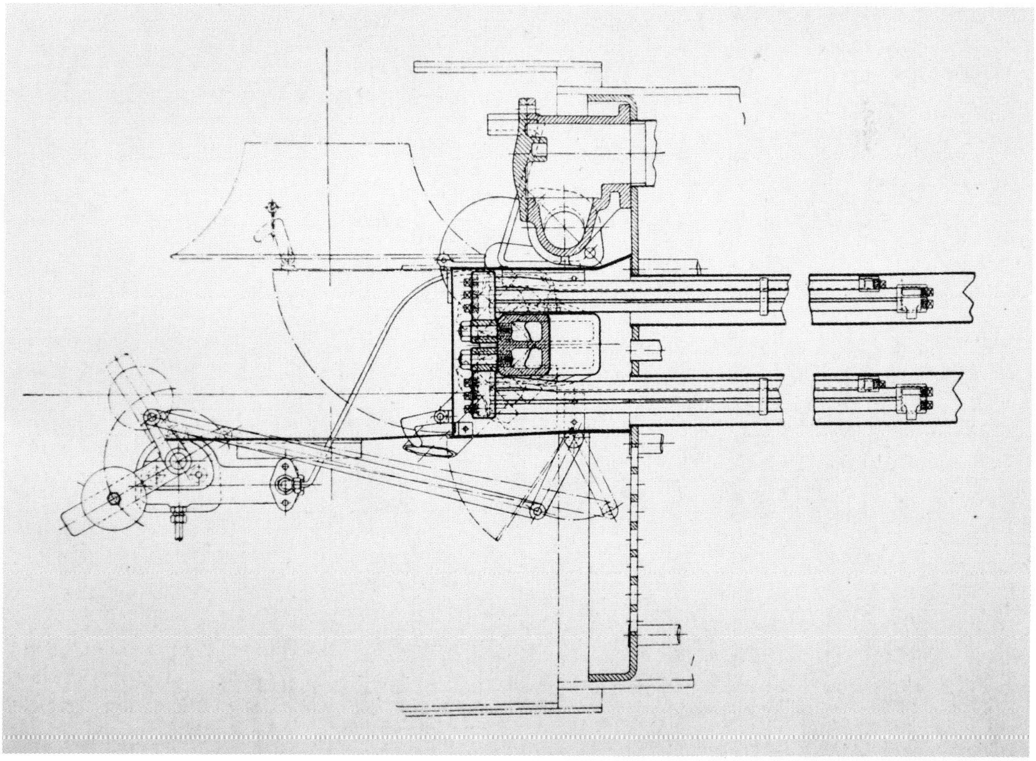

to get the best optimum performance. This became his guiding principle when assessing which options to pursue.

So, engine No. 2901 was fitted with a Schmidt superheater which contained three rows of eight elements, with 307sqft of superheater surface. Then in 1907, a four-cylinder Star class engine, No.4010, Western Star, was fitted with a Cole superheater with 269sqft of heating surface, containing three rows of six units, with an internal flow and external return arrangement; the flow tubes went through a gland between the saturated and superheated steam spaces of the header and the return tube was expanded onto the superheated steam space.

Having evaluated these designs Churchward believed he could do better and three versions of a Swindon superheater were designed and then fitted to engines between 1907 and 1909. The first of these was installed in locomotive No. 4011, Knight of the Garter. This had three rows of six units with internal flow and external return tubes, but here it was so designed that the complete unit could be withdrawn through the smokebox so making maintenance much easier. The superheater tubes were 1⅜in diameter with 300sqft of hearing surface. The second one was fitted to engine No. 2922, *Saint Gabriel*, during 1909 and had the same number of units, but they had return bends instead. The header had some resemblance to the Cole model with 1¼in tubes and 275sqft of heating surface.

The third Swindon superheater, which was fitted to engine No. 2913, Saint Andrew, in 1909 had two rows of seven units, 1in tubes with 248sqft of heating surface. The units were expanded into cast steel unit headers, which were fixed to the main header by stud fastenings and also had return boxes at the far end which were later superseded by 'U' bends.

All the early superheater headers were encased in damper boxes, the damper doors were opened by steam cylinders on the side of the smokebox closed when the steam was shut-off. This was introduced to prevent gas flow through the superheater flues when the units were empty, but several years later it was dispensed with. It was this model that was found to meet Churchward's needs best and became, in due course, the standard Swindon superheater.

The only real problem found with the superheated engines concerned the need for more frequent lubrication. This was caused by the higher temperatures carbonising the oil which then restricted the steam passages, valves and pistons. To help overcome this problem and keep the amount of extra lubrication to the minimum Churchward decided, after experimentation, to apply only a moderate degree of superheat. Once again it was a case of trying to achieve an optimum balance between an engine's operating performance and its maintenance needs.

Although the development of superheaters was key to the success of the Stars, as well as the improvement of other classes, it was only one part of Churchward's continuing standardisation programme. However, there were other important issues still being resolved at this same time, first amongst them was the range of standard boilers. By 1906 a programme that commenced when Churchward was appointed to be manager of the locomotive works in 1896 still had some way to run and would continue to undergo further refinements and additions long after Churchward had left the scene. But by the time the Stars appeared, his work had advanced sufficiently to produce the boilers he needed for his immediate needs.

Apart from the boilers, the design of smokeboxes continued to be an area of continuing interest for Churchward. It was here that the test plant so recently commissioned proved useful. Here data could be gathered and different options evaluated, especially those relating to the way gases flowed, hopefully in a uniform, balanced way, through the tubes. According to Cook, Churchward believed that 'getting the proportions of the smokebox right was of the greatest importance', then adding that this probably explained why 'Great Western engines were fitted with smokeboxes larger than the dimensions prevailing elsewhere at the time'.

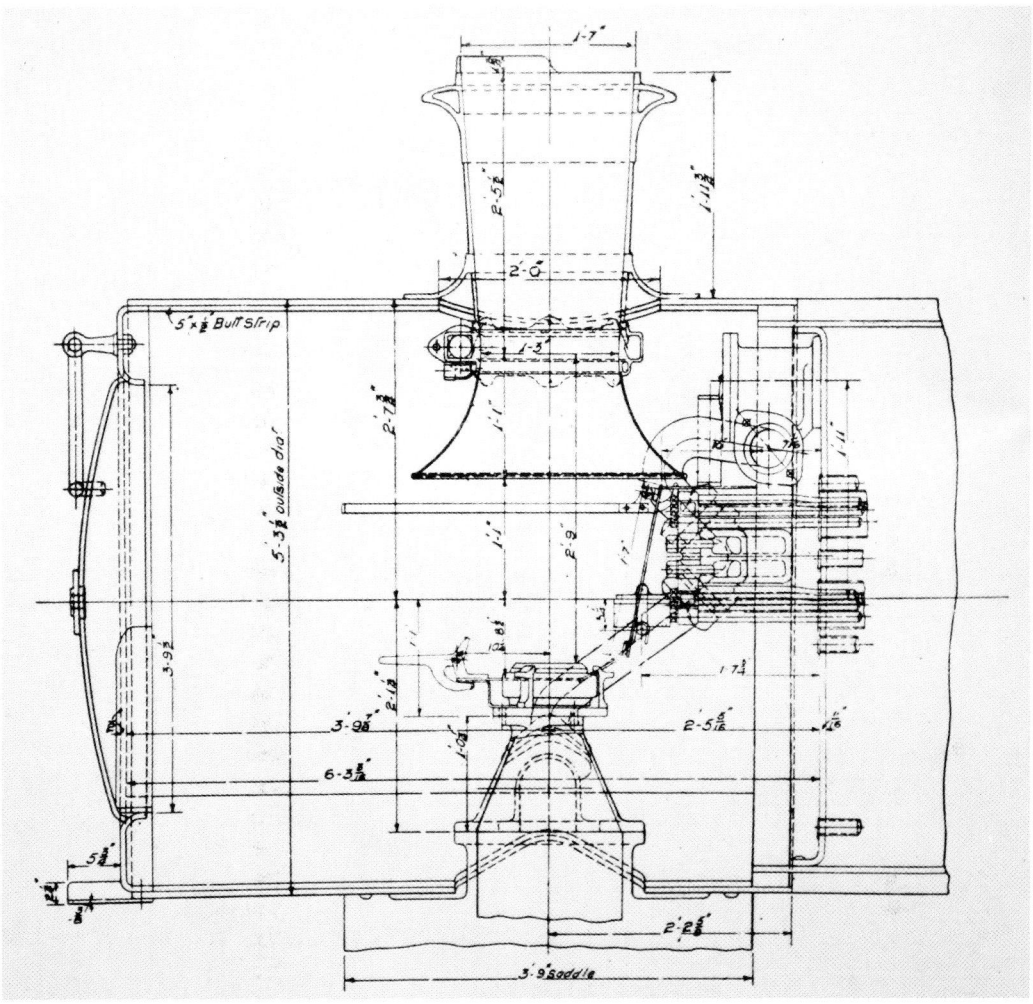

A typical GWR smokebox of the time, in this case with a Standard No. 1 boiler and superheater fitted. Churchward placed great emphasis on 'getting the proportions of the smokebox right' and during a number of experiments his team carefully evaluated the relationships between the blast pipe tip, chimney height and choke diameter. In doing this they were able to produce a formula that balanced the dimensions of each of these elements to achieve optimum performance for each type of locomotive. (KC/IMechE)

As a result of the experiments carried out at Swindon, the relationships between the blast pipe tip, chimney height and choke diameter were very carefully evaluated. This, in time, led to a standard formula that embraced these dimensions, being calculated and then used in producing smokebox designs to achieve optimum performance for each type of locomotive in use. This formula underwent periodic review, to take account of the development of such things as the jumper top being introduced into the blast pipe in 1910, but essentially remained the same so proving its worth as a design tool for years to come.

Earlier in this chapter we saw how Churchward was prepared to standardise the valve gear he used whenever possible and the reliance he placed on a derived version of the Robert Stephenson and Co solution, which first appeared in 1842. Then we observed how he successfully adopted a modified version of Egide Walschaerts 1844 introduced valve gear specifically for his four-cylinder Star Class.

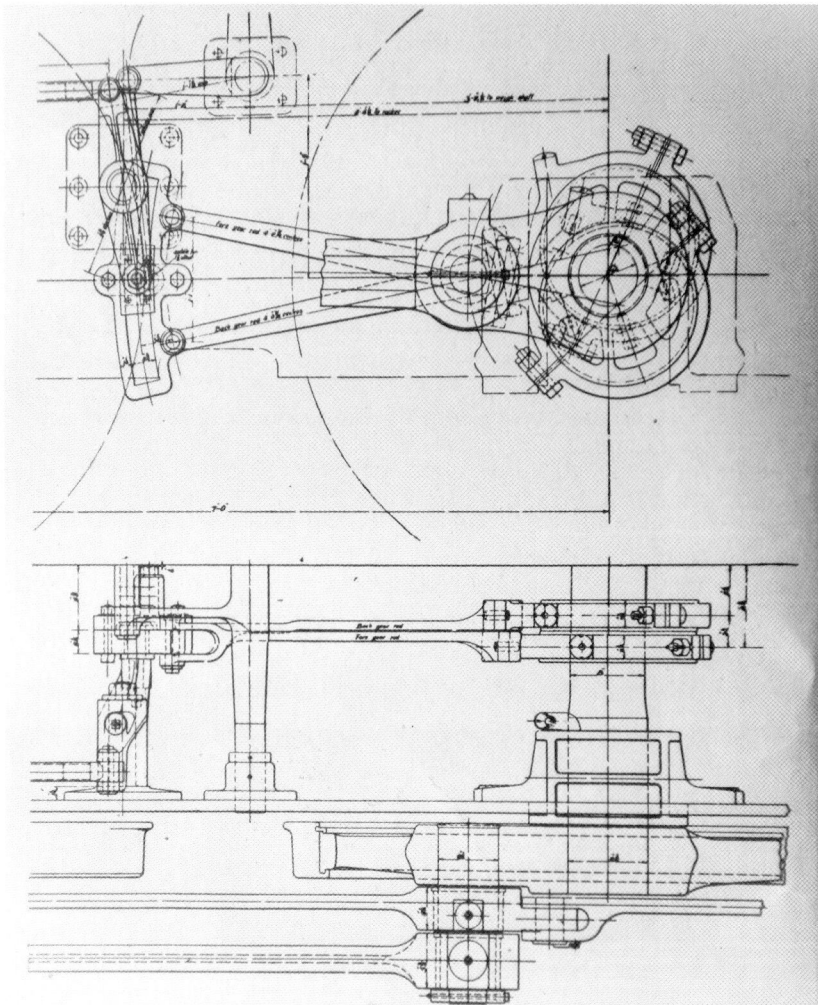

The evolution of valve gear under Churchward was, as one might expect, a process that involved studying what was on offer around the world, adding his own ideas plus those of his staff, then producing solutions that would work best on his locomotives. Once this was completed he tested and measured the extent to which they succeeded, going back to the drawing board if necessary and then putting it into regular service where it would be tested in even more trying conditions. These four drawings demonstrate how this process worked in practice. (Above) The GWR Stephenson & Co derived valve gear which was fitted to the Dean/Churchward prototype 4-6-0 engine No. 100 which appeared in 1902 four months before Churchward became Superintendent. (Opposite above) By the time the second prototype 4-6-0, No. 98, left the Works in 1903, the valve gear had undergone further modification. In this form it would be used on the third prototype, engine No. 171, then the remainder of Saint Class when production commenced in 1905. (Opposite middle) The arrival of the first four-cylinder 4-6-0 No. 40, later named *North Star* (though initially built as a 4-4-2) in 1906 called for a different solution. This version came to be known as the 'Scissors' gear. This unique arrangement derived, according to Cook, 'from a compound motion from the two inside crossheads, the left-hand crosshead driving an extension of the right-hand quadrant and obtaining also a combining motion from the inside valves direct and through a rocking lever to the outside valves on the same side of the motion'. This model was only fitted to No. 40, the remainder of the Star Class, which began appearing in 1907, received the modified version of the Walschaerts valve gear (Opposite bottom) This proved to be remarkably effective and helped add to the Star's reputation of being extremely free running engines. (KC/IMechE)

Changing Times and Competing Expectations 179

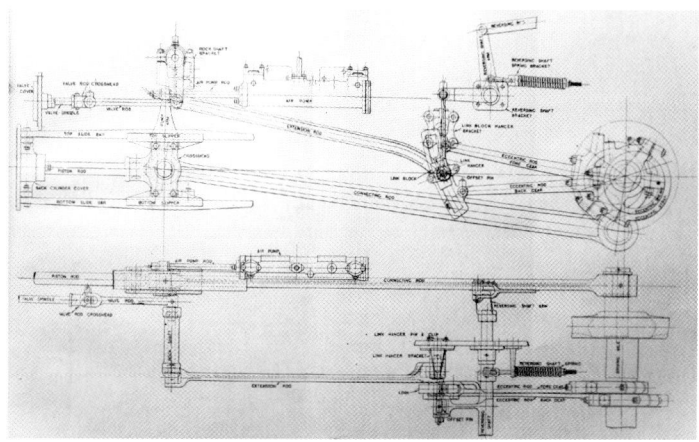

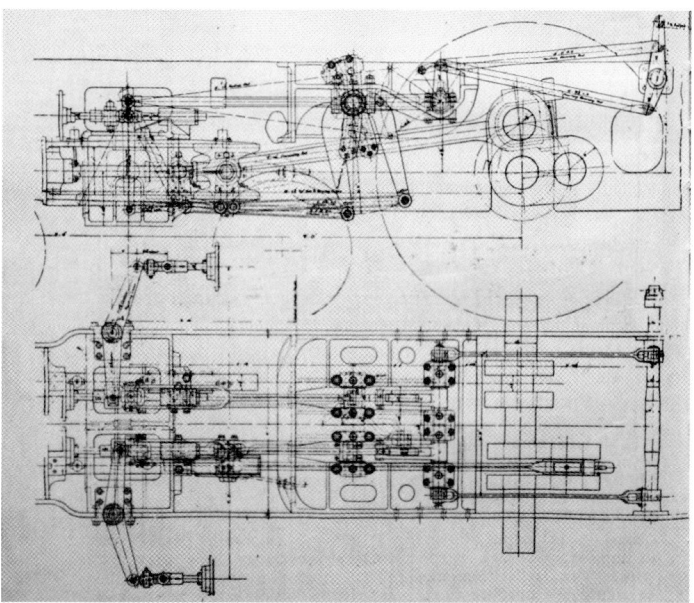

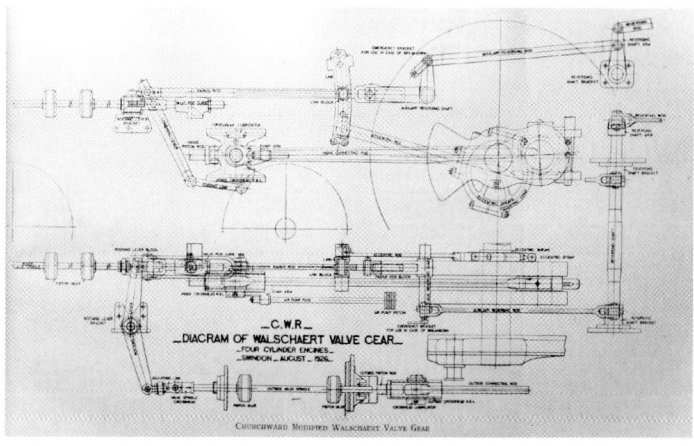

Churchward Modified Walschaert Valve Gear

Whilst this was happening similar attention was being paid to piston valve design as Churchward sought to improve the way they admitted steam into the cylinders. For the GWR this resulted in two types of valve being used across the standard range of engines and, as Cook recorded, these:

> Went up in oversize steps of $\frac{1}{16}$in up to $\frac{3}{8}$in. One significant improvement was introduced when a semi-plug type of valve was introduced, in which steam was admitted into each cylinder head. This expanded the rings to the size of the port bushes and locked them at that dimension. When the regulator was closed these rings contracted to their normal size. As a result of this Churchward was able to indicate a wear figure of .030in at which point the steam chest needed to be re-bored (an expensive and time consuming operation) It is interesting to note that research into piston valve design some years later, long after Churchward had retired, confirmed both the angles of the rings and that the limit of wear, which he had been laid down, was, in fact, the ideal.

The same might be said of his work on cylinder lubrication, which became more critical with the advent of superheating, and top feed. For the latter, the question was how could the risk of thermal shock, which occurs when cold feedwater mixes too quickly with hot steam, be reduced or eliminated. In finding a solution to this particular problem Cook recalled that:

> Churchward always had an eye towards what he used to refer to as 'tapping the latent' and to achieve this many experiments were carried out on the delivery of the water into the top feed trays and its outflow from the trays to be split up into finely diffused, less damaging streams. The result was that it actually mixed with the existing water in the forward half of the barrel. This system did not eradicate the problem but it reduced it significantly.

By 1906, when the first of the Stars was built, all this work, which also included improvements to the braking systems – achieved by combining the ejector and a crosshead-operated pump together to produce an efficient system that consumed less steam – had progressed to a very advanced level. Nevertheless, no effort was spared in pursuing further efficiencies and, in the process, improving the breed even more.

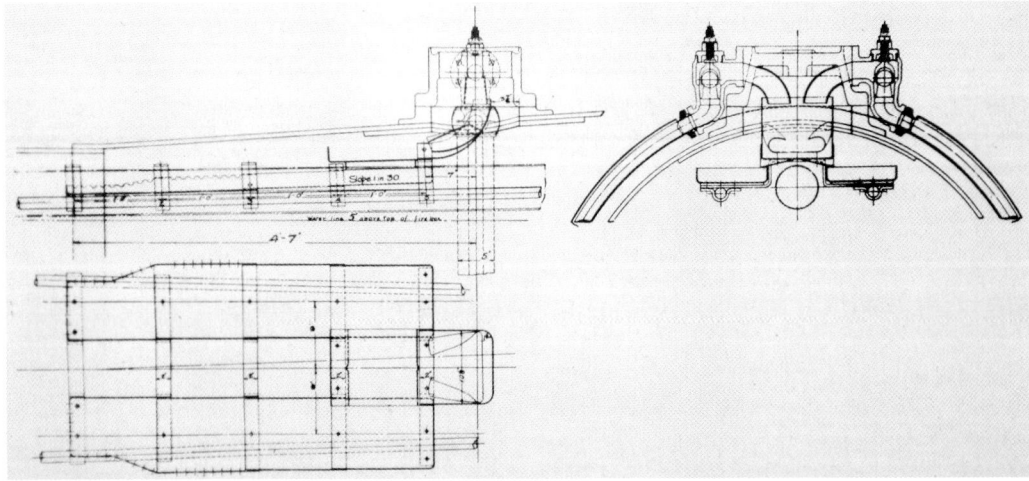

The issue of thermal shock when cold feedwater mixes too quickly with hot steam was an issue that concerned all locomotive engineers. Churchward successfully adopted the above arrangement which then became a standard part of his standardisation development plan. (KC/IMechE)

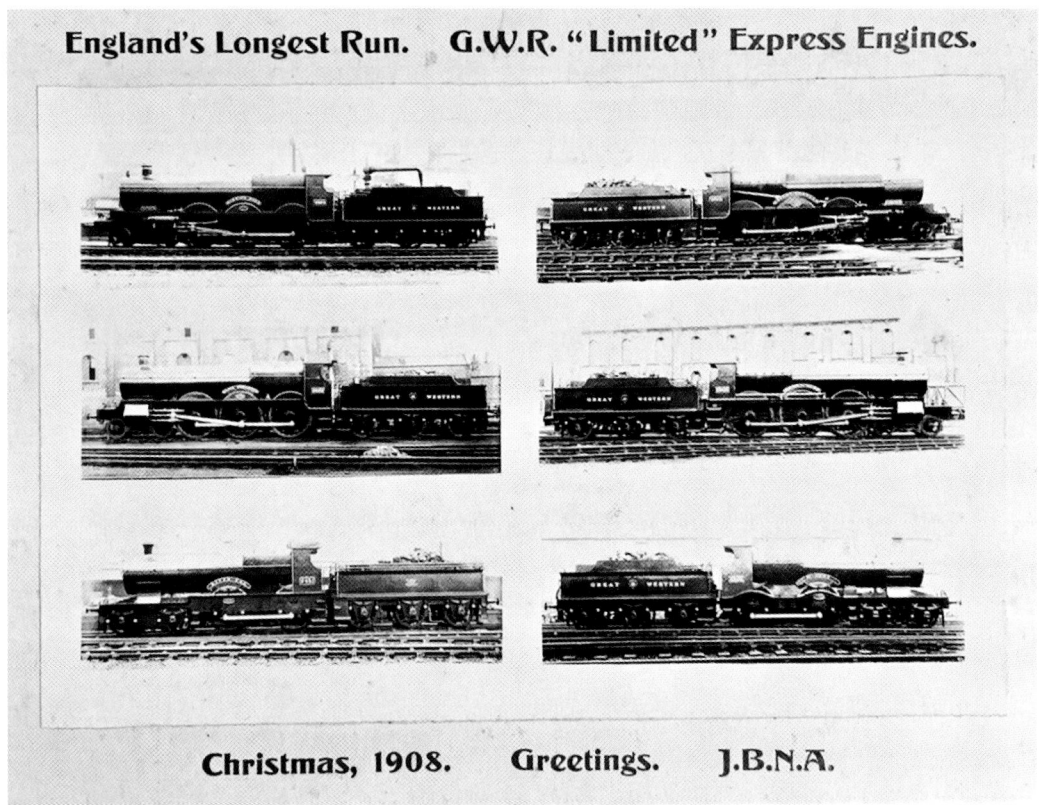

Each year, as its locomotive fleet grew, the GWR would send out Christmas Cards proudly celebrating its achievements, all of which Churchward could justifiably claim credit. (Author's collection)

One might have thought that the production version of the Stars, which began entering service in 1907, marked the high point of Churchward's career and might have led to some slackening of effort. Yet as the new year dawned there was much more to drive him on although some of it might not always be to his liking. As we have seen, he would find the struggle in trying to meet or quell rising demands for better working and living conditions, increasingly absorbing much more of his time. To make matters worse, the political situation in Europe was worsening year by year as rival nations sought to protect themselves from implied threats from their neighbours. Very soon a timetable to conflict would overtake the peacemakers and the continent would slip into a war of unparalleled violence. If the Edwardian era was seen as a golden age for some, the years that followed were the polar opposite. Luckily for Churchward he'd had twelve years to achieve his ambitions and bring locomotive, carriage and wagon design into the twentieth century before the clouds of war obliterated much that he and many others held dear.

Chapter 7

A Passing Age

By 1908 Churchward reigned supreme at Swindon, so his Chairman and James Inglis, who became General Manager in 1903, having been Chief Engineer before that, were less likely to question his decisions as long as he continued to deliver success, or so it seems. But he had played a very astute game in achieving this. A methodical, measured approach, which has checks and balances built into it and is presented rationally to those with the power to provide funds and authorise change, always tends to succeed. And it did so now in the corridors of power at Paddington. At such a level in a big industry there will always be lively debate, arguments and tough, uncompromising words spoken at times, but this is as it should be. In this way strategy is formed and funding agreed, with disputes, if they existed at all, being swept under the carpet, to be mulled over in private, if considered at all. So, as he looked ahead Churchward could do so with a degree of optimism.

Yet, even allowing for his many successes, in the wider railway world he was less well-known and his reputation as a design engineer of great standing had yet to be confirmed. Certainly he was still seen as 'a coming man', as the phraseology of the time described it, even though he was 51 so hardly just starting out. However, there were other engineers of note who had fostered equally, if not stronger reputations by then. These included, in Britain, both Gooch and Dean at Swindon, and men such as John Aspinall, Henry Ivatt, James and Patrick Stirling, William Kirtley, Dugald Drummond, William Stroudley, George Whale and Francis Webb amongst others. But Churchward's ideas, though long in the making, had not been fully implemented by 1908 and so the product of his work may not have been available in sufficient numbers to promote his reputation above the others. Still there were fifty-two Saints, thirty or so 2800s, ninety plus

Churchward's Star arrives, in this case engine No. 4037 *Queen Philippa* which was one of ten built at Swindon in 1910/11. However, with all the new developments contained in the Star's design, any hope that the cab might be improved to provide better cover and a slightly better working environment was unfulfilled. Such refinements would have to wait until Charles Collett was in charge. (DN)

2-6-2Ts, of both the light and heavy varieties, twenty 3800 Class 4-4-0s, ten 2221 Class 4-4-2Ts and twenty-one Stars to underpin the good work he was doing. So, it was a good start, added to which his ideas on standardisation were gaining ground within the GWR and the wider railway community, as his membership of the Association of Railway Engineers (ARLE), to which he was elected in 1902, could bear witness.

The ARLE, which was first formed in Scotland in 1868 only to lapse for a time until revived in 1876 by Stroudley and James Stirling, brought together as many of the Locomotive Superintendents and CMEs of the day as possible. The purpose of this association was a simple one, namely to 'discuss locomotive practice in force on the Railways with which the members are connected, and for other purposes'. It was a very broad brief indeed but in this way became a valuable means of sharing knowledge and ideas for the benefit of all. It was here as a member, then later as its chairman, that the forceful and astute Churchward was able to give voice to his ideas, particularly on standardisation, and achieve wider recognition in the industry as a result – all backed up by the appearance of his new classes of locomotives.

Despite this impressive start, Churchward's, and the learned papers he produced describing his work, wider acknowledgement required something more if he were to reach or exceed his predecessors at Swindon, let alone the wider world. Inevitably, one requires a good press and very public successes for this to happen. And it was in furthering his cause that the huge expansion of newspapers and magazines, all eager for news of the most spectacular kind to sell their products, proved a godsend. Here *Lord of the Isles'* memorable but rumoured 100mph record run of 1904 proved to be important and newsworthy.

The changing face of Edwardian Britain here on display at Paddington. This photograph captures many things but three are particularly noteworthy. First of all, we can see the growing influence of Churchward's standardisation programme at least on carriages. Secondly, there is the sheer weight of passengers using the railway then suggesting that they had more money to spend – particularly the rapidly growing middle class. This certainly provided a boost to passenger numbers while the major source of revenue, goods traffic, held firm. Finally, in the style of dress, there seems to be a loosening of the rigidness of Victorian standards suggesting that society is, to a certain extent, progressing in a more liberal direction. (Author's collection)

For a company such as the GWR such recognition was their life-blood and would be embraced and exploited whenever possible. Just such an opportunity arose in May 1906 when a newly built Saint Class engine, No. 2903 (a year later named *Lady of Lyon*), was a put through her paces with dramatic consequences. Although reports of what happened were soon circulating around the railway industry, it took some years for a fuller account to appear in the Railway Magazine:

> During January last a statement obtained wide currency in the daily press that Mr H.J. Robinson, then just about to retire from the position of Chief Locomotive Inspector on the Great Western Railway, had been responsible for driving a locomotive in this country at a speed of 120 miles per hour. It is needless to say that readers of The Railway Magazine who are familiar with all the speeds hitherto claimed as railway records, and in particular with the figure of 102.3mph achieved down Wellington Bank of the GWR on May 9, 1904, which from that day to this has had an unchallenged supremacy, are interested to know on what authority this new claim has been made, as is evidenced by the extensive correspondence we have received on the subject.
>
> We therefore wrote to Mr C B Collett, the Chief Mechanical Engineer of the Great Western Railway, who communicated to us an interesting account of what actually occurred. It appears that in May 1906, No 2903 - one of the newly introduced 2-cylinder 4-6-0 locomotives and herself fresh from the shops - was taken for a trial run light from Swindon to Stoke Gifford, with the intention, after running the engine round the Filton-Patchway triangle, of having "a sharp run" back. Signal checks were experienced, however, and No 2903 was then stopped at Chipping Sodbury until "line clear" had been obtained through to Wootton Bassett, after which she was re-started, and there was evidently some running of very startling order down the 1 in 300 from Badminton to Little Somerford.
>
> The purpose of the run was to demonstrate that an engine taken straight from the shops could be run at over 100 miles per hour. Those on the footplate included Mr Collett, who was then Assistant Manager of the Locomotive Works, Mr G H Flewellen, the Locomotive Inspector, and the Foreman of the Erecting Shop, Mr Evans. The timing for some distance by the mileposts with a stop watch was given as 120 miles per hour, and the clocking between the signal-boxes of Little Somerford and Hullavington was booked as two minutes for the 4½ miles.

For many years rumours circulated that in May 1906 a brand-new Saint Class engine, No. 2903 (above), had achieved the colossal speed of 120mph during a running in turn. Word of this 'unofficially' recognised event soon reached the ears of those in the know and undoubtedly enhanced and broadened Churchward's reputation in the railway industry. (Author's collection)

Mr Collett points out that, while the object of running a new engine on its first trip at over 100 miles per hour was achieved, the timing could not be regarded as accurate and that the 102.3mph record of 'City of Truro' in 1904, made under the personal observation of one of the most careful recorders of his time - the late Charles Rous-Marten - with the aid of a chronograph reading to one-fifth parts of a second, must remain the best duly authenticated railway speed record that this country has yet witnessed.

One wonders whether Churchward knew of this special run or even authorised it? Either way, when word got out, as it tends to, it would have had a polarising effect on the railway world. Rumour, then and now, has a tendency to spread more quickly than official statements and to those interested, in and outside the industry, attaining such a speed would have been thought an extraordinary leap forward. In the event the man or the men responsible would have gained great kudos and their work considered the stuff of dreams. This would have been especially so for a public relations department eager to exploit any opportunity they could to boost the reputation of the company. If so, the years ahead, as we shall see, opened up many other possibilities for them to explore.

In the meantime, the next phase of Churchward's development plan was coming to fruition, though speculation suggests it may well have been forced upon him by a Chairman and General Manager eager for another good story to parade. This might well be true because the engine that emerged at Swindon very early in 1908, a 4-6-2 Pacific, seems to be an odd choice to have made. This was especially so for a company very heavily committed to building 4-6-0 fast passenger express locomotives when modernising its fleet. So, why a Pacific at this stage of the game especially as it was the first to appear in Britain and would remain so until 1922 when examples built by Nigel Gresley and Vincent Raven were unveiled? In my book *Princess Royal Pacifics*, I described how Churchward and, later on, other British designers were probably influenced by developments overseas and came to the conclusion that a Pacific offered advantages over other wheel configurations for fast passenger services:

> It is believed that the Pacifics grew from 4-4-2 Atlantic Classes and the 4-6-0 configuration, with the two earliest examples being developed in the USA. In 1887 the Lehigh Valley Railroad discovered that in mounting a new firebox on to a 4-6-0 design that the extra weight could only be carried if the frames were extended. To provide balance and stability, the designers hit upon the idea of adding 2 trailing wheels. In 1897 the Chicago, Milwaukee and St Paul Railway also found it necessary to add a set of trailing wheels when developing a 4-6-0 design so that axle loading would be reduced. However, neither design found favour and were not continued.
>
> In 1901 the New Zealand Railway Department commissioned the Baldwin Locomotive Works of Philadelphia, Pennsylvania to design and build thirteen new engines. The specification called for fireboxes capable of burning poor grade lignite coal. As design work proceeded Baldwin's realised that the engine would require a much larger firebox than normal and the extra support this needed could be best provided by a 4-6-2 configured locomotive, rather than a 4-6-0.
>
> The success of this work soon reached the attention of engineers around the world and the model began to be explored in depth. Designers were intrigued by the potential of this concept and saw in it a means of producing greater stability at speed and higher tractive effort. It also encouraged the addition of bigger, wider fireboxes and larger boilers to enhance an engines efficiency and output. And so, a massive building programme got underway, particularly in the USA and Canada, where more than 6500 Pacific locomotives were in service by the 1930s. Soon they were a global phenomena and appeared on railways across all Continents as the century progressed. In Europe, the first prototypes of note

Although the first examples of 4-6-2's appeared in the USA in the last years of the nineteenth century, the first engines of this type of note appear to have entered service in New Zealand. In 1901 the Chief Mechanical Engineer of the New Zealand Railway, Alfred Beattie, issued a specification to Baldwin's for thirteen new engines. Having considered this requirement, and concluded that the boiler and firebox could only be mounted effectively if a trailing bogie was fitted, engineers in the States suggested that 4-6-2 solution be adopted. In the negotiation that followed Baldwin's managers seem to have persuaded Beattie that it would be prudent to do so and allow them to build the new engines as Pacifics. From these discussions the first major class of 4-6-2's emerged. (RH)

An inventory of main-line steam locomotives in the United States completed in 1904 identified 233 Pacifics in service across the country. Other than this broad summary the information provided is very slight so giving few guides to the design of the engines involved. One of these, a Union Pacific Railroad Pacific No. 119 that entered service in 1904, is pictured here. (JC)

appeared in France in 1907. It was a four-cylinder compound, designed for the Compagnie du Chemin, by George Solacroup, with the support of Alfred de Glehn. This was followed by an example being built in Germany, though design work had begun 2 years earlier."

Ever watchful, Churchward and his team undoubtedly read the limited material available that described these new engines and been intrigued by what was happening overseas. This was particularly so of de Glehn's work, especially with three of his compounds already at work on GWR metals, but it was not an experiment to be repeated this time by the acquisition of one of his Pacifics. However, there is always a pressing need for stronger more powerful engines and a 4-6-2

A Passing Age 187

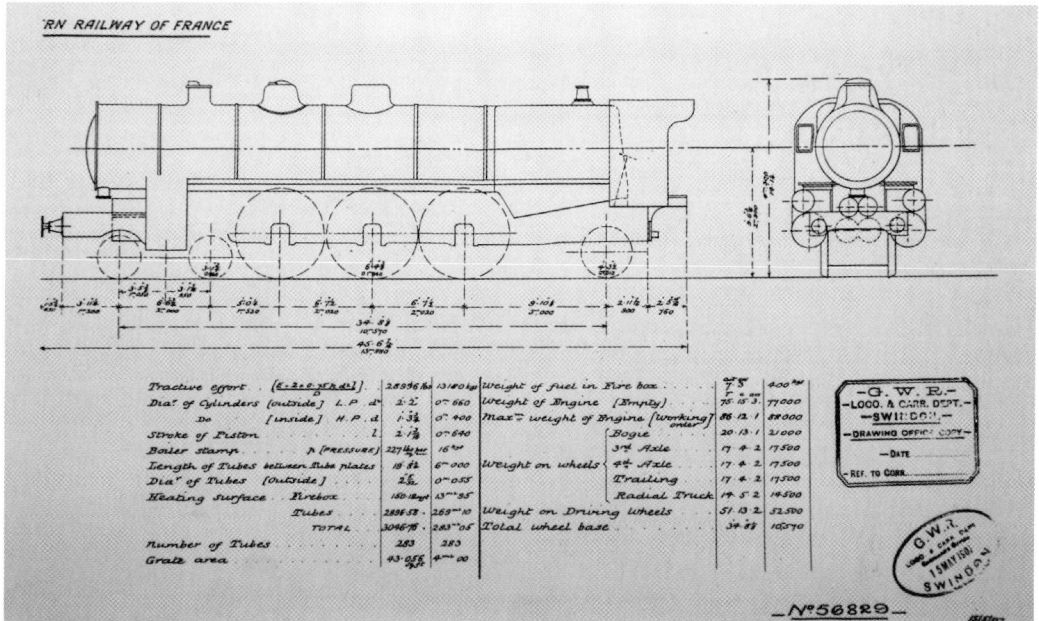

In 1907 the French engineer George Solacroup, with the help of Alfred De Glehn, introduced the first European 4-6-2s, on this occasion two prototype Pacifics for the Compagnie Du Paris-Orleans, of which he was Chief Mechanical Engineer. These four-cylinder compound engines (above, captured in an early drawing that was acquired by Churchward as the GWR stamp bears witness) proved so successful that the Paris-Orleans would go on to build another 277 Pacifics, while other French companies would produce an additional 1087 4-6-2 engines (below one of the Solacrouop engines as built). (BS)

may have been seen, by those at Swindon or Paddington, as a way of achieving this, but needed to be assessed and proven before a change of locomotive policy might be sanctioned.

In many ways this development worked towards the targets Churchward had described in his 1905 paper to the Institution of Mechanical Engineers and his hypotheses that the 'modern locomotive problem is principally a question of boiler'. Greater capacity was a primary aim and the Pacific design could achieve this, but would the greater weight and length of such locomotive prove a disadvantage on the GWR's railway system and would it perform better than their 4-6-0 engines on fast passenger services or fast goods for that matter?

So, a GWR Pacific came into existence, to be called the *Great Bear*, with its development following a well-trodden path – produce a prototype then undertake a detailed evaluation and attempt improvements before deciding whether to construct more or not. But did Churchward build this engine of his own volition, in which case he would probably have been filled with enthusiasm for the project, or was it undertaken on the whim of GWR senior managers eager to have such a large prestigious engine to publicise the success of the company? Even now this is an issue clouded by speculation and a degree of uncertainty which is difficult to break through.

This may well be so, but it was Churchward who engaged the editor of the prestigious and widely read *Engineer* journal in January 1908 and made sure that the locomotive's arrival was 'spun' effectively, with his name prominently appearing at the top of an article that bore the headline 'The GWR Four-Cylinder Non-Compound Express Locomotive'. It is also more than likely that he provided many of the words used by the editor in the write-up, as well as photographs and drawings. If so, he may not have been the unenthusiastic supporter that some believe, but a very willing participant. Either way the report contains much of interest about his latest project:

February 14th 1908.
The Great Western Railway has on its system many particularly difficult pieces of road from the point of view of gradients. Of late years the problem of taking increasingly heavy loads over these gradients, at the high speeds now demanded by the travelling public, has become more and

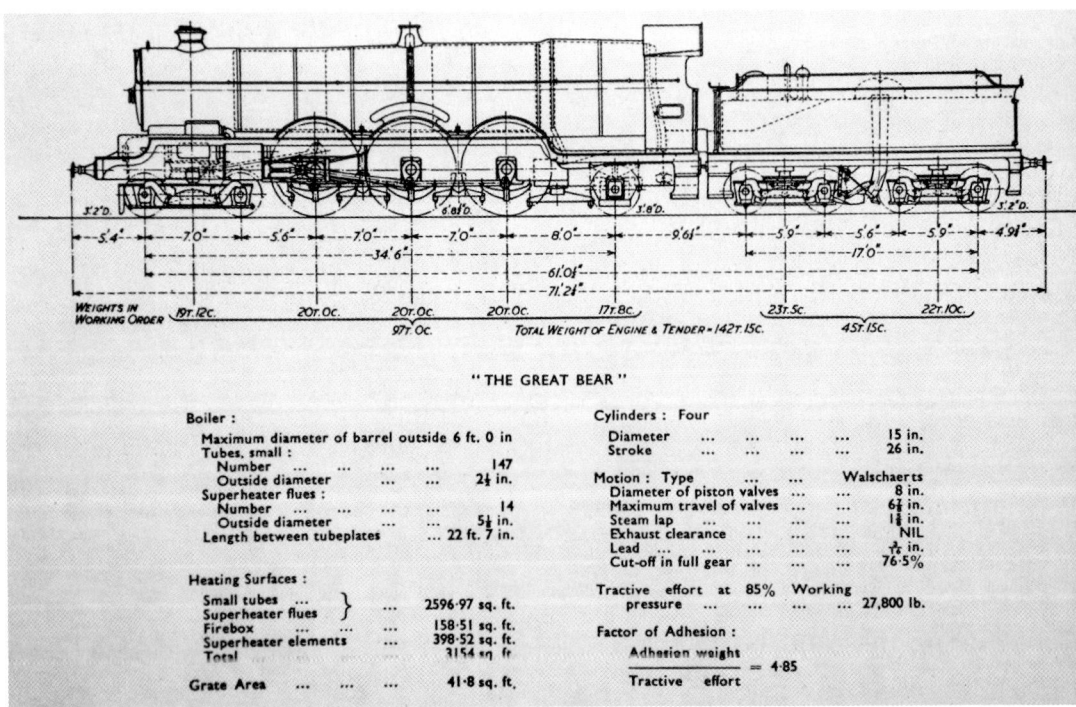

Churchward's first and only 4-6-2 Pacific as conceived in 1907. Although No. III, *The Great Bear*, must have seemed to some a significant departure from the central themes Churchward was exploring, some considered it to simply be a stretched Star Class. With the same cylinder, motion and wheel arrangement, except for the trailing truck, this comparison is not an unreasonable one to have been made. (DN/Author's collection)

A Passing Age 189

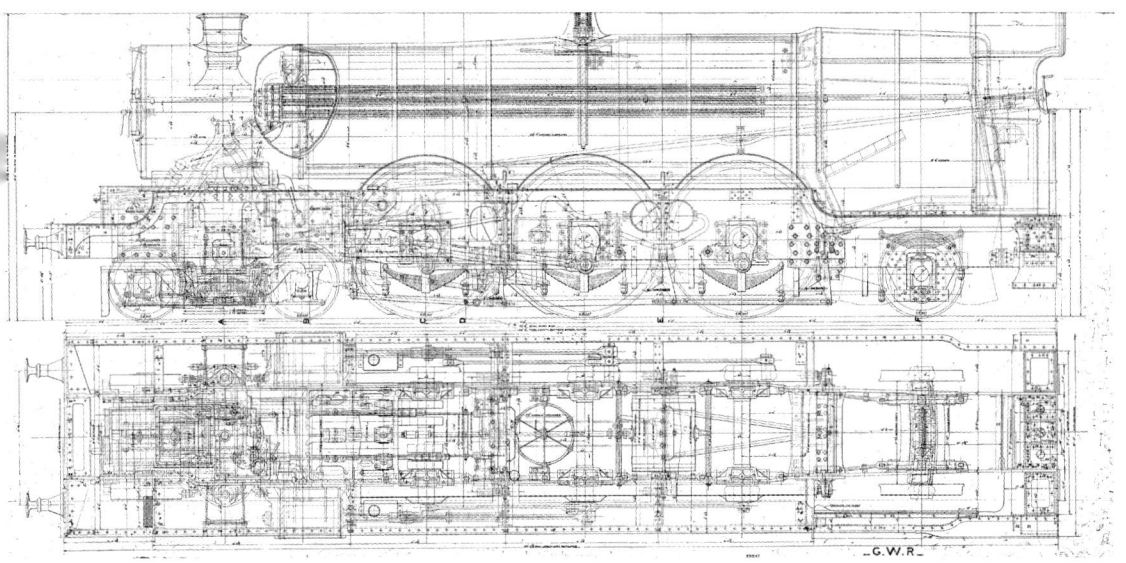

(Above) The general arrangement drawings of No. III as originally designed and (below left and below right) forward and aft views showing the superheater, cylinder and cab layout, amongst other things. (DN)

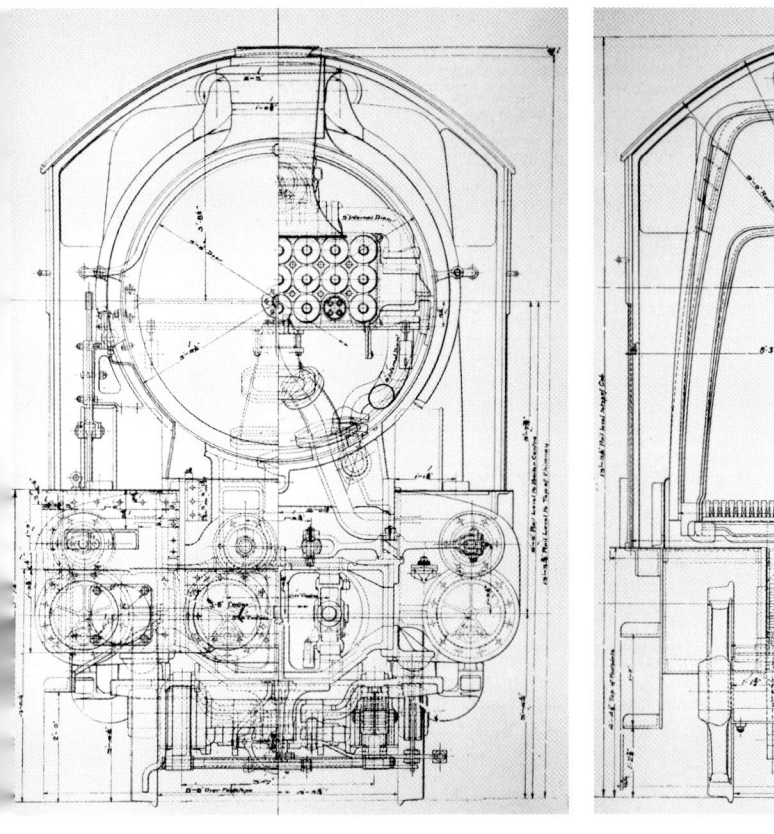
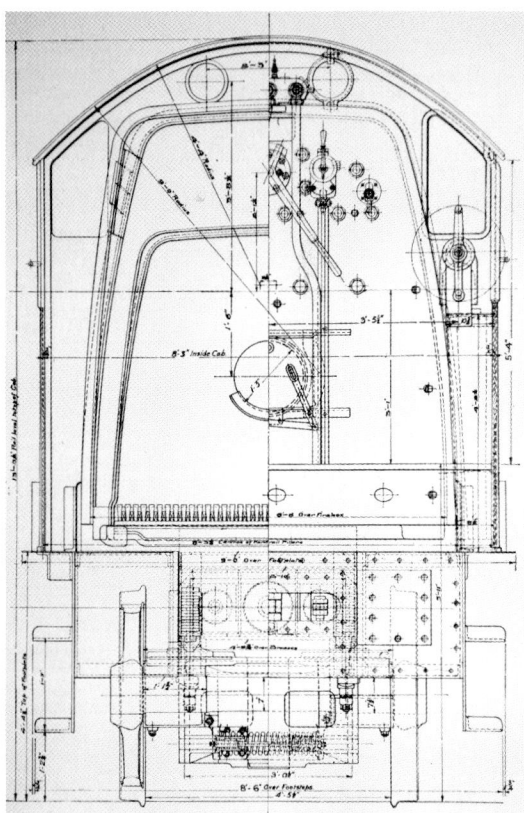

more difficult. We have referred at times to the progressive steps being taken by the company's chief locomotive engineer, Mr G.J. Churchward – who is particularly enterprising – to cope with the difficulties he has encountered, and we are now enabled by his courtesy to place before our readers' engravings showing the latest developments in locomotive engineering on this railway, which is celebrated for its high speed, long distance, non-stop runs.

The engine is question is called *Great Bear* and we believe it to be the heaviest locomotive which has yet been put to work in this country, its total weight being 96 tons. It cannot, we imagine, lay much claim to beauty, but at all events it has the appearance of great strength and capability. It is truly an enormous engine, and no one looking at it casually would imagine that each of the driving wheels is 6ft 8½ inches in diameter. This, however, is a fact, and from it some idea of the immense size of the locomotive may be gained. Each of the main axles carries a load of 20 tons and the four wheels of the bogie, which are 3ft 2inches in diameter, support a like amount. The trailing wheels are 3ft 8inches in diameter together and account for 16 tons.

The detail of the boiler also bears testimony to the size of the engine. The barrel is 23ft long and has a diameter varying from 5ft 6 inches to 6ft. The firebox, which is of the Belpaire type is 8ft by 5ft 9 inches and 6ft 9in. outside and 7ft 2⅜in by 4ft 11⅛in and 5ft 8⅝in inside, the height varying from 6ft 5⁵⁄₁₆in to 5ft 2⁷⁄₁₆in There is a superheater (a Swindon type No. 1 based on the Cole design) – a comparative rarity in British engines – containing 84 tubes 1¾in, diameter and 21ft 4in long and producing a low degree of superheat. The fire tubes are of two diameters. There are 141 of the smaller size, which are 2½in diameter; and 21 of the larger – measuring 4¾ in…..The heating surface is made up of:

Superheater tubes	545.00sqft.
Fire tubes	2673.45sqft.
Arch tubes	24.22sqft.
Firebox	158.14sqft.
Total	**3400.81sqft.**

This we believe to be a record figure in this country. The area of the fire grate is 41.79sqft, and the working pressure is 225lb on the square inch. There are four-cylinders, each 15in diameter and 26in stroke, and the tractive effort is 29, 430lb.

A new departure for the Great Western is having the tender carried on two four-wheeled bogies. The water capacity is 3500 gallons and a pick-up apparatus is fitted so that water can be scooped up when the engine is in motion.

We understand that the 'Great Bear' was taken for a run with a train on Wednesday of last week, and that it came out of the trial most successfully.

So, Churchward took the lead in publicizing the engine's development, which, to me, suggests a strong level of patronage and minimal coercion on the part of his leaders. He was after all a scientist who was fascinated by the evaluation of new ideas and concepts, so I believe his imagination was piqued, initially at least, by the possibilities inherent in the 4-6-2 configuration and he was more than happy to initiate then proceed with the project. So he sought approval from his managers and was allocated £4,400 in January 1907 to build this experimental engine; a further £860 being added later to cover additional, unspecified costs that arose during construction.

As work progressed he and his designers soon decided that the boiler should be built in three rings, the middle section being coned. It would contain 141 x 2½ inch fire tubes, against 176 x 2in tubes in the `Stars`, but with the same number of superheater flues (18), though ⅜in wider. To enhance the engine's performance significantly the firebox, a Belpaire type, had to produce more heat, so the firegrate was built proportionally larger, with greater capacity than those attached to the Star Class. When completed this new boiler was designated Swindon Standard No 6.

(Above left) No. III's well laid out but cramped cab. Here the crew would have had little protection from the elements. (Above right) A rare photograph of one the engine's tender bogies, which seems to have been identical to a standard locomotive bogie. The tender body is partially visible in the background. (Below) The engine as it appeared in 1908 when new and ready for testing. Some thought it ugly or unbalanced in shape. For myself I think it an elegant design that might have been improved by a longer cab and, as Kenneth Cook wrote in a 1965 letter, 'trailing wheels that were boxed in with outside, not inside frames. In which case it would have strongly resembled Stanier's most handsome Princess Royal Class 4-6-2s that began entering service in 1933'. (DN/Author's collection)

The remainder of the locomotive drew heavily on the `Star Class` design. There were four cylinders, two middle ones set well forward between the frames and the outer ones covering the tops of the rear wheels of the leading truck. Harold Holcroft, the draughtsman responsible for producing the cylinder design for this engine, described in his book `Locomotive Adventure` how Churchward was involved in each stage of development, often disagreeing with the draughtsman's proposals:

> Churchward insisted that the `Star` class arrangement should be adopted without modification, other than in cylinder diameter, and the only point outstanding was as to how the diameter could be increased above the 14 ¼ inches of the `Stars`. The longer wheelbase increased the bogie side movement and the angle taken by the trailing wheels of the leading truck behind the cylinders. For this reason, a 15 inch diameter was the largest predictable in the limited space.

Due to its weight and length No. III's route availability was severely limited, so the line from Paddington to Bristol became its stamping ground and here it was found, according to Cook, that the engine 'ran satisfactorily and worked vey exacting passenger services of considerable size'. These three pictures capture *The Great Bear* in her natural element. (Top) Backing on to her train at Paddington soon after construction. (Left) Looking large and brooding when on shed, according to notes that accompanied this photo, at Old Oak Common. (Below) At speed passing through Sonning Cutting with a fairly light load of eight coaches towards the end of her service. (DN/Author's collection)

This was explained on Churchward's next visit. I pointed out that GWR tyres were 5¾ inches wide, and that if narrower tyres were used the increased clearance behind the cylinders would allow a diameter of 16 inches. The Chief would not agree to a departure from the standard width of tyre, and seemed quite satisfied with 15 inch cylinders.

With only a small increase in diameter size the tractive effort produced was marginally better than the 'Star' Class. Consequently, many of the potential gains from adopting the Pacific design were not fully exploited.

In January 1908, *Great Bear* was ready for trials to begin. Sadly, though, most records for this period of her life no longer appear to exist. If these papers had survived they might have confirmed how extensive the testing regime was and whether the engine hauled a dynamometer car at some stage or was processed through Swindon's purpose built test plant. Armed with such material we might have been able to determine in which direction Churchward's thoughts had been going, what his intentions were in respect of the Pacific and why he chose not to build more. What is left is sketchy at best and only marginally helped by several contemporary reports that appeared in the press. These included one written by the Reverend W.J. Scott for the *Railway Magazine* in June 1909:

> A trial one Sunday morning with the fast express goods to Stoke Gifford yard, the train being specially made up to 100 wagons, or a load of over 1,000 tons, showed conclusively how great the engine's hauling power is, though the hoped for inclusive speed of 40mph was not achieved. Once the pace rose to 50mph, but with so vast a load on the gentle rise, from Brinkworth to near Badminton, soon made itself felt and time was lost. Still enough was done to show that the biggest passenger trains of Easter and August holidays – 400 to 430 tons – could be handled with ease by the *Great Bear*.

He then added a brief report based on his own recollections of the engine in action:

> The only run I have had behind *The Great Bear* was not an interesting one, as just one minute was lost on the booked time between Bristol and Paddington, via Badminton,

No. III was much photographed in her early days, here at Old Oak Common, her permanent shed. (DN)

without any signal check and a load of barely 200 tons. The work up Filton Bank (1 in 75) was especially disappointing but – as the inspector on the footplate told me afterwards – she was worked throughout under easy steam to avoid any overheating of the axles. On another occasion, however, with over 400 tons behind the tender, she covered the same stretch in about 117 minutes – or 3 minutes inside the schedule.

W.A. Tuplin, in his 1958 book *Great Western Steam*, referred to an even heavier test train being pulled by No. III when new, but first he alluded to a problem the crew encountered with the engine:

> The difficulty with bearings (of the trailing truck which could overheat because of their close proximity to ashpan above) and indifferent steaming associated with long fire-tubes (which resisted the flow of the gases from the fire) are sufficient to explain why The Great Bear was never regularly employed on the 'crack' trains. There is certainly no record of any attempt to demonstrate exceptional ability by hauling, for example, a 600 ton test express train at express speed as was done by a Gresley Pacific later on. (However) as a special demonstration, *The Great Bear* hauled a freight train weighing 2,300 tons from Swindon to Acton at an average speed of 24mph, but this could only have produced a melancholy satisfaction for the designer of an engine that might have been expected to take 600 tons over the road at 70mph.

Years later O.S. Nock, the railway historian, added to this meagre fare when he referred to a run made by No. III between Paddington and Bath on 3 February 1913. On this occasion her load was 310 tons and one E.L. Bell was on hand to record her performance. To this Nock added a brief note giving some more information:

> The load of 310 tons was not heavy, but the engine started briskly from Paddington at 1830 hrs and after a leisurely acceleration after Ealing ran well until a slight check nearing Reading hindered progress. The recovery was good, with speeds ranging from round 66-68mph on to Didcot. But there was a sudden falling off after that presumably because the train was by then on time. The average speed after Wootton Bassett indicated a maximum of close to 70mph on Dauntsey bank and despite very easy running after Chippenham the train would have been comfortably on time – a 112 minute schedule – but for a final signal check.

So, when assessing the success or failure of this engine there isn't much to go on in official records or eye witness accounts, though what there is suggests that the engine did show promise. But in entering service it faced one insuperable barrier – her size was thought too great and her route availability too limited. As a result, she spent her life running between Paddington and Bristol where the track and bridges were thought strong enough to bear her weight. There was also the success of the Stars, and to a slightly lesser extent the Saints, to consider. Here was an expanding fleet of 4-6-0s capable of doing much that No. III could do but without the restrictions imposed by the 20 ton 9cwt axle loading of *The Great Bear* on parts of the network where 20 tons was considered the absolute maximum.

In the event the 4-6-2 probably doesn't seem to have added anything special or uniquely useful to the GWR fleet except, perhaps, as a publicity vehicle. Yet even here it was a role she only seems to have fulfilled up to a point, if the content of newspapers and magazines of the period are anything to go by. In this sphere speed and performance were the headline grabbers, and a new super large locomotive would only have been newsworthy when achieving something special – a very fast run or an exceptionally heavy passenger load pulled in trying conditions. This No. III never did, or so it seems, and any excitement generated by her appearance soon dissipated and dissolved.

6.40 p.m. PADDINGTON—BATH

Load: 310 tons (less 25 tons slipped at Chippenham)
Engine: 4—6—2 No. 111 *The Great Bear*

Dist. Miles		Actual m. s.	Av. Speed m.p.h.
0·0	PADDINGTON	0 00	
1·3	Westbourne Park	3 28	
5·7	Ealing	9 25	44·3
9·1	Southall	12 59	57·2
13·2	West Drayton	17 14	57·8
16·2	Langley	20 09	61·8
18·5	SLOUGH	22 17	64·3
22·5	Taplow	26 06	63·0
24·2	Maidenhead	27 48	60·0
31·0	Twyford	34 22	62·2
—		sigs.	
36·0	READING	40 22	50·0
38·8	Tilehurst	43 07	58·8
41·5	Pangbourne	46 01	
44·8	Goring	49 03	65·2
48·5	Cholsey	52 26	66·5
53·1	DIDCOT	56 42	64·8
56·5	Steventon	60 05	60·3
60·4	Wantage Road	64 07	58·8
63·9	Challow	67 48	57·1
66·5	Uffington	70 42	53·8
71·5	Shrivenham	76 09	55·0
77·3	SWINDON	82 12	57·5
82·9	Wootton Bassett	87 33	62·8
87·7	Dauntsey	91 46	68·3
94·0	CHIPPENHAM	97 15	69·0
98·3	Corsham	101 57	54·9
101·9	Box	105 45	56·8
—		sigs.	
106·9	BATH	113 38	

Cost of checks: Reading 1½ min.
Bathampton 2 min.
Net time: 110 min.

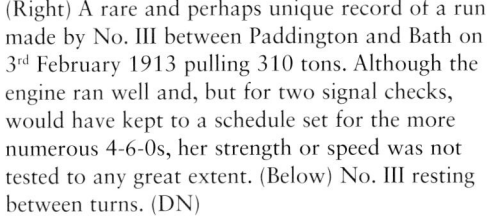

(Right) A rare and perhaps unique record of a run made by No. III between Paddington and Bath on 3rd February 1913 pulling 310 tons. Although the engine ran well and, but for two signal checks, would have kept to a schedule set for the more numerous 4-6-0s, her strength or speed was not tested to any great extent. (Below) No. III resting between turns. (DN)

The Great Bear was considered by some to be a perfect vehicle for the GWR's Publicity Department at Paddington to exploit. This may be so but reports in periodicals and adverts of the time are not extensive enough to confirm this either way. However, this publicity photo, taken at Swindon early in the engine's life, was certainly eye-catching and worthy of coverage in the press. In another sense this picture hints at a problem experienced with the engine – her rumoured preponderance to derail on the tight curves around the Works at Swindon, in sidings or Old Oak Common. Does this photo, in fact, contain a wry dig highlighting this apparent shortcoming? (Author's collection)

So, was *The Great Bear* a missed opportunity or a 'white elephant' of a project with no purpose other than to test a theory close to Churchward's engineering heart – the capacity of a boiler to produce the highest possible level of energy? With so little to go on debate by historians has been dogged by speculation and rumour.

In some ways Kenneth Cook, who played little or no part in *The Great Bear's* life, may have come closest to the truth when writing much later that:

It seemed to me that The Great Bear probably evolved as an idea to be explored as an exercise in what was possible within the technology then available. Churchward would have seen what was being attempted overseas, most of which was in an early stage of development, and been intrigued by the possibilities inherent in a 4-6-2 configuration. However, I do not believe that at any stage it was a project designed to produce more than a prototype. Once satisfied that the Stars could equal or better No. III in day to day service his interest waned quite quickly. After that he was happy for the draughtsmen to seek ways of improving its performance, but at no stage, I believe, did he consider building more.

Over the years much was made of this engine's high axle loading and the restrictions this imposed on its operation. There was talk that No. III might have been used more widely if Churchward had known that beginning in 1902 a programme of improvements, initiated by James Inglis when Chief Engineer, had gradually raised the axle loading limit on track and bridges beyond Bristol to something above 21 or 22 tons. If so, the engine might have found wider use so encouraging the powers that be to build more. It was implied by some that this knowledge may have been deliberately kept from Churchward by Inglis who was promoted to General Manager and consulting engineer in 1903.

If rumours are to be believed, they had fallen out over some never fully explained disagreement and this soured their relationship in the years up to Inglis' death in 1911. If so, it was a problem that was exacerbated by Inglis who unsuccessfully attempted to rein in Churchward's access to the Chairman and board by placing the Superintendent under his direct control, a move that Churchward strongly resisted. In my opinion such disagreements at very senior level are not unknown, but it would have been remarkable indeed if this had been carried so far as to keep Churchward in ignorance of such a significant change in the operating conditions that prevailed at the time. In any event he was far too astute and aware of what was going on around him to have had the wool pulled over his eyes so completely as this rumour implies. Consequently, I do not believe that, even if true, such an impasse between these two powerful men played any part in the decision to restrict the Pacific Class to one. It was, to my mind, simply an experiment.

It has also been said that Churchward was greatly saddened when in 1924 *The Great Bear* was scrapped. Yet, here again, knowledge of the man makes this a questionable assessment. He was above all else a hard-headed, practical engineer and businessman to whom such an emotional attachment would have been most unlikely. He did not live in the past, but looked to the future. Proof of this is not hard to find, with the scrapping of two historic locomotives – Gooch's broad gauge *North Star* and *Lord of the Isles* – in 1906, ostensibly because they took up too much space in the workshops, being one example.

The truth of all that happened seems likely to remain a mystery, but one that will continue to intrigue railway historians because there will never be an answer to the eternal question why? All we will ever know with any certainty are the bare bones of the story, with the rest remaining speculation. But having set the 4-6-2 project in motion, and perhaps been disappointed by the outcome, Churchward did allow the story to run on and in doing so saw No. III gradually undergo a series of modifications before her life was drawn to a close by his successor in 1924.

Some of these changes were fairly straightforward in the making. For example, the engine was fitted with a new cast-iron chimney and a steel cab roof at some stage. Then when entering Paddington for the first time in 1908 her leading left side step fouled the platform which led to the removal of the steps on both sides of the smokebox. Then there were operational issues to be addressed, particularly in the way the footplate crew handled such a powerful engine. It was here that the wide firebox presented a problem, as Churchward himself had predicted it might when presenting his paper to the IMechE in 1906:

> The wider firebox evidently requires a higher standard of skill in the fireman, for unless the grate is kept fully covered, there is a tendency to have an excess of air, reducing efficiency and increasing tube trouble.

With the Great War at its height and maintenance reduced No. III still managed to look good in 1917, however, she has just completed a period of maintenance at Swindon so this is hardly surprising. Her wartime record does not appear to have survived but an engine of this size was probably rostered to the heaviest loads. (Author's collection)

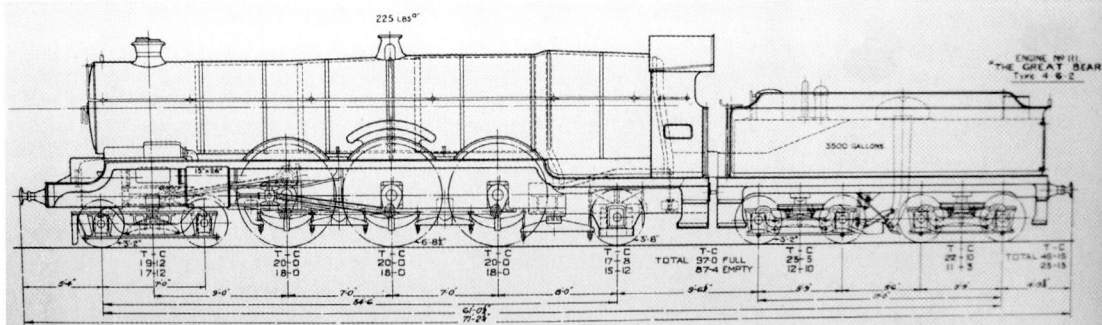

This Swindon drawing shows the Pacific in her final, post Great War form. She had undergone a number of modifications by this time, including the removal of her special number 3 superheater and its replacement by an 'ordinary' No. 3 type in which each flue was given three not four elements. At the same time a new four-cone injector, to supply water to the boiler, and a new steel cab roof were fitted. (DN)

No.III still looking in good condition although she will soon be withdrawn from service. However, in Charles Collett's hands she found a new life of sorts when, in 1924, parts of her were used in the construction of a new Castle Class 4-6-0 – No. III, *Viscount Churchill*. In this guise she remained in service until July 1953. (DN)

This did indeed come to pass and soon No. III's firemen were complaining that the engine didn't steam as effectively as it might. In time a new firing technique was developed that seems to have overcome the problem, but there were other more complex issues that had to be resolved which, in some cases, had to wait for the engine's first major overhaul in 1913 to be addressed.

Amongst the list of modifications undertaken that year was the removal of her arch tubes and the fitting of the top feed system that had been successfully applied to other GWR express locomotives. Then, at about the same time, she was fitted with a four-cone ejector and the Swindon No. 1 superheater was removed and replaced with a No. 3 'special' version, which had four pairs of elements extended back through each flue. This created more room for the passage of hot gases and so improved the efficiency of the flow. In 1920, at the engine's next overhaul, the No. 3 'special' was itself removed and replaced by an 'ordinary' version of the same type, though in this case each flue contained three elements, not four. This had the effect of reducing the superheating area somewhat, but, at the same time, further improved the flow of gases. And so the list of adjustments went on, all mostly minor in nature and with varying degrees of success.

One issue that doesn't appear to have been resolved satisfactorily was the overheating problem associated with the trailing truck. Nevertheless, this doesn't seem to have presented an insuperable

(Above) *The Great Bear* towards the end of her life and still performing well. In 1924 Charles Collett, when faced with the need to build a replacement boiler for this engine, chose instead to end her life and use what might be salvaged to build a new Castle Class locomotive. (Right) No. 111 in its new Castle Class guise and named after Viscount Churchill who was the GWR's Chairman from 1908 until his death in January 1934. This engine ran with the *Great Bear's* unique four-wheeled tender for a while, but it was then used on other engines including (below) 2916 *Saint Benedict*. (Author)

problem, even though it must have taxed the crew at times with the need to constantly check for overheating. However, if the engine's maintenance records had survived they might have told a different story, as they would about the frequency of returns to the Works for repairs and adjustments, rumoured to have been a frequent occurrence.

So in a prototype state, then in more regular service, the time of the GWR's Pacific slowly passed – an experiment never to be repeated. Nevertheless, in its own modest way the engine had probably told Churchward a great deal about the 4-6-2 concept and the wider issue of boiler capacity. A failed experiment? Probably not if the purpose had been simply to test and evaluate a theory. If adopted more widely would it have added something missing from the GWR's developing fleet of locomotives? Here views will always differ, but in seeing how other companies forged ahead with 4-6-2s with great success, who is to say whether more *Great Bears* would have been better for the GWR than the 4-6-0 Castles and Kings they favoured? As the LNER and LMS later discovered, there was more than enough room for 4-6-2s and 4-6-0s.

When *The Great Bear*'s end came it was an event that became mired in controversy. On face value it can be viewed as a simple business decision – a new boiler and cylinders were required as part of a costly major overhaul. In such a situation an accountant will always question whether it is better to scrap a costly singleton locomotive or build a new standard engine instead. With the new Castle Class 4-6-0s under development, and likely to dominate the network for the next 30 to 40 years, the choice would seem to be an obvious one. But life is rarely that simple especially when, as Kenneth Cook later reported:

Collett disliked Churchward, some said, intensely – they were men cut from entirely different cloth. As a result, it was suggested that Collett may have borne a grudge against Churchward for some historic slight and the premature demise of No.III gave him the opportunity to vent his feelings. I was certainly aware that the 'old man' took the matter personally.

Once again conjecture fills a void created when a lack of information fails to provide a definitive answer. However, if this story is true, and the evidence is slight at best, it paints an interesting picture of a business at work and the often petty issues and jealousies that can colour judgement, effect a legacy and distort the actions of normally objective men or women. Either way, though, the Pacific was consigned to history and whatever parts could be salvaged were used in building a new No. III, in this case a 4-6-0 Castle Class engine, named *Viscount Churchill*, in honour of the GWR's new chairman who took office in 1908. So, in a way some of the Pacific lived on until, that is, the new No. 111 was itself scrapped in the early 1950s.

As the end of the first decade of the twentieth century approached, there was still much going on at Swindon, in terms of new locomotives, carriages and wagons, but it seems that the pace of change may have been slowing. With so much having been achieved in Churchward's first eight years in charge this probably came as no surprise. The time had undoubtedly come to take stock of all that had happened, review the way the company was moving and consider how the balance between profit and capital outlay was holding up. With a new Chairman in place, who may have been more cost conscious and possibly less accommodating of Churchward plans than his predecessors, Viscount Emlyn and Alfred Baldwin, this was, perhaps, inevitable. And if the Superintendent had indeed fallen out with Inglis as General Manager, Churchward may well have had far less support at the top table when arguing any case he wished to make in support of new initiatives he had in mind.

The times were changing and the need for greater economy seems to have become the order of the day. This is, perhaps, unsurprising because by 1910 the locomotive programme, and the projects Churchward had inherited from Dean, were completed or well-advanced and producing engines that seemed to be achieving all that was hoped of them. And these production programmes still had some way to run, with Saints, 2800s, 3800s, 4-4-2Ts, Stars, 2221s and 4500s being built as the company entered the new decade. In this situation, a more cautious approach to new or additional expenditure was, perhaps, inevitable.

The one apparent exception to this was the soon to appear 4200 Class of mineral tanks locomotives. Ever aware of the importance of the mining industry to the GWR, Churchward and his team, having first considered building a 2-8-2T class of engine to haul very heavy coal trains from pithead to ports and other distribution points, then chose to construct a 2-8-0T instead. This change came about because it was realised that the longer wheel base of the 2-8-2T might prove too restrictive. So the design was finalised and a prototype, No. 4201, was built at Swindon in 1910.

The engine was fitted with Stephenson valve gear and two cylinders measuring 18½ x 30in, a superheated boiler with a total heating surface of 1566.74sqft to which the superheater contributed 215.80sqft. All this helped produce 200 psi of working pressure and a tractive effort of 31,450lb, making this type of engine ideally suited to the task for which they were designed. However, even though the principles of top feed had been well rehearsed by then the prototype was not equipped in this way, for reasons that aren't clear, though production models, that began to appear in 1912, were.

Like the 2800s before them the leading wheels were 3ft 2in diameter and the coupled wheels 4ft 7½in, though, in this case, the engine enjoyed a slightly different spacing which had the effect of

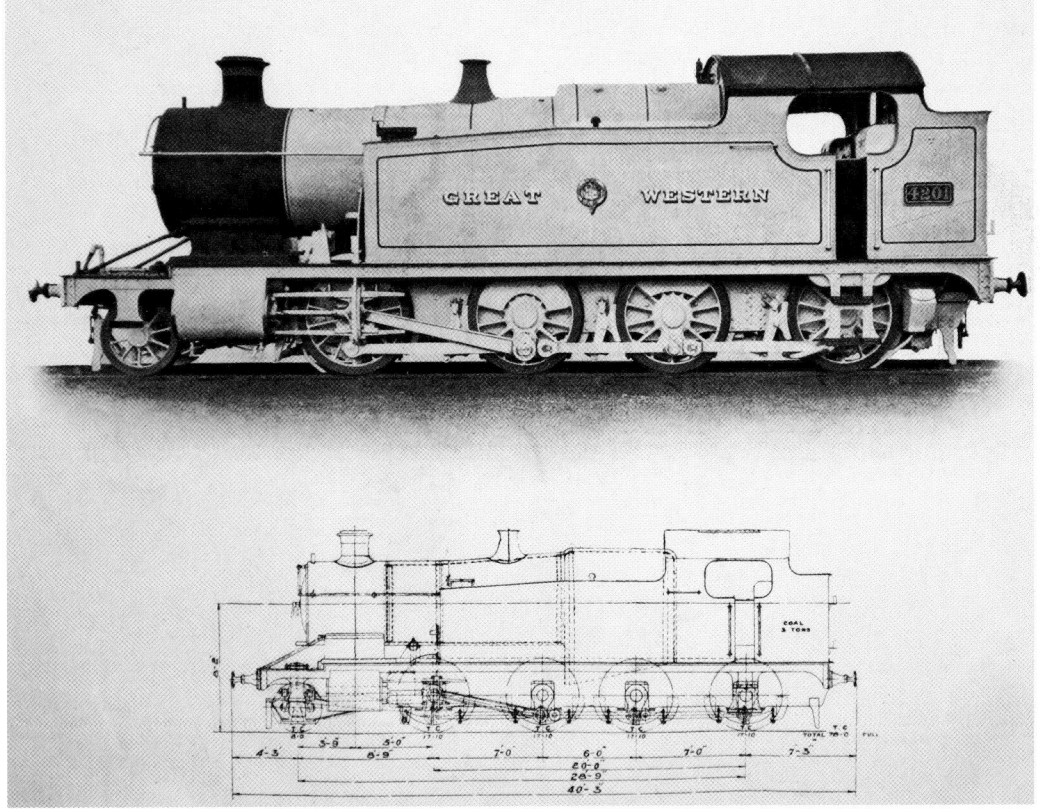

The prototype of the 4200 Class 2-8-0T mineral locomotive as built at Swindon in 1910. It was a type of engine specifically designed for use on short haul, heavy duties in the mining areas of South Wales. Production continued until 1940 by which time 205 had been built. (Author's collection)

placing the rear axle directly under the cab. This according to one report 'gave them good adhesion but a hard ride at times, though this was far less noticeable at low speeds'. The prototype was also fitted with a bunker holding three tons of coal and 1800 gallons of water. Trials revealed that this didn't give them a sufficient range and production models were modified to carry half a ton more, then, later on this was increased to 4 tons 2cwt. And in this form the engines went into production to do valuable service into the 1960s.

By the time the first of these engines appeared Churchward's reputation, although well established in GWR circles with echoes of his achievements rippling out into the wider world, had

The 4200 Class, (above) here represented by No 4227, seen here near the Superintendent/CME's office at Swindon, and their derivatives had long and useful lives with many seeing service on the GWR until the end of steam in that region. When a design was being considered for a powerful tank engine Churchward thought in terms of a 2-8-2T locomotive, but this idea was dropped when it was realised that its long wheelbase might prove too restrictive. As a result, a 2-8-0T design became the order of the day. In due course, and long after Churchward's departure, the 2-8-2T design was resurrected and fifty-four 4200s were rebuilt as 2-8-2Ts so that more coal and water could be carried and their operating range increased. (Below) The 7200 Class, as these new engines became, is represented here by engine No. 7242. Both classes saw service into the 1960s with eight 2-8-0Ts and three 2-8-2Ts surviving into preservation. (DN)

still to reach the legendary status it would eventually enjoy. True, his contribution to engineering had been immense and the speeds achieved by Lord of the Isles in 1904 and by No. 2903 in 1906 had grabbed the attention of professionals and press alike, but something more was needed to propel his status to even greater heights. An opportunity for this came in 1910 in the form of a competition, something that in a sporting country such as Britain will draw a crowd and grab the attention of the media.

For such an extremely competitive business any success over a commercial rival had to be exploited to the full and had been this way since the well-publicised 'Race to the North' of the 1880s where express trains from different companies tried to be the quickest over the highly prestigious routes between London and Scotland. This rivalry ended in a fierce, and some might say, dangerous competition, but one that made headlines before being brought to a halt on safety grounds. However, in the early twentieth century there was a revival of sorts in such practices, but now encouraged by a desire to evaluate the work of other engineers to see what might be applied more broadly.

To a certain extent such interaction had become something actively encouraged by the ARLE, the Institutions of Civil and Mechanical Engineers and the soon to be formed Institution of Locomotive Engineers. And, as we have seen, it was a practice which included purchasing examples of 'foreign' engines or paying a patent fee for some element of a design to avoid any accusation of sharp practice or plagiarism. So in a spirit of learning, but also of 'gentlemanly' competition, some companies had begun arranging interchange trials where each would test and compare each other's locomotives.

The first exchange of any real note in this period took place in the summer of 1909 initiated, or so it seems, by Charles J. Bowen Cooke, who had become the LNWR's CME earlier that

The GWR made much of their engines' participation in the exchange in the summer of 1910, as this group of photographs taken at Euston, which received wide coverage, makes clear. (Author's collection)

year when George Whale retired. Being a noted theorist on locomotive design and an author of note on the subject, he saw great value in comparing the performance of his company's 4-4-0 Precursor Class with a contemporary locomotive at work on a neighbouring line, in this case a Henry Ivatt, GNR designed large-boilered Atlantic class engine. Once completed this led to other comparability trials taking place involving a Caledonian Railway 4-6-0 Class engine, two LNWR Experiment Class 4-6-0s and a London, Brighton and South Coast Railway 4-4-2 express passenger tank locomotive.

At this point another exchange of engines was mooted, but on this occasion, Bowen Cooke wanted to broaden the scope of the trials and engage Churchward in the programme. His reasons for doing so are easily explained.

Swindon had by then undertaken a massive programme of modernisation and standardisation of its locomotive fleet, all of which had been chronicled in the press. But there was a growing belief that many of the GWR's technical innovations had been given little publicity as though secrecy was of paramount importance – concepts were undoubtedly understood but there was little first-hand knowledge of the specifics of their design. The esteemed railway historian Cecil Allen gave voice to this suspicion in 1949 when he wrote, "Thus, in the race for superiority in locomotive capacity and efficiency there was something of the 'dark horse' about Swindon products."

As with any engineering or scientific 'dark horse' there will always be a desire to seek more information and deepen ones understanding of what has been achieved. From this, lessons might be learnt and absorbed then applied to your own work or, at the other end of the scale, be rejected because it might not be as good or as cutting edge as expected. Either way, Bowen Cooke was sufficiently interested to want to learn more about Churchward's work and in August 1910 he reached an agreement, seemingly with his opposite number at Swindon, to conduct a series of exchange trials. So a seemingly quite simple collaborative exercise was set in motion which, perhaps surprisingly, would have significant and lasting effects on Churchward reputation as an engineer.

It was decided very early in the process that two 1907 built Star Class engines – Nos. 4003, *Lode Star*, and 4005, *Polar Star* – would be allocated to the trials though the reason for their choice is unclear. Perhaps, they had just completed a period of maintenance so would be in the best possible condition for the trials, or they were simply considered the best of the thirty-one members of the class then in service. In any event, none of the new engines built in 1910 was selected which suggests Churchward wasn't prepared to risk locomotives that had barely been run in. Meanwhile, Bowen Cooke had no such qualms and selected two new members of the LNWR's Experiment Class of 4-6-0s – Nos. 1455, *Herefordshire*, and 1471, *Worcestershire* – which were built in 1909 and 1910 respectively.

In the event, no matter which engines Bowen Cooke chose they proved ill-matched to the cream of Churchward's fleet. So when No. 4005 was compared with No. 1455 over LNWR metals and No. 4003 against No. 1471 on the London-West Country route the result was never, at any stage, in doubt. Cecil Allen, who personally witnessed part of the trials, later remarked that:

> In retrospect, it seems astonishing that Crewe should have dreamed that an engine such as an Experiment could ever hope to compete on level terms with a Star. The former with 6ft 3in driving wheels, 19in by 26in cylinders, 175lb of pressure, 46¾ tons of adhesion and a tractive effort of 18,615lb, was to attempt the same duties as the GWR 4-6-0 with 6ft 8½in wheels, four cylinders, 225lb of pressure, 55½ tons of adhesion, and a tractive effort of 25,090lb. How could the result be anything but a foregone conclusion?

The GWR trains chosen on the first day of a week of trial running were the 9 am semi-fast from Paddington to Bristol returning with the 5.5 pm two hour non-stop express to London. On the second day it was the 11 am two hour Bristol down express, and the 5.54 pm back.

(Above) 4005 *Polar Star* awaiting departure from Euston and (below) then at speed when pulling a Glasgow bound express through Bushey Troughs on 20 August 1910. (DN)

On the third day there was the redoubtable 10.30 am down Cornish Riviera Limited and on the fourth day the 8.30 am from Plymouth to Paddington and so on. Lode Star took the corresponding workings in the opposite direction with the programme precisely reversed in the second week.

Throughout the test weeks whilst Lode Star equalled or bettered the timings over each route comfortably (and here even the non-superheated GWR Saints, let alone the Stars, could keep time without difficulty with trains of over 400 tons), the Experiment had to be flogged unmercifully in an attempt to keep time, her coal consumption being tremendous, and finally returned to Crewe in a badly strained condition. On the LNWR, on the other hand Polar Star performed every allotted task with the utmost ease and at appreciably lower coal consumption than that of the competing Experiment Herefordshire.

So there you have it, two contemporary locomotives designed for the same task proving unequal, seemingly, in every respect. It was, in truth, a battle between a true heavyweight and lighter weight opponent, but the Experiment Class, so Kenneth Cook believed, 'was probably the best other companies had to offer at the time, and would do for some time, and even they could not compete on level terms with a Star, let alone a Saint or *The Great Bear*'. Nevertheless, it would have been interesting to have run comparability trials against the Caledonian 4-6-0s of the Cardean Class or even a large boilered Ivatt Atlantic, used the previous year, for that matter. Something of the sort did take place in 1925 when Nigel Gresley was drawn into another exchange trial by the GWR. Here he found his 1922 introduced, state of the art, iconic A1 Class Pacific bested by a descendant of the Stars, the 4-6-0 Castle Class. Here again it was left to Cecil Allen to give a public voice to what happened during these later trials and, in so doing, pay homage to Churchward's exceptional skill as an engineer and leader. 'There could hardly be any dispute as to which engine had 'won'; the contest was a resounding triumph for the Swindon principles of design which from Churchward's time had been a quarter of a century ahead of British locomotive practice in general.'

If anything, 1910 proved to be the high spot of Churchward's career. However, his work was far from over and there were still many challenges to meet and problems to be resolved; ever worsening industrial relations being just one. But all these would pale into insignificance when compared to the cataclysmic world events that would soon unfold and the slaughter that would follow.

One of the two LNWR George Whale designed Experiment Class 4-6-0s which competed with two of Churchward's Stars. In this case No. 1471, *Worcestershire*, which was photographed, or so the notes accompanying this print reveal, at Paddington. During the comparability trials the Experiments were found to be no match for the Stars. (DN)

Chapter 8

Drawing to a Conclusion

When Edward VII died in May 1910 he left behind a world almost unrecognisable from the one his mother knew. There was only nine years between the two events, but the reformists in society had begun a movement that was rapidly gathering pace and gaining many influential supporters. The old guard, happily enjoying the strict conventions of a society that left them unchallenged, sought to hinder progress, but the once submissive masses were now developing a strong will for change. Managing workers, who for so long had been turned to silence by so little legal protection, were beginning to find their voice and were prepared to turn words into deeds whenever necessary. But while the desire for change was becoming an irresistible force it was met by an immoveable object. This was none more so than in Swindon, where the police, local authorities and employers, particularly the GWR, found their patience and their resources stretched at times by the increasing level of protest.

So all was not well in the last decade of Churchward's time at Swindon and he seems to have been poorly equipped to deal with the ever growing demands for better living and working conditions, except, that is, in a dogmatic, uncompromising way. He was not alone in this, though. Many others leader in politics and industry also found the customs and practices formed over centuries hard to give up and rebelled against a system based on the themes of equal rights and a fair share for all.

In reality, Churchward seems to have found it difficult to cast off his autocratic, take it or leave it approach to staff management. When workers' representation by trades unions was in its infancy and having little effect this was bad enough, but as they grew in strength this could only end badly. Here a more conciliatory approach might have borne fruit, but like many at the time he found it difficult, if not impossible, to shrug off a long established, almost dictatorial way of working. The end result was, inevitably, more conflict at a time when appeasement might have achieved much more.

It was a problem long in the making, so probably came as no surprise to those around him who, if they had dared, might have suggested a less bellicose approach. And yet he does not seem to have been an unjust man, only one hidebound by the traditions and culture of his age. This was an attitude that served him ill especially in a situation where the working and living conditions of his employees could only be described as poor at best, or dire at worst. With the cost of living rising during Edward's reign, with no meaningful increase in wages to offset this inflation, the situation, if anything, became more acute. When representations were made about this by fledgling unions, particularly the 1870s formed Amalgamated Society of Railway Servants, the GWR and Churchward failed to recognise them officially. As a result, when a grievance became too much to bear, as it did in 1908 when short time working was re-introduced, backed up by another savage round of discharges, there was an explosion. Alan Peck, in his authoritative book *The Great Western at Swindon Works*, described what happened next:

> Mass meetings were held on 7th July 1908 outside the town hall and a petition was sent to the Board, but to no avail, and much hardship became apparent. It was now that the unions confirmed commitment to the Labour party. Churchward being an autocrat is reported to have replied to a union man that 'if you and those you represent are not satisfied with the conditions in my department, I shall be pleased to receive your notice.

To give him his due it must be said that Churchward was probably under great pressure, from his recently installed Chairman, Victor Spencer, to rein in costs and make savings, and James Inglis as General Manager, ever eager to bring the Superintendent under his control. However, the company's books at this time do not reflect a dire financial position and could probably have

In May 1910, Edward VII died and with his demise came the end of, what for some, had been an exciting era. After a ceremony in London the GWR had the responsibility for transporting the King's body and mourners to Windsor for the burial service. It was a duty they had undertaken for Victoria in 1901 and would do so again for George V in 1936. Ever aware of the obligation as well as kudos attached to such an event Paddington (top left) and Windsor Stations were prepared very carefully, and ostentatiously, with the colour black abounding. The engine chosen for the task was Star Class *King Edward*, which was, in military parlance, dressed overall (above), with the locos crew (top right) smartly attired as befitted such an occasion. Interestingly enough, this was an age when it was quite common, and expected, for drivers and firemen to wear collars and ties as a matter of course each day. In the poor working conditions they faced, this must have added an unnecessary degree of difficulty and discomfort. The Stationmaster at Windsor's formal dress also differed little from his normal working clothes (opposite below) and, with his 'topper' helped pick him out as a figure of some authority. (DN/Author's collection)

Drawing to a Conclusion 209

borne an increase in what were pitiful levels of pay even by the standards of the age. If so, the greater efficiency of the standard classes of engine then in mass production would have made for a healthier operating profit, but this could be a double edged sword as far as the workforce were concerned. Once again Alan Peck caught the essence of this issue when writing that:

> As far as the Works was concerned the great economic success of Churchward's policy of locomotive design was crucial. These engines were now capable of running longer periods between repairs, particularly to the boilers. The rapid introduction of inter-changeable parts meant the store holdings could be drastically reduced, not having to maintain separate spares for each class of locomotive, carriage or wagon. The issue of notices was, to say the least, unfortunately timed, appearing a few days before the annual holiday outings, spreading much bitterness amongst the staff. They thought it a poor reward for producing such engineering wonders as the Stars and *The Great Bear*.

So, the workers were bullied into submission, yet, in doing so, Churchward and Co probably ensured that the unions would grow in size and strength and return to the scene of battle with greater determination. In the circumstances one can hardly criticise them for this, because the level of injustice they witnessed beggared belief. But Swindon was not alone in this; if anything the mining industry and the mills were even worse.

The reaction of the railway unions was slow in coming, It took until August 1911 for the first major railway strike to be called, following a series of minor stoppages earlier in the year. This national walkout was serious enough to warrant the intervention of David Lloyd George, then

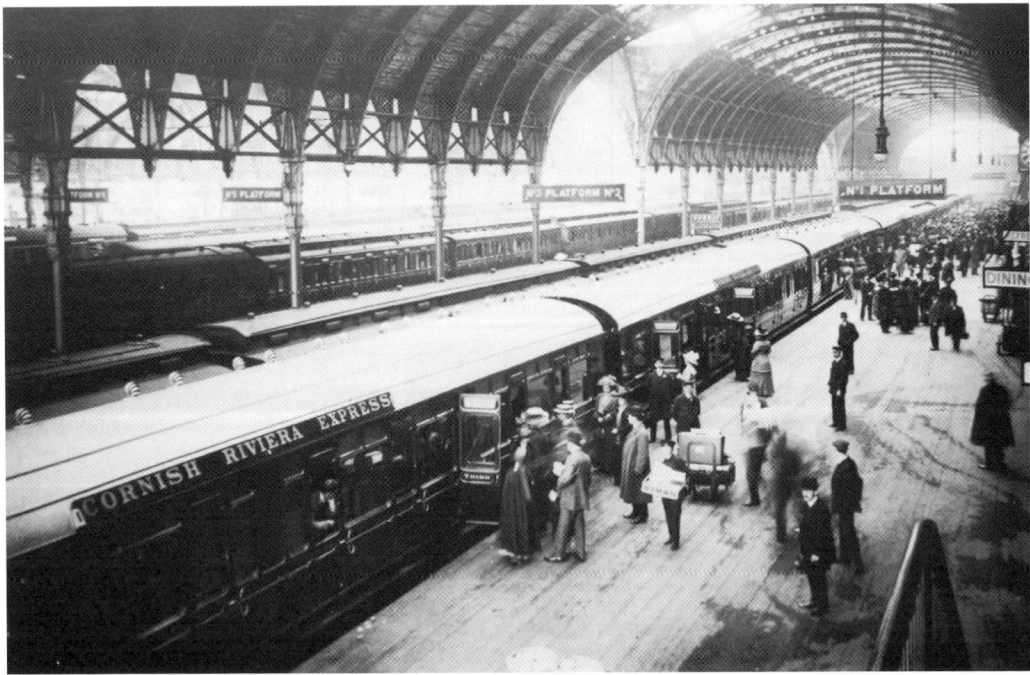

While the GWR's industrial workforce suffered from poor pay and, consequently, poor living conditions, the company's glamourous express services and their many new engines continued to drew much attention. The attraction of travelling on the Cornish Riviera Express and the comparative wealth of those able to enjoy such a service, in this case just before the Great War, lays plain this disparity in living standards then existing. (DN)

Chancellor of the Exchequer, who helped bring it to an inconclusive and unsatisfactory end. But in doing so he and industry leaders only increased the resolve of the unions to step up the battle for better pay and working conditions and led to the creation of the National Union of Railwaymen (NUR) in 1913 and a rapidly expanding membership of the Associated Society of Locomotive Engineers and Fireman (ASLEF). With an ever growing membership they felt empowered to take industrial action more often and began to do so. The NUR with 180,000 and more members in their ranks soon took the lead in this campaign and only the coming of war in 1914 bringing some temporary relief to besieged managers, who, if truth be told, only had themselves to blame.

For any commercial concern good publicity is essential and companies such as the GWR became very adept at marketing their products in the first decade of the twentieth century. (Above left) Each station was covered with billboards and noticeboards, such as this displayed here at Paddington in about 1911/12, advertising holidays and much more. (Above right) In 1911 the GWR produced this montage for their in-house magazine showing a few examples of that Summer's press articles and releases and adverts. (Below) To this was the regular release of photos, such as this to the press, just to remind possible customers of what was on offer. In this case it is Saint Class engine No. 2928, *St Sebastian*, leaving Paddington on a Bath Spa and Bristol express. (GWR/Author)

It is often the case that someone suffering under the huge pressures Churchward had to bear each day finds solace in the support of their family. In his case the life of a bachelor, whilst having some compensations, could be a lonely existence which his involvement in local politics and the duties of a JP may only partly have assuaged. Perhaps he was content to live this way in his large GWR house a short walk from his office supported by a housekeeper, Mary Gray, maids Grace Bull and Matilda Shatford, and a manservant who lived out and it seems doubled up as his driver. But a close family to surround him – sadly not.

Within the property he'd created a fully equipped workshop, which allowed him to practice his craft, and a billiard room and shooting range to practice slightly different forms of marksmanship. And with his love of fishing and shooting to engage him he continued to immerse himself in these gentlemanly pursuits accompanied by his friends. These included some of his 'bright young men', but also Benjamin Hale, who began as an apprentice in April 1880, when barely of age, who then rose to become Foreman of the Locomotive Shops.

Hale was known, according to Cook, as a:

Great and eccentric character around the Works who was very skilled on a variety of machine tools. Early in his career he went to the United States while accompanying the on loan *Lord of the Isles*, which he was tasked with others to erect. When in charge of all the machine shops he made sure the Chief always received up to date lathes to equip

Although considered a strict disciplinarian by some, Churchward was always attentive to the educational needs of the men he employed. For example, in 1907 he introduced a scheme that allowed apprentices to attend technical classes without loss of pay. At about the same time he successfully persuaded the chairman to sanction payment of college fees by the company. He also sought to allow particularly distinguished men to spend part of their apprenticeship in the drawing office or chemical laboratory where their specialist skills might be further honed. In addition to encouraging further education through what was on offer in Mechanics Institute he introduced such things as Improvement Classes, which helped developed skills and allowed workers to benefit from slightly better pay. The 1911 'graduation' ceremony of the Enginemen and Firemen's Class is captured in this picture. Of particular note is the appearance of the 35-year-old William Stanier at the centre of the group. At this stage he was Assistant to the Divisional Locomotive Superintendent in London and would, in 1912, return to Swindon as Assistant Works Manager before becoming Churchward's Works' Manager eight years later. (Author's collection)

his workshop at Newburn. They would often spend many hours together discussing any engineering idea that occurred to either of them. Although Ben never overstepped the bounds of propriety Churchward treated him as an equal and clearly enjoyed his company – in his workshop or when out fishing. He was, I believe, frequently entertained by Ben and his wife at their home in nearby Dean Street and this remained the case until his death by which time Ben had, himself retired.

By this stage of his life Churchward's father was long dead having passed away in 1891. Following his demise, the family farm passed to George's brother John, who was later described as 'an eccentric and rather peculiar man' and his wife Gwendoline (Frederick Churchward's daughter and so a first cousin). They, so it is reported, seem to have developed a resentment of George due to his success, position and wealth. They came to believe that he had received a better education than his brothers which greatly boosted his chances in life. With hindsight they appear to have been a fractious, divisive pair who happily bore a grudge. This was something that could have been magnified by the stress caused by having only one child who was born with many serious health problems, both physical and mental. Whatever the cause, the result was a family feud which, ultimately, led to an estrangement that appears to have lasted to the end of George's life.

Luckily he remained close to sisters Mary and Adelina, who never married and lived in a house together in St Andrews Road, Paignton, where they were joined by their mother, who would live on with them until her death in 1922. Over the years it became a regular feature of George's life to spend holidays with them, motoring down or taking the train to Devon as he saw fit or as his health allowed. Meanwhile, brother James, with whom George seems to have remained on close terms, chose at quite an early age to emigrate to the USA to make a life for himself there. There were undoubtedly occasional reunions, as witnessed by at least two forays George made across the Atlantic, to catch up with James and also witness first hand all he had read about when studying Stateside locomotive practices. So he had a family life of sorts, though undoubtedly a disjointed one in which distance played a significant part in how closely relationships could be conducted. But, perhaps, he preferred it that way.

As trouble continued to brew in the workshops a situation arose that, if anything, made things even worse. In 1912/13 a time recording system, created to allow specific jobs to be measured and costed more accurately, was introduced. Inevitably, perhaps, employees, grown used to being exploited, translated this as a means of comparing one person's performance against another's, so allowing management to speed up work so increasing production and allowing personal performance to be monitored. When a complaint about this new practices was made public, Churchward felt moved to issue a formal denial, but few, it seems, believed his words to be true. With short hours regularly being worked and many hundreds of redundancy notices being issued any other reaction would have been unlikely. Faced with such an impasse, it is likely that Churchward turned towards the production of two more new locomotives with a certain amount of relief.

The first of these engines was the 4300 Class of 2-6-0s, which, at the time it appeared, was still something of a novelty in Britain, but not so in North America where two examples, built by the Baldwin and Norris Locomotive Works, appeared in 1852/53. For the remainder of the century, 2-6-0 designs continued to be developed, built by various companies, including the Baltimore and Ohio, Louisville and Nashville and the New Jersey Railroads. So successful did they prove to be that by 1910, when production is believed to have ended, more than 11,000 had been built with some being purchased by three British Companies – the Midland, Great Northern and Great Central Railways – from the Baldwin and Schenectady Locomotive Works. Such arrivals would have soon come to Churchward's notice, but until 1909/10 he appears to have made little effort to produce a 2-6-0 of his own.

This may have been a change sparked by Harold Holcroft, who moved to Swindon in 1906 to work for George Burrows as a draughtsman. He seems to have impressed those around and

By the time Churchward considered it necessary to build a class of 2-6-0 tender engines for the GWR, the type had become a common feature on railways across North America. In 1909 a party of engineers, including Harold Holcroft from the Swindon Drawing Office visited Canada and the States to view locomotives there. (Above) Holcroft was particularly impressed by the 2-6-0s operated the Grand Trunk Railway of Canada of which No. 326 is one of many examples. (Author's collection)

During a period when insufficient production capacity existed in Britain some companies turned towards US manufacturers for help. In the process ten 2-6-0s were acquired by the Midland Railway from the Schenectady Works in New York in 1899/1900. Churchward would undoubtedly have been aware of their presence in Britain. (Author's collection)

was soon marked down as a designer of some note. So, it probably came as no surprise when in July 1909 he joined a party of engineers visiting North America to view and assess locomotive developments across the continent. Whilst there he was impressed by the strength and versatiity of the 2-6-0s he saw. This was particularly so of those employed by the Grand Trunk Railway, which operated trains across the Canadian provinces of Quebec and Ontario, down into the US States of Maine, Connecticut, Michigan, Massachusetts, New Hampshire and Vermont. Any engine successfully employed on such a large and testing network would inevitably draw the interest of engineers and on return to Swindon Holcroft reported his findings to Burrows, as he recalled later:

> Churchward, who had apparently been told by Burrows of my observations on the use of the 2-6-0 in Canada as a general purpose locomotive, returned and on reaching my board he addressed me saying, 'Very well then, get me out a 2-6-0 with 5ft 8in wheels, outside cylinders and the No. 4 boiler and bring in all the standard parts you can'. With that he departed.

Unusually, Churchward chose not to build a prototype of the two-cylinder 4300 Class presumably because of his extensive experience of its standardised parts and the performance of the 3150 Class 2-6-2Ts on which it was based. (Above) This picture and diagram were produced in the Drawing Office at Swindon in late 1910 and capture the second of the class, No. 4302 as built the following year (one of twenty in an initial batch of engines) So successful did the class prove to be that by 1932 342 had been built with some remaining in service until 1964. (Author's collection)

By the time the 4300 Class 2-6-0s entered service, standardisation of loconotives on the GWR had reached a very advanced level. With such a cleverly thought out mix and match philosophy instilled into Churchward's designers the chances of producing a poor product were far less likely. The 4300's were a perfect example of what such a system could produce. Here the 1911 built engine No. 4317 (though it may be No. 4312 of the same batch under all that grime) is captured at an unidentified location towards the end of her life. (Author's collection)

It did not take long to outline the new design, and in order to keep down the overall wheelbase of the engine and tender to enable it to turn on the shorter turntables on branch lines, I made use of the Saint cab...Few more detail drawings were necessary, so it was possible to order all material for twenty engines straight away. After that I thought no more about it.

As things turned out, Holcroft's suggestion had come at an opportune moment. Churchward, having reviewed his standardisation plans, had come to the conclusion that what was needed was a powerful mixed traffic engine with the widest possible route availability, including the many branch lines on the network. The 2-6-0, as specified by the Superintendent, and schemed out by Holcroft, fitted the bill and soon approval to build a first batch of twenty in 1911 was given. By 1915 this number would rise to 80 and when production ended in 1932 a total of 342 were in service.

Later on, when the first engines had proved themselves, the Assistant Chief Draughtsman, Oscar Deverell, took time out to compliment his young designer on his work, adding an interesting rider in the process:

Deverell came along to tell me that Churchward was satisfied that with the addition of the 4300 Class he had all the standard types necessary to operate the entire GWR system and

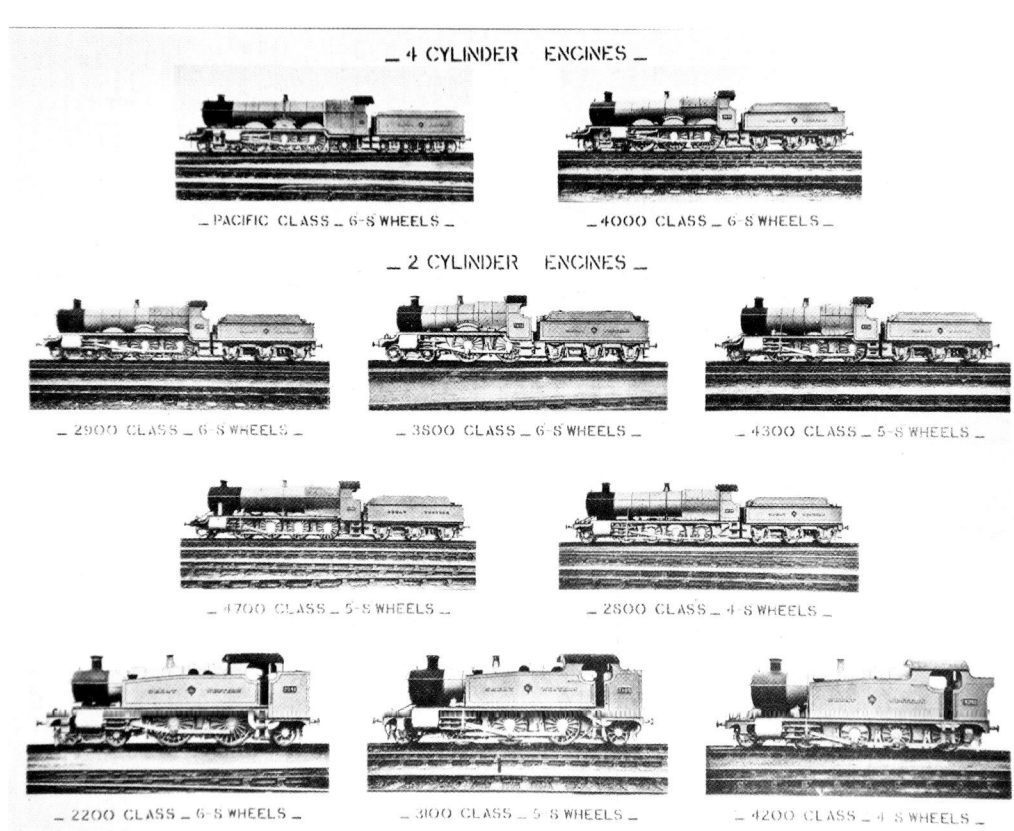

Over the years it became common practice to celebrate Christmas with cards displaying all the new engines built under Churchward's regime. 1912, when this picture appeared, was no different. There was, indeed, a great deal to celebrate in these years, though, with a restriction on new designs coming into force, the card probably represented the peak of Churchward's achievements. (Author's collection)

that no new designs were likely to be undertaken for another ten to fifteen years apart from one or two for some special duty. All new construction would be to existing designs with, perhaps, some minor modifications or improvements from time to time. Deverell went on to say that there would be no more development work for me in the locomotive drawing office and that they could make better use of me on the general side, where there were some problems outstanding, awaiting solution… My object then was to look out for some vacancy on the locomotive side on another railway and early in 1914 I moved to the South Eastern and Chatham Railway as leading locomotive draughtsman.

One wonders whether Churchward was deliberately being restrained by his Chairman on cost grounds or simply as a means of reining him in, as Inglis had tried to do for a long time. If the

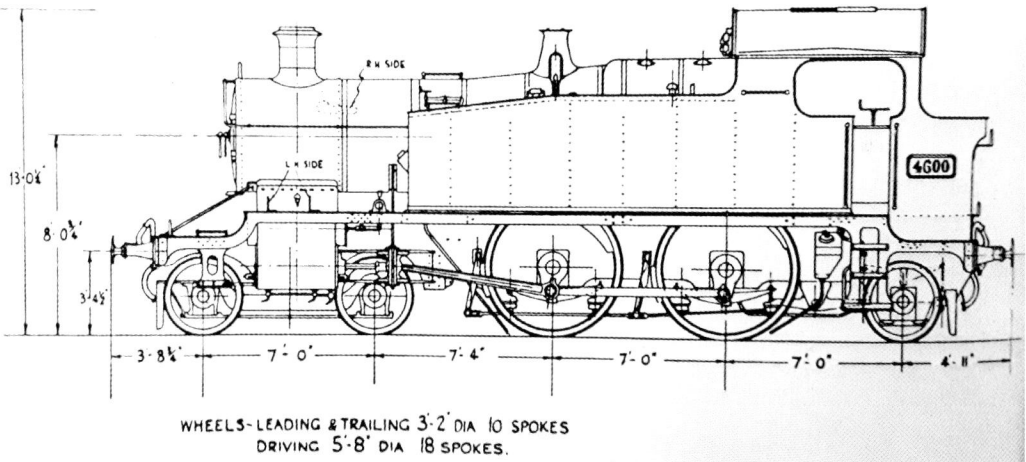

The 4600 Class 4-4-2T was an attempt to provide the running department with an alternative to the light 2-6-2T design that had proved so successful. But in this case Churchward wished to make the engine capable of pulling local suburban trains at higher speeds. To do this, it was decided to fit larger, but two fewer, coupled wheels. (Above) As a result, the drawing office produced this diagram and (below) the first of the class as it appeared when new in 1913. As a prototype, the engine underwent the usual evaluation and, in so doing, was found to offer few, if any, advantages over what was already available. Not surprisingly no more were built and the engine was eventually scrapped by Collett in 1925. (Author's collection)

218 *George Jackson Churchward, 1857–1933*

latter, it was a problem lessened when Inglis died in December 1911 leaving Churchward to deal with his replacement on perhaps more favourable terms. As there was no change to the policy outlined by Deverell following Inglis' demise, it is probably safe to say that standardisation had, in fact, achieved its primary aim and produced the best possible fleet for the company's needs and so little more was required. If so, was there sufficient creative work left to do for a man of Churchward's stature or did he feel, as Holcroft did, that his time at Swindon may have been coming to an end? For such an inventive man this must have been a frustrating period, but in

Some came to see the 1914/18 War as the birth of a new age where many of the trappings of the old world were discarded in favour of a more egalitarian, democratic state. If so many Britons died or were crippled to make it so. Yet the decade before it began came to be seen, by some at least, as a sort of elegant, but advancing golden age. The way the GWR developed during these years helped complete this picture, with Churchward's beautifully proportioned, functional, powerful and headline grabbing locomotives, supported by equally modern carriages at its core. These two pictures capture a little of the character of this vanishing age. (Above) Engine No. 40, *North Star*, with her white collared driver and a bowler hatted manager on board. (Left) An equally impressive Star Class No. 4023, *King George*, awaiting departure from Paddington attended by top-hatted officials in a show of pomp and circumstance. (DN)

1914 he would, as did many in Britain, face a far greater challenge. For someone much younger than he was the coming years would present insuperable difficulties, but for someone fast approaching 60 they would be an even sterner test of his leadership and engineering skills. Would his energy and determination to succeed stand up to the trials that lay ahead?

Only time would tell, but in the meantime he carried on as best he could and occupied himself with the day to day business of running such a vast organisation. Nevertheless, he still dabbled whenever he could in any locomotive project that fell within any limitation imposed by the Chairman. It was quite meagre fare by comparison to what had gone before, but was not without its interest, especially when it involved modifying existing engines. Perhaps, the most noteworthy of these was the 4600 Class of 4-4-2 tank engine.

Here Churchward's intention was a simple one – to produce an engine generally based on the light 4500 Class 2-6-2Ts that would run at higher speed when pulling suburban trains and produce greater tractive effort in doing so. To achieve this it was decided to do away with 4ft 7½in coupled wheels and fit 5ft 8in wheels instead. However, this change could only be realised in the space available by adopting a 4-4-2 configuration, with the rest of the engine following a well-established standardised path by then. The cylinders measured 17 x 24in coupled to 10in piston valves. A No. 5 boiler was fitted which produced a total heating surface of 1271.86sqft, 200lb of pressure and a tractive effort of 18,360lb. The water tank could carry 1100 gallons, a slight increase over the 4500s, and the bunker was designed to hold 3 tons of coal, 14 cwt less that the 2-6-2Ts. On paper the changes seemed justified but when this prototype was compared to the 4500s it was found to offer few, if any, advantages, as Kenneth Cook later reported, 'It was

The Great War was received in each warring nation by large celebrating crowds as shown here in Central London – a reaction replicated in towns across Britain, including Swindon, where many men quickly volunteered for service. A lot of them, perhaps surprisingly, saw it as a release from the burden of stagnating and poor lives and others simply as a great adventure. Sadly, the reality of the bloodiest war in history, until then, would soon change these naive attitudes. (Author's collection)

soon proved that the 45xx class with 4ft 7½in wheels was so versatile that the larger wheeled four-coupled engine was not really required.'

Initially the engine was used in South Wales and was then transferred to the Birmingham area where it supplemented the 2-6-2Ts employed there. As time passed, and with no benefits to be gained from its presence, No. 4600 gradually slipped from view and was withdrawn from service in 1925. For the small outlay on design and production the exercise, though ultimately unsuccessful, was a valuable one in engineering terms. Trying to push back boundaries and explore other possibilities is an essential part of a design engineer's work. However, in doing so it is likely that there will be some development work that might prove to be fruitless though still adding something to the overall theme of collective knowledge. The sole 4600 was, I believe, just such a case, undoubtedly one of many pursued at Swindon over the years in the struggle to produce the most effective engines possible.

All this work soon paled into insignificance when war came in August 1914, though the commonly held belief at the time that it would 'all be over by Christmas' seemed overly optimistic. As the German Army swept westwards and began occupying France and Belgium, it soon became apparent that a short, victorious war was simply a vain, misplaced hope. Conflict had come a long way from the nineteenth century with advances in science and heavy industry contriving to make war much more brutal. So, by its first Christmas, both sides had fought themselves to a standstill, took to their trenches which quickly spread from the coast to the French border with Switzerland. And so, the business of blow then counter blow began and with it slaughter on an industrial scale with millions soon dying or wounded. Little would change over the next four years as one side then the other sought to achieve an increasingly elusive victory.

Although Britain had reformed its Army under the direction of Richard Haldane, the Secretary of State for War between 1905 and 1912, by the time Germany invaded Belgium it was a very small force by comparison to the vast army the enemy could put into the field. However, it was far better prepared than it might have been and Haldane made sure that industry and the railways, in particular, were included in all mobilisation plans. With Britain's vast industrial strength to be exploited and such an extensive railway network to support the effort, this was a shrewd and sentient act of great foresight.

As a result, the Railway Executive Committee was set up in 1912 and the general managers of the nine largest companies were enrolled as members, with the President of the Board of Trade, Sydney Buxton MP, in the chair until February 1914. He was then followed by John Burns, then Walter Runciman and Albert Stanley as the war progressed. Soon it was agreed that the railways, whilst peace lasted, would run as before, but when war came they would come under the direct control of the Railway Executive Committee. In August 1914 this change was quickly enacted. For Churchward this meant that all his energy and workshop capacity would be focussed on meeting all movement requirements for military and civilian traffic across his region. But to this was added a more telling, unspecified obligation – to produce armaments as and when specified by the War Office to do so.

Very quickly, and despite many railway workers being given reserved status, large numbers soon volunteered for front line service. This left huge gaps in the ranks of trained engineers and workers. It would be a haemorrhage of men that went on until 1918 with no like for like trained replacements being forthcoming. The one untapped source of labour, which was unlikely to find favour with Churchward, lay in the employment of women in the workshops and sheds, though not on the footplate. However, although these willing workers soon made up the numbers, it took some time for them to acquire the necessary skills to fully replace the trained men now in uniform or dead.

The demand on those who remained must have been intense and while long hours working could paper over some of the cracks, the law of diminishing returns prevailed as exhaustion set in. Inevitably, maintenance standards soon deteriorated as did the condition of locomotives and

Above and overleaf: The GWR and Swindon in the Great War. The GWR being easily the biggest employer of trained engineers in Wiltshire, let alone Britain, and possessing great industrial muscle, inevitably played a significant part in the Great War. On one level a reducing number of skilled workers, as men left to join the services, had to keep the trains running and pulling much heavier wartime loads. And then the same people had to take on the many extra manufacturing tasks assigned to them by the War Office – weapon assembly and maintenance, armaments production, construction of vehicles for wartime use such as hospital trains and much else besides. The task list must have seemed to severely stressed managers and workers as being endless and hugely challenging. This group of photographs captures some typical scenes of wartime as it affected the Works. (Top) Throughout the war the many thousands of GWR employees who volunteered or were conscripted into the services died in huge numbers with their photos appearing each month in the company magazine or the local press to highlight the level of sacrifice. (Author's collection) (Next page top) With so many men going to war, despite their reserved status, women were drafted in to the workshops and, as they acquired technical skills, contributed greatly to keeping production going. This photo shows a group of Swindon women employed on the manufacture of munitions. It has been said that their massive and essential contribution to the war effort did more for the suffrage movement than the pre-war efforts of the Suffragettes and Suffragists. (Author's collection) (Next page middle) Part of a hospital train built at Swindon. (Author's colelction) (Next page bottom) Even the local swimming pool, in the GWR Medical Fund building on Milton Road, was turned into a makeshift hospital as seen here. (DN)

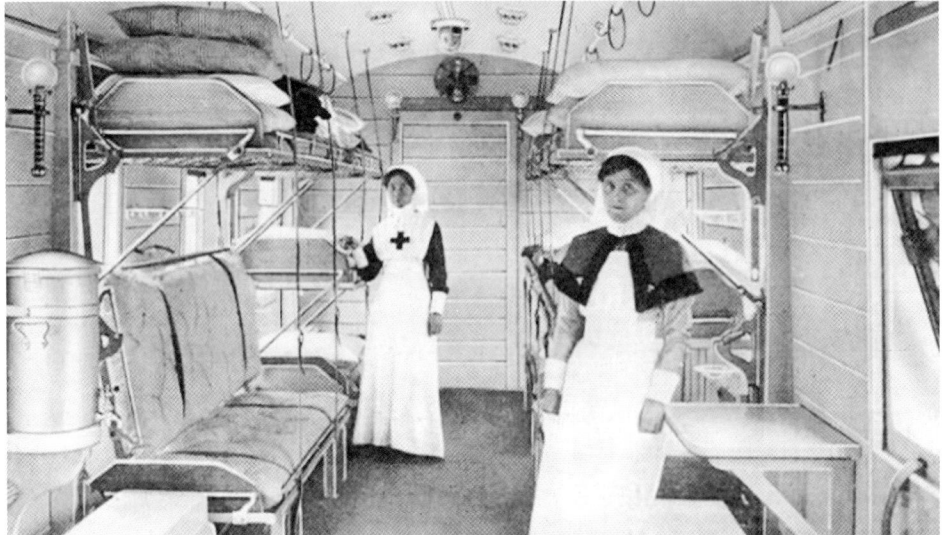

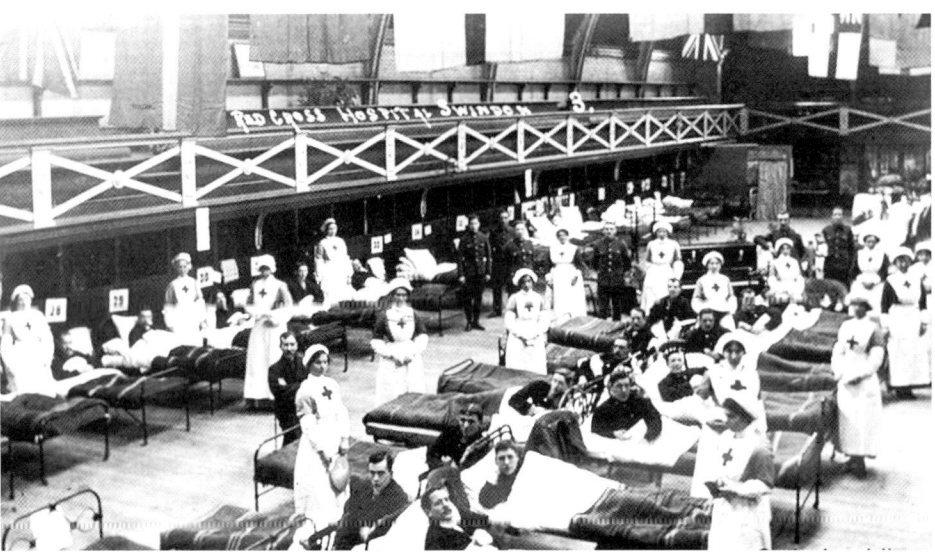

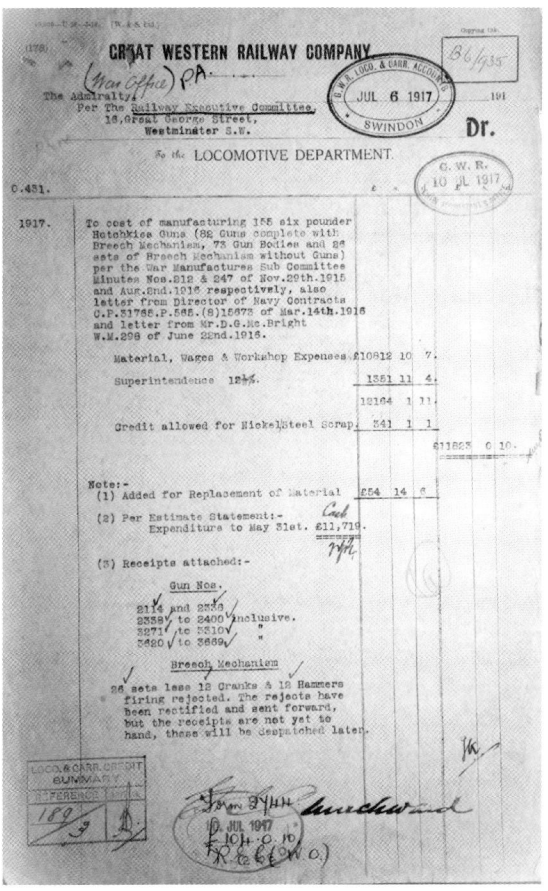
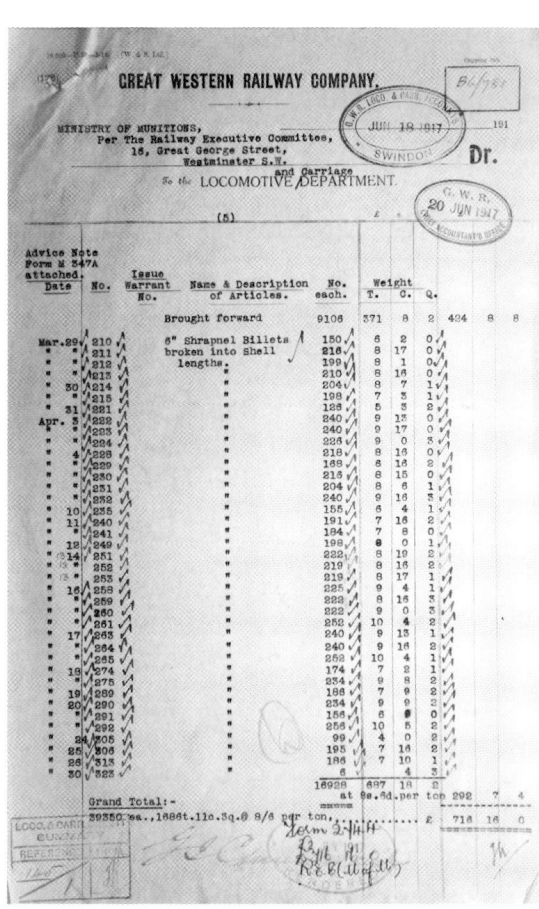

For Churchward, who took a direct hands-on approach to work, the war added many new tasks to fill the void left by having no new locomotive projects to involve him. A few years ago, his personal finance ledger for January to June 1917 was offered on eBay and bought for the princely sum of £34. These personal records, which now reside in the National Railway Museum, York, reveal much about how closely involved in day to day wartime business he was. (Above left and above right) These invoices, signed and approved by Churchward, for the production of armaments, provide only two out of hundreds of examples of the level of control he exerted on all that happened. (Author's collection) (Below left and below right) And the end result of his endeavours – armaments produced by the GWR. (DN)

rolling stock. Nevertheless, the pressure didn't lessen and for Churchward, now given the title of CME, and his managers, the load they had to bear must have been intolerable at times. This was especially so as the armament tasks gradually increased in volume as the war demanded more men and materiel to be committed to the conflict. Here the task list was a long and complex one and included guns, both large and small calibre, battlefield tanks, water carts, ammunition wagons and limbers, aircraft dropped bombs, ambulance trains, locomotives for service with the Army, and providing support to munition factories.

To make matters worse during the war years, when the need for a fully committed workforce was at its height, the demand for better pay and conditions grew more intense, with unions gradually taking a more direct part in this process. These claims they then pursued with a growing level of aggression and intransigence not seen before the war. For an autocratic manager such as Churchward this must have been a particularly difficult time, where compromise and a loosening of the purse strings was necessary and unavoidable. And once this particular genie was out of the bottle there was no going back – the path to reform and equality being paid for by the sweat of those labouring in the workshops and the blood of millions suffering and dying on the battlefield. Change would not be stopped, but it would still take several decades before the old order finally accepted the inevitable. For those who couldn't move with the times, and I suspect Churchward was one of them, the time to leave the stage may have arrived, but only time would tell if this was so.

When the war finally came to an end it was greeted with joy and relief, albeit tinged by a deep and profound sadness at the loss of so many young lives, compounded by the influenza pandemic that killed many more. All in all, it would take a long time for each warring nation to recover as it would the organisation Churchward managed. If indeed he wished to stand aside, a man of his quality wouldn't do so until all the survivors had returned to work. And while this happened, the hiatus would have allowed him to begin restoring his department, plus the locomotives and rolling stock to something nearer their pre-war level of efficiency. But this would prove to be a very difficult task, made more challenging by the growing power of trades unions and the general desire for change. It was a time when the cry 'a fair share for all' was heard in many quarters, but in a near bankrupt country still run on intransigent lines this would prove to be a struggle lasting many more years yet.

For his efforts in the war, Churchward was elevated to CBE, then in 1920 became a Freeman of Swindon. At the same time, OBEs were awarded to the stalwart Locomotive Works Manager, Charles Collett, and his opposite number on the Carriage and Wagon side of the business, Frank Marillier. For Churchward these must have been pleasant consequences, but ones dogged by the increasing management problems he was facing as both the NUR and ASLEF flexed their muscles.

There had been a number of disputes during the war, but these appear to have been settled quite quickly. With the threat of intervention by the army and of prosecution this was inevitable, but peacetime meant that these sort of tactics were no longer effective, especially against the battle hardened veterans who had survived the war to return to work. Procrastination and pitiable wages would no longer suffice and a new breed of manager, who understood and reflected these changes in society were needed. Sadly, these were, as yet, few and far between and with many stubborn,

Churchward photographed in 1918 when the stress of running such a large industrial concern in wartime was clearly etched on the 61-year-old's face. It is small wonder that exhaustion didn't consume him, as it did many others, and force him to retire as soon as the war ended. (DN)

Churchward's certified Balance of Accounts for the period January to June 1917. Judging by the papers that have survived he was meticulous in recording all expenditure, no doubt to ensure that the Chairman and Board were satisfied with the way he ran his department. This accounting document, possibly the only one to survive, reveals that in that six-month period he authorised a total expenditure of £4,568,663 10s 8d on salaries, maintenance and renewals of rolling stock and locomotive running expenses. However, he does not specify how much of this outlay went purely on war work except £34,682 spent on the supervision of that work for which payment would have been sought from the War Office. (Author's collection)

backward looking men, still in charge battle lines were soon drawn and a more profound conflict commenced.

In September 1919, for example, the NUR called a national railway strike when the government, which still had oversight of the network, announced their intention of arbitrarily reducing the 'wartime' wages, so carefully negotiated by the NUR and ASLEF, to 'pre-war' rates. Trades Union action proved effective and after nine days it was agreed to extend the agreement for another twelve months to allow more negotiations to take place. As a result, and after much hard bargaining, there was a standardisation of wages across the railway industry, highlighted by the introduction of a maximum eight-hour working day. Pressure had been applied and seems to have paid off, but this was only the start of the disputes which would go on for many decade and reach a toxic head with the 1926 General Strike.

While these disputes raged, Churchward took the opportunity to build one last, significant class of locomotive, in this case one capable of handling heavy vacuum braked freight trains. Here managers in the running department appear to have asked for an engine more capable of handling these loads than those already available. It is said that the successful use of *The Great Bear* on services such the 'Cocoa' vacuum braked train from Bristol to London was a critical factor in deciding upon the design of a purpose built engine specifically for this sort of work. Following analysis, it was decided to build an engine which was, to all intent and purposes, an eight-coupled wheel version of the 2-6-0 as Kenneth Cook described:

> It was an extremely easy matter to develop the 4300 Class by the addition of another pair of coupled wheels. The general type of extension frames remained with cylinders enlarged to 19in. diameter by 30in. and the saddle radius to take the smokebox of a higher capacity

With roughly a third of the GWR's work force of nearly 80,000 joining the services, heavy losses were inevitable. The company's war memorial at Paddington records that 2,524 of them were killed, with, if war statistics are to be believed, another 6,000 or so being wounded, with many crippled for life as a consequence. So, it is hardly surprising that when counting the cost of the war the GWR, in particular, commemorated this appalling sacrifice with many memorials. In due course, each workshop or office at Swindon had beautifully produced wooden memorials listing their dead mounted on their walls. (Above) In this case Churchward, now 65, leads one of many ceremonies to remember the dead. It is inevitable that he would have been deeply moved on these occasions. (DN)

Drawing to a Conclusion

![A.S.L.E. & F. and N.U.R. SWINDON BRANCHES. 1919 STRIKE COMMITTEE]

F. Scott, H. Chamberlain, W. Sansum, F. Sly, J. Hill, A. Waldon, J. Loveday, T. Sansum, C. Humphries, A. J. Day, W. Beckingham, C. Lawrence, J. Godsell, F. Eyres, W. Perry, C. Wilkins, G. Bowen, C. Caswell, C. Pickering, W. Parsons, W. Blackwell, F. Bishop, D. Birkett, H. Haines, G. Whitbread, E. Price, J. Slade, E. Payne, J. Mayell, J. Bennett, F. Beavis, Sn. C. Price, Chairman, A. Wentworth, R. Hobbs, W. Walker, C. Ayris, C. Holland, W. Hollaway, W. Steele, C. Westlake, J. Giles, F. Russell, F. Stone, G. Pulker, A. Bradfield, W. Evemes, H. Ruck.

The pent up frustrations that built over any years, exacerbated by extreme losses in the war, erupted in September 1919 into major strike action on the railways. An arbitrary decision by the government to ignore a TU negotiated agreement on pay led to a nine-day walkout across the industry. In taking this action the now well organised NUR and ASLEF successfully flexed their muscles and negotiated improved working conditions for their members. It was the beginning of a long and often bitter struggle. (Above) The TU officials who faced Churchward and his managers just after the war. (Below) Star Class engine No, 4004, *Morning Star*, stands at a near deserted Paddington waiting to depart with an express service to Plymouth at the height of the strike. (DN/Author's collection)

boiler in this case a No.1 standard boiler with lengthened smokebox for the prototype until a new design, the No. 7, was built and fitted to the later engines. This version had a total heating surface of 2556sqft, which included 323.90sqft within the superheater, all of which produced 225lbs of pressure and a tractive effort of 30,460lb. The leading, driving and intermediate axle-boxes, valve gear, crossheads, slide bars and piston valves remained the same and the axle-boxes with inclined planes in the trailing position fitted to the 2-8-0 and 2-8-0T engines, were provided in the new trailing position.... They were very fine engines.

Very interestingly, and in a valedictory way, he then concluded with the words, 'This design provided a fitting fruition to Churchward's reign in showing the general foresight inherent in his original standardisation plan.'

Nevertheless, only one of these engines appeared before Churchward retired and it was left to Collett to complete the task when eight more were built in 1922/23, all of which would see useful service for forty years or more.

As Cook reported, they did indeed provide a fitting end to a long and distinguished career and, although Churchward carried on until the end of 1921, there would be little more of note in design terms to savour. On the other hand, his contribution during these final years undoubtedly helped the GWR recover after four years of the most appalling war. In the process he left a valuable legacy for his successor to enjoy and exploit in a rapidly changing world. To this end it isn't surprising that towards the end of his career Churchward is reported as saying 'it is time the old man retired'. This he chose to do shortly afterwards, remaining at Newburn, with his staff around him, from where he could continue to keep an eye on what was happening around his old stamping ground.

His exit at 65 may also have been spurred on by the departure of two old friends and colleagues at Swindon. First of all, Henry King retired in March 1920 and Frank Marillier a little later. Over the years these two men, who had occupied very senior ranks under Churchward, had been steadfast in their support, and it is probably safe to say that without them he may not have achieved so much as he did, especially in wartime. Then in June 1921 Felix Pole was appointed General Manager and where Inglis had failed in bringing Churchward under his control, Pole succeeded. In that year he pushed through a change, presumably with the Chairman's agreement, that saw the CME reporting to him directly. Although there were undoubtedly some operational benefits to be derived from this, it did have the appearance of reducing Churchward's standing in the organisation and at the same time taking away his direct link to the Chairman.

When Churchward's retirement was announced, his managers organised a collection to mark the event. It isn't reported whether his workers voluntarily contributed money from their meagre wages to the fund or were pressed to do so. This was something that appears to have been the custom and practice at time, and well into the 1970s for that matter, in military circles at least, for such things as gifts for members of the Royal Family at major events such as Coronations or Royal Weddings. Either way, a 'substantial amount' was collected and when asked what he would like as a retirement gift, he chose a fishing rod, which was then presented to him by the Chairman of the Works Committee at a ceremony in the Mechanics Institute. Such a simple, low value present left a substantial sum to be used for other purposes and Churchward chose, in a well-received gesture, to create a trust fund to provide annual prizes to be awarded to particularly hard-working and successful apprentices. And with that the 'old man' departed the scene.

For such an energetic, creative leader it must have been very difficult to finally release the reins and begin playing such an inactive role. After the cut and thrust of business and civic life it must also have been difficult to adjust and, without a large family around him, possibly a lonely existence as his health and hearing declined. Nevertheless, he remained keenly interested in all that was happening on the railways and was often visited by old boys whose careers he had helped nurture. These included William Stanier, who would soon leave Wiltshire for the LMS and even greater glory, taking with him much he had learnt from the 'old man' over many years.

Drawing to a Conclusion 229

Kenneth Cook believed that all Churchward had worked so hard to achieve in locomotive design came together in the 4700 Class of 2-8-0s. Although only nine were built they were, as Cook related, *'very fine engines'*. (Above) The Swindon diagram showing the 4700's substantial dimensions and (below) one of the class on shed possibly at Old Oak Common. (Author's collection/DN)

Many others remained with the GWR, including William Pellow, who in 1933 had one final and poignant meeting with his former leader. Pellow, who by then had reached the rank of Divisional Locomotive Superintendent, received a message from someone in the running department at Swindon to the effect that Churchward was travelling to Devon and would be changing trains at Bristol. Clearly concerned for the wellbeing of an increasingly fragile, elderly man, Pellow was asked to ensure that he made it safely across the station to the connecting train for Newton Abbott. He later wrote in a letter that:

> When his train from Swindon arrived Churchward slowly disembarked saw me waiting and he raised his hand in greeting saying, at the same time, 'I know you. I remember you from your drawing office days. How are you getting on? He was obviously pleased to see me and as we had 30 minutes to wait I asked him if he would like to walk as far as the sheds which were close

On a misty morning in December 1933 Churchward was hit by engine No. 4085, *Berkeley Castle*, seen here pulling a mixed load of carriages sometime in the 1930s. He had wandered too close to the track and undoubtedly didn't hear the fast approaching train. In his funeral eulogy the Bishop of Barking referred to the accident in a rather black way with the words, 'here he lived and here he died the engineer hoist by his own petard, killed by what we might call his own children or by their cousin…' As an old friend he probably understood Churchward's sense of humour and realised that the 'old man' might have found this funny. (DN)

by. 'No let's find a seat where we can sit and chat'. We did so, and he fired off question after question, asking how various types of locomotive were behaving and what we were doing about this and that problem. The time passed too quickly and as the train by which he was travelling from the north ran in, I picked up his overcoat to escort him to his compartment. 'Hey!' he yelled, 'Go easy with that coat, my flask and sandwiches prepared by my housekeeper are in the pockets'. Just typical of him! When I put him on the train he badly wanted me to travel on with him, 'Just as far as Taunton, say. I wish you would, we have had such an enjoyable yarn'. Unfortunately, I had an important meeting to attend in Bristol and it could not be managed. That was the last chance I had to talk to this grand old man, which I greatly regretted a few months later when I heard of his tragic and wholly unnecessary death.

And so the months passed with Churchward passing the time in his large rambling house at Swindon still looked after by housekeeper, Mary Gray, and staff, now including three retired labourers to attend to the gardens. Most days, it seems, he would walk, when he felt able, beside then cross the tracks to visit the works to see what was going on and talk to old friends. He, according to Cook, had:

Mellowed considerably by then and the once fearsome reputation he had 'enjoyed' had faded quite considerably. With this any ill-feeling caused by his autocratic way of working seems to have given way to a genuine affection for a frail and increasingly gentle old man who seemed so pleased to see and chat to everyone he saw.

It was during once of his sojourns to the Works that he met his death, on a typically wet and misty December morning, as Cook again related:

It was the nineteenth of the month and I was in the 'A' Erecting Shop half under a locomotive when Ted Plaister, the Chief Foreman, tugged at my sleeve and almost pulled me over. I was slightly annoyed but he tugged at my sleeve again and said 'you must come quickly; the Old Man has been knocked down on the main line'. I hurried out to find the first-aid man Drinkwater with him as he lay dead, his head very badly crushed. It later transpired that he had been struck by engine No. 4085, *Berkeley Castle*, which was pulling the 8.55 am Paddington to Fishguard Express which passed through Swindon at about 10.22.

It appears that he was interested in the track alongside his house which was almost due for relaying and was leaning over it looking at the sleepers. With sight and hearing failing, and in the murky conditions that morning, he evidently did not notice that the express was approaching. The old men he employed as gardeners had tried to tell him on a number of occasions that he ought not go along the path by the main line, but he seems to have ignored the warning and allowed curiosity to get the better of him and died.

Not surprisingly, his funeral, a few days later, was attended by many of the great and good from the railway industry, including Stanier, Nigel Gresley, Collett and James Clayton, representing Richard Maunsell of the Southern Railway. There were also many senior civic leaders, members

Above left: One source suggests this photo of George Churchward was taken towards the end of his life, but Kenneth Cook recorded on the back of this print 'GJC in 1921 – a formal retirement photo'. He has then added 'by the 1930s this once dynamic man was a mere shadow of his former self with failing eyesight and hearing and very stooped and slow when walking. He came to rely very heavily on his manservant, who doubled up as chauffeur, in the last few years of his life'. Old age comes to us all and the extreme trials of Churchward's life had clearly exhausted him. (KC)

Above right: Churchward's legacy centred on the workshops under his control as much as the locomotives and rolling stock he built. He modernised whenever he could and kept production rates high in peace and war, but he drove his workforce autocratically and ruthlessly at times, diplaying, in the process, a poor regard for their health and welfare. As this picture reveals these workshops were dangerous and dirty places to inhabit, as consistsly poor accident rates and industrial illneeses could bare witness. Conditions only really began to improve post the Great War when the generation who had fought and died demanded much more for their sacrifices. (Author's collection)

of the Institutions he graced, GWR employees from all departments, as well as a plethora of friends and admirers. Sadly, though, none of his family seem to have been able to attend, so executor, John Kelynack, who was the CME's Chief Clerk, and his staff from Newburn acted as substitute mourners in their absence.

Before the service at Christ Church, in Swindon's Old Town, where he appears to have worshipped, Churchward's coffin was drawn round the town with many thousands turning out to pay their respects as the cortege passed by, according to press reports. His old friend James Inskip, the Bishop of Barking, led the service. Before laying him to rest he tried to sum up Churchward's life in an understanding and sympathetic way:

> A man in his position requires an extraordinary degree of technical knowledge and a powerful inventive faculty, with considerable organising and administrative ability. He may be brilliant in all these respects and yet be unsuited for filling a post in which one mistake in dealing with a staff of men running into thousands may spell disaster. To fill such a position a man requires an intimate knowledge of human nature and a true sympathy with his fellow men. George Churchward was strong on all these points.
>
> So we take leave of him. His influence will still live amongst us. You are the richer for having had him amongst you for nearly 60 years. You cannot emulate his achievements, but you can all emulate his devotion to duty and his interest in the services of his fellow men.

When his will was published in February 1934 the level of his wealth was revealed. He had accumulated a total estate valued in the region of £62k, which today would be worth more than £3.5 million. And when dispersing these assets, he proved generous to friends such as Sir Cuthbert Wallace, the famous surgeon, and those who worked for him at Newburn. Mary Gray received £3,000, Mabel Scrivans £800 and Ada Warwick £400. Meanwhile his 'chauffeur-valet', Frederick Northover, son of Robert Northover who for many years had been Churchward's driver, and later married and became a butcher, calling his own house in Cricklade Newburn, along the way, received £4,000 - plus 'his lathes, rifles, fishing gear, car and his wearing apparel'. And, finally, his head gardener, Lot Mildenhall, received £1,000 and his two assistants, Jack Hatherall and Tom Pope, £400 each. The residue of his estate was inherited jointly by his sisters Mary and Adelina, which allowed them to see out the rest of their lives in great comfort; Mary died in 1940 and Adelina eleven years later at 85. For John, who appears to have died in 1949, there was nothing, which suggests their estrangement had continued to run deep. But for James there was nothing either, although they appear to have remained on good terms throughout their lives.

So, Churchward's substantial estate was wound up leaving only his engineering legacy to remind the world that he had existed. But what a legacy it was; arguably without parallel in Britain's railway industry before or after with some very stiff opposition to consider when judging such an issue. Even overseas his name was greatly revered, as another great locomotive engineer, Andre Chapelon, made only too clear when recalling, later in his life 'it was he, and Gaston de Bousquet, who laid down the foundations of efficient locomotive performance which all who followed were guided by'. This was view with which William Stanier wholly agreed. At the end of Kenneth Cook's presentation in 1950 he summarized his late leader's contribution with the words:

> I have a great regard and affection for his memory. As Mr Cook has said, 'His soul goes marching on'. That is true because all his engines, which are still of the most modern types, were built before 1910. Those who have come afterwards have tried to follow in his footsteps ever since.

He was not alone in his praise because Nigel Gresley felt the same. Following Churchward's death, he, as President of the Institution of Locomotive Engineers, paid a very public tribute to

Drawing to a Conclusion 233

Churchward has been dead for some time when this photograph was taken and his successor, Charles Collett, had chosen not to occupy the house built for the Superintendent, so Newburn lay empty. With no real purpose to serve the house was demolished to make way for new carriage sheds and this last physical link with Churchward's time at Swindon came to an end. (DN)

someone he had met quite often and came to regard as a friend, albeit a rival as well. 'He was without doubt one of the most eminent railway engineers of recent times, and we see evidence of his influence in the designs of the most up-to-date engines of each of the great railways of this country.

A month later, at another Institution meeting, he hinted at the closeness of his relationship with Churchward and the influence he could and did exert:

> The practice of stretching ordinary boiler tubes has been introduced by the Great Western Railway and has been a very good one indeed. I myself have copied it, as I have copied many GWR practices. I remember an occasion when I went down to Swindon and got Mr Churchward to lend me the drawings so I could make a stretching bench myself.

Coming from three such eminent engineers this is high praise indeed, but it is a view supported by a great deal of evidence, beginning with his skill in getting such a large organisation moving in the right direction so effectively. This he began to do when becoming William Dean's deputy in 1895 and then his successor. During this time, he analysed and rationalised his department then initiated a massive expansion of the facilities available at Swindon. Before then it appears to have lacked the sense of purpose such a large and developing business needs. Churchward had a clear, uncluttered view of the future and understood how the business needed to change and made effective in meeting all future needs.

All these tasks ran in parallel and the complexity of what was planned required a master of organisation and administration so they might be brought to a successful conclusion. Churchward was just such a man. But to achieve all this he needed to gain the support of his Chairman and Board of Directors; normally a most risk averse group, especially when there were investors and shareholders in the background demanding a cautious approach to protect their dividends. In convincing a Chairman to invest in such a situation requires someone who is a master of persuasion, someone who understood the economics of big business and could present a complex proposal for approval. Churchward proved himself particularly adroit and accomplished in doing all these things, taking senior managers with him then delivering all that was promised and more at minimal risk.

These are skills that few possess. As a result, each programme he pursued, be it infrastructure, locomotive or rolling stock based, he did so successfully. Later on, when the regime in charge at Paddington changed, he had to deal with a far less supportive, sympathetic, more cost-conscious senior team. Under Churchill, as Chairman, and Inglis, as General Manager, bureaucratic obstacles appear to have been placed in his way, with lack of ambition, a power struggle and petty jealousies seeming, at times, to take the place of reasoned argument. They seemed content with what they had and so reined in experimentation and speculation. Churchward stood his ground and continued to seek improvements where he could, but in his last decade in charge he didn't reach the heights of his early years. Luckily, as Stanier and Gresley made clear, he had provided them with the strongest, most modern fleet of locomotives and this met their needs for the foreseeable future. But if Churchill, his Board and successive General Managers, had remained supportive and ambitious where might their talented CME/Superintendent have taken them?

Then the war came and everything changed. Suddenly a whole list of high priority tasks bore down upon him and any chance he might have had to pick up the pace of locomotive development again quickly disappeared. Nevertheless, the task he faced was central to Britain's

Churchward's locomotive legacy would be hard to equal. In a long and stimulating career he produced a fleet of engines nearly all of which served the company, and then British Railways, in a most efficient and effective way. Even those produced by Collett, his successor, adopted the principles Churchward had so cleverly expounded and developed over twenty years or more. In the picture above it is a Saturday in July 1926 and the General Strike is over. Here a strong line-up of GWR engines, led by No. 4056, *Princess Maragret,* back down towards Paddington ready to pulling no less than five portions of the prestigious Cornish Riviera Express. The Group includes three of Churchward's Stars and a Saint, plus a Star derived Castle Class engine. (DN)

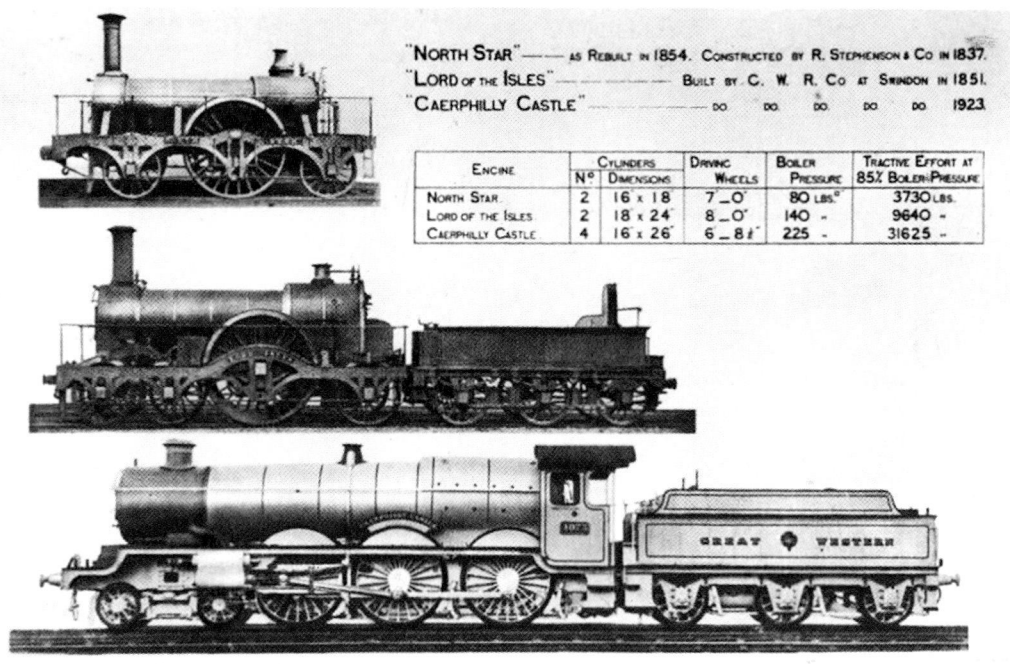

Not long after Churchward's retirement, this picture card appeared showing the way GWR engines had evolved since *North Star* appeared in 1837 and seems to pay homage to the part played by Churchward. Interestingly, a 'Collett' Castle Class engine of 1923 is used to complete the picture rather than the Stars from which it was derived, so the supposed homage is a little skewed. In addition, the two older engines in the picture were both scrapped by Churchward despite their historic nature and it was left to Collett to authorise a replica of the first be built in 1925. One wonders whether the card is, in fact, a subliminal criticism of the 'old man', who Collett is thought to have disliked despite the way Churchward encouraged his career. (Author's collection)

war effort and for four years this astute, strong manager made sure that the GWR played its part to the full; despite the loss of staff to the services and the addition of numerous tasks linked to the production of armaments and munitions. Many would have buckled under such pressure. Churchward, backed by senior managers cut from similar cloth, did not. Nevertheless, this shouldn't have come as a surprise because he had demonstrated his resilience, an ability to think on his feet and a wide range of technical skills since the beginning of his career in the 1870s.

When he took charge in 1902 these were all honed to near perfection, helped by John Wright at Newton Abbott and then Joseph Armstrong and William Dean at Swindon. During this time, he learnt the basics of his trade and developed an ability to look more widely at practices and ideas being cultivated elsewhere as he considered in which direction his design work should go. To do this he looked overseas, to the United States and France in particular, for inspiration, but at the same time didn't forget the principles and practices tried and tested by his forebears on the GWR. These he respected, absorbed and adopted where he could as a sound basis for the designs he then produced. To this he then added his own ideas with results that still astound us today and which touched the work of the leading designers who came after, as Gresley was only too pleased to admit.

So, the years that followed were full of great endeavour with his standardised fleet of engines, and there many contributory innovations, being at the centre of all he and his team attempted to do. In the process the engines he produced became the beating heart of his great legacy and were a cleverly planned mix and match arrangement in which superheating, top feed, a standardised range of boilers, piston valves, cylinders and much more were tried, tested and accepted in one form or another. And it was a system that seemed to work well. If there was a failure, which some considered *The Great Bear* to be, the intention was always greater efficiency until another class of locomotive was proven to do the job just as well, or even better. So, not so much a failure as an essential scientific exercise in pushing back boundaries to see what is possible. For a true engineer, such as Churchward, this was an essential process to be followed. If not, he might simply have stood still like lesser men or, at best, he hardly advanced at all. His continued inventiveness, to which his many development programmes bear witness, confirm that he remained a man of science and discovery to the end of his days.

Where he was, perhaps, less successful was in the business of managing a large, diverse workforce at a time of great social change. For traditional Victorians, such as he, it had long been a matter of master and servant when it came to the treatment of industrial labour, with servitude the result. In this class ridden society, which had its origins in Britain's medieval system of serfdom, workers had few rights and what there was had no legal backing. As a result, great wealth and power were vested in a tiny minority and the rest had to scratch around as best

Churchward was a key figure in the development of the GWR's classic 4-6-0s and the company's rail cars and lived to see both continue to be developed under Collett. The scene, captured here in the 1950s, shows how diesel railcars evolved post 1933 from Churchward's steam railcars, before being progressively replaced by British Railways more modern Diesel Multiple Units, and steam, here represented by King Class four-cylinder engine No. 6001, *King Edward VII*. (Author's collection)

These photographs of two GWR 4-6-0s in full flight do to my mind make a perfect end-piece to a book about Churchward, underpinning, as it does, the extent and potency of his legacy. (Above) Castle Class engine No. 5086, *Viscount Horne*, was a 1937 rebuild of a Star Class locomotive, No. 4066 of the same name. As a Castle she will remain in service until 1958. (Below) A King Class engine, No. 6008 *King James II*, caught at high speed from a passing car. This locomotive was built at Swindon in 1928 and was reduced to scrap there in 1962. Luckily three others survived to remind us that those who followed Churchward remained influenced by his ideas and his achievements. (Author's collection)

they could to eke out a most basic living. True, they were helped to a certain extent by the construction of the Mechanics Institute, medical facilities and some company houses. Plus, they were encouraged to pursue further education where they could, and some were occasionally sponsored to do so. Nevertheless, this was hardly sufficient for a work force approaching 12,000 in number and, to be honest, most of it was achieved by staff subscription, not major company investment or patronage.

Social reformers in the late nineteenth century began the process of change, but it wasn't until the post-Great War years that true progress began to be made. However, it was a process met by an old order loth to give up their long enjoyed privileges. As Superintendent, then CME, Churchward demonstrated a similar level of intolerance to the spread of industrial democracy and failed to treat workers' representatives fairly or responsibly. The result was that they remained a commodity to be used or caste off as suited the business. And while they remained in harness the pay was poor and working conditions challenging to say the least. This created a cycle of poverty and abuse which wasn't broken during Churchward's career, and was sustained by his autocratic style of management and commitment to maintaining the production flow. The end result was hardly edifying or charitable and does him little credit and yet when he retired a staff collection produced a substantial amount most of which he presented to a fund to help his employees. So, unless the workers were obliged to contribute to this gift, he seems to have had their respect, though whether this was from fear or genuine affection, I leave others to decide. In truth, he was the product of his age and clearly found social change difficult to cope with in a charitable, inclusive way. In the event, it was probably to his benefit that he retired when he did.

So, how do you sum up the life of this great man and do justice to everything he contributed to the GWR and the Swindon community? He was, undoubtedly, a man of his age with all the assets and shortcomings of the Victorian era. On one side of the balance sheet we have his strength of character, sense of purpose, his desire to lead, his will to succeed and his ability to work hard and to good effect in peace and war. Then we have his clever, creative, incisive, mind, his scientific curiosity and his desire to experiment wherever possible. And last, but not least, we have his indomitable spirit and his great organisational skills.

However, to counter-balance this we have his apparently unyielding sense of autocracy, which even Stanier felt moved to mention in a brief speech at Churchward's funeral. Then there was his apparent acceptance of the appalling living and working conditions his industrial workers and their families suffered, so truthfully and movingly captured by Alfred Williams. But he was not alone in this. For centuries, as Britain evolved from a farming to an industrial economy, with mass migration from the country to towns and cities taking place, it had been this way. Many employers turned a blind eye to the problem and did nothing until forced to do so by Central Government and others simply played lip-service to reform. However, there was a small third group, mostly made up of a few far-seeing religious based businesses, who attempted to alleviate the problems in a generous and noble way. The GWR, at best fell, into the second category with little or no effort being made by senior managers, including Churchward, to follow the example of the better employers, siting insufficient funds to do more. This lack of action would eventually rebound on all those companies who sought to hold on to the past, when embracing the future would have served them far better in the long term.

Nevertheless, Churchward did achieve great things for the company and railway history and is rightly feted for all he achieved as an engineer, a designer and a production manager. For this alone he is rightly lionised, for without his skill and drive the story of the exceptional fleet of modern locomotives, carriages and wagons he led in producing might have turned out very differently.

References Sources

The National Railway Museum (Search Engine)

Records Consulted
The G.J. Jackson Collection (some items donated by the author)
The R. Bond Collection.
The E.S. Cox Collection.
The R. Riddles Collection (donated by author)

Other Collections Consulted
Institution of Mechanical Engineers, London.
K.J. Cook
R.A. Hillier.
D. Neal.
T.F. Coleman/M. Lemon.
B. Spencer.

Books and Other Publications
Swindon Engineering Society Journals.
GWR Junior Engineering Society Journal.
IMechE/ILocoE Journals.
The Engineer.
The Gazette.
The Mecanno Magazine.
Steam World.
The Stephenson Society Journal.
Backtrack (Various Editions)
The Railway Magazine Archive .
The GWR Magazine .
The Railway & Travel Monthly Magazine.
The Locomotive, Carriage and Wagon Review.
Allen & Bursley, *Heat Engines*, McGraw 1941
Bannister, E., *Trained by Sir Nigel Gresley*, Dalesman 1984
Bond, R., *A Lifetime with Locomotives* (1975)
Bowen-Cooke, C.J., *British Locomotives*, Whittaker & Co 1899
Bradley, R., *GWR 2-cylinder 4-6-0s and 2-6-0s*, David & Charles 1988
Brown, E.A.S., *Nigel Gresley. Locomotive Engineer*, Ian Allan 1961

Bulleid, H.A.V., *Bulleid of the Southern*, Ian Allan 1977
Bulleid, H.A.V., *Master Builders of Steam*, Ian Allan 1963
Chacksfield, J.E., *Sir William Stanier*, Oakwood Press 2001
Chapelon, A., *La Locomotive a Vapeur*, Bulliere, 1952
Chappell, H., *Life on the Iron Road*, Bodley Head 1924
Cooke, K.J., *Swindon Steam*, Ian Allan 1974
Cox, E.S., *Chronicles of Steam*, Ian Allan 1967
Cox, E.S., *Speaking of Steam*, Ian Allan 1971
Dalby, W.E., *British Railways: Some Facts and A Few Problems*, 1910
Dalby, W.E., *The Balancing of Engines*, 1920
Durrant, A.E., *Inside Portrait of the Great Western Works*, Runpast, 1989
Foxwell, E. & Farrer, T.C., *Express Trains* (1889)
Gibbs, K., *The Steam Workshops of the GWR*, The History Press 2014
Hardy, R.H.N., *Steam in the Blood*, Ian Allan 1971
Haresnape, B., *Gresley's Locomotives*, Ian Allan 1981
Haresnape. B. and Swain, A., *Churchward Locomotives*, Ian Allan 1975
Hillier-Graves, T., *Gresley and His Locomotives*, Pen & sword Transport (2019)
Hillier-Graves, T., *Gresley's Master Engineer – Bert Spencer*, Pen & Sword Transport (2023)
Hillier-Graves, T., *Peppercorn. His Life and Locomotives*, Pen & Sword Transport (2021)
Hillier-Graves, T., *The Princess Royal Pacifics*, Pen & Sword Transport (2018)
Hillier-Graves, T., *Thompson. His Life and Locomotives*, Pen & Sword Transport (2021)
Hillier-Graves, T., *Tom Coleman. His Life and Work* Pen & Sword Transport (2019)
Hillier-Graves, T., *Turbomotive – Stanier's Advanced Pacific*, Pen & Sword Transport (2017)
Holcroft, H. *Locomotive Adventure Vols 1 and 2*, Ian Allan 1962
Holcroft, H., *Locomotive Adventure* (two volumes), Ian Allan 1962/1965
Hughes, G., *The Construction of the Modern Locomotive*, E & F.N. Spon 1896
Hughes, Geoffrey, *Sir Nigel Gresley*, Oakwood Press 2001
Langridge, E.A., *Under 10 CMEs* (2 volumes) Oakwood Press, 2011
Maidment, D., *Eight-Coupled Heavy Freight Locomotives*, Pen & Sword Transport 2015
Matheson, R., *Doing Time Inside*, The History Press, 2011
Nock, O.S., *Sixty Years of Western Express Running*, Littlehampton 1954)
Nock, O.S., *The GWR Stars, Castles and Kings* (1970)
Nock, O.S., *William Stanier – An Engineering Biography*, Ian Allan 1964
Rogers, H.C., *G J Churchward – A Locomotive Biography*, (1975)
Rogers, H.C.B., *The Last Steam Locomotive Engineer* George Allen & Unwin 1970
Rutherford, M., *Castles and Kings at Work*, Ian Allan 1982
Sixsmith, L., *The Book of the Princess Royal Pacifics*, Wild Swan 2000
Tuplin, W.A., *Great Western Steam* George Allen & Unwin 1958
Williams, A. *Life In A Railway Factory*, Duckworth, 1915

Photographic Sources

The photographs reproduced in this book come from many sources and are credited as follows:

Kenneth Cook (KC), Ronald Hillier (RH), Tom Coleman (TC), the GWR Magazine (GWR), the Institution of Locomotive Engineers (IE) and the author.

Copyright is a complex issue and often difficult to establish, especially when the same picture may exist in a number of collections – public and private. Checks have been strenuously made to ensure each picture has been correctly attributed, but no process can be flawless, especially when most of the pictures are more than 100 years of age and the photographers long gone. If an error has been made it was unintentional. If any reader wishes to affirm copyright, please contact the publisher and an acknowledgement will be made in any future edition of the book, should a claim be proven. We apologise, in advance, if a mistake has been made.

Index

Adams, William – 75
Allen, Cecil – 204, 205
Amalgamated Society of Railway
  Servants – 207
American Locomotive Co – 174
Armstrong, Joseph – 28, 29, 36, 44, 46, 48,
  51, 235
Aspinall, John – 173, 174, 182
Associated Society of Locomotive Engineers
  & Firemen (ASLEF) – 211, 224, 226, 227
Association of Railway Engineers
  (ARLE) – 183
Atmospheric Railway – 31
Avonside Engine Co – 31-33

Baldwin, Alfred – 200
Baldwin Locomotive Works – 185, 186, 213
Baltimore & Ohio Railroad – 213
Beattie, Alfred – 186
Bell, E L – 194
Belpaire firebox – 7, 5-59, 97, 190
Boilers (GWR):
  Standard No 1 – 78, 169, 177, 228
  Standard No 2 – 60, 62, 137
  Standard No 4 – 60, 141, 142, 214
  Standard No 5 – 138, 142, 219
  Standard No 6 – 190
  Standard No 7 – 142
Boulton Williams – 9
Bousquet, Gaston du – 61, 100, 103, 168, 232
Bowen-Cooke, Charles – 203, 204
Bristol and Exeter Railway – 22, 24, 31, 33,
  36, 43, 48, 56, 86, 87
Brunel, Isambard Kingdom – 8, 9, 22, 31
Bull, Grace – 212
Bulleid, O V S – 95
Burns, John – 220
Burrows, Henry George 83, 91, 213, 214
Buxton, Sydney – 220

Caledonian Railway – 204
Campbell, Frederick – 54, 55, 61, 62
Carlton, Samuel – 36
Carriage Development Programme – 125-128
Chamberlain, Joseph – 54
Chapelon, Andre – 232
Chicago & Milwaukie Railroad – 185
Churchill, Viscount – 199, 234
Churchward, Adelina (mother) – 16, 18, 19
Churchward, Adelina (sister) – 17, 19,
  213, 232
Churchward, Charles – 19
Churchward, Frederick – 17-20, 25, 26, 213
Churchward, George (father) – 16, 213
Churchward, George Jackson – 7-9, 1-16
  Childhood – 16-24
  Premium Apprentice – 24-37
  Draughtsman – 37-40, 44, 46, 48, 51, 53
  Asst Manager – 55, 59, 61, 62, 65
  Dean's Assistant/Deputy – 67-69
  Locomotive and Carriage Supt – 69,
    71-79, 81-83, 86, 89, 91, 93-99,
    102,-104, 120-130, 132, 134-137,
    140-149, 153, 155-157, 162,
    165-168, 172, 174, 176-183, 185, 187,
    190, 191, 196, 197, 200-207, 210,
    212-215
  During the First World War – 218-220,
    225, 228
  Retirement and death – 228, 230-233,
    236-238.
Churchward, Gwendoline – 213
Churchward, James (brother) – 17, 19,
  213, 232
Churchward, John (brother) – 17, 19,
  213, 232
Churchward, Mary (sister) – 17, 19, 213, 232
Churchward, Paul – 19
City of Bath (loco) – 62, 65

City of Truro (loco) – 64-66, 185
Collett, Charles – 83, 86, 140, 146, 149, 182, 184, 185, 198, 200, 224, 231, 235
Compagnie du Chemin – 186
Compagnie du Paris-Orleans – 187
Cook, Kenneth – 7, 33, 47-50, 51, 55, 62, 63, 65, 66, 72, 88, 97-103, 123, 125, 128-133, 144, 149, 164, 168-172, 174, 176, 180, 196, 200, 206, 212, 226-233
Cornish Riviera Express – 102, 206, 210
Cross, J W – 83

Dean, William – 7, 28, 29, 36, 44, 46, 48, 51-59, 61, 62, 66, 67, 69-71, 73, 77, 95, 97, 121, 142, 156, 162, 165, 166, 178, 182, 235
Deverell, Oscar – 216, 218
Drummond, Dugald – 128, 182
Duchy of Cornwall – 16
Dynamometer Car (No. 7) – 122-125

Earl of Devon – 16
Edward VII's Funeral – 207-209
Emlyn, Viscount – 54, 162, 200
Engineer Journal – 188, 190
Evans, Edward – 31

Factory and Workshop Acts – 155, 156
Fairburn & Sons – 31
Farrar, Frederick – 21
First World War – 149, 155, 168, 197, 218-224
Flewellen, G H – 124
Flying Dutchman – 21, 45

Garbe, Robert – 82
'Gauge Wars' – 41-45
Geach, Charles – 31, 32
General Strike 1926 – 226
Gibbs, Alfred Wolcott – 96, 97
Gibbs, Joseph – 9
Gibson, John – 53
Glehn, Alfred de – 61, 82, 95, 96, 98, 100, 103, 168, 172, 186, 187
Gloucester Railway Carriage & Wagon Co – 129
Gooch, Daniel – 31, 39, 40, 43, 46, 54, 56, 122, 170, 182
Gray, Mary – 212, 230, 232

Great Central Railway – 213
Great Exhibition – 8, 9, 20
Great Northern Railway – 213
Grenville, Robert – 34, 35, 36
Grenville/ Churchward Steam Carriage – 34, 35, 36
Gresley, Nigel – 30, 71, 78, 95, 185, 206, 231-233
Grierson, James – 125

Hackshaw, John – 39, 40
Haigh Foundry – 31
Haldane, Richard – 220
Hale, Benjamin – 212, 213
Hatherall, Jack – 232
Hawksworth, Frederick – 83, 86
Highland Railway – 67
Hill House, Stoke Gabriel – 18, 19
Hiring Fairs – 14
Holcroft, Harold – 68, 88, 191, 193, 213, 214, 216-218
Holden, James – 75, 77, 125
Huxham-Watson, R – 24

Improvement Classes – 212
Industrial Revolution – 9, 149
Ince Forge Co – 32, 33
Inglis, James – 182, 196, 208, 218, 234
Inskip, James – 232
Institution of Locomotive Engineers (ILocoE) – 28, 232
Institution of Mechanical Engineers (IMechE) – 28, 73-81, 83, 95, 173, 187, 197, 203
Ivatt, Henry Alfred – 77, 182

J & C Rigby of London – 164, 165
Johnson, Samuel – 57, 75

Kelynack, John – 232
Kerr, Stuart & Co – 129
King Edward VI's Foundation School – 19-23
King, Henry C – 78, 83, 86, 228
Kirtley, William – 182

Lancashire & Yorkshire Railway – 173, 174
Lehigh & Mahoney Railroad – 134, 185
Lloyd George, David – 210, 211

Locomotives
  Caledonian Railway 4-6-0 – 204
  Great Northern Railway – Class C1 – 77
    A1 Pacific – 206
  GWR – (Broad Gauge) – Iron Duke 4-2-2 – 22, 49
    Rover Class 4-2-2 – 44, 45
  GWR – (Standard Gauge) – 157 Class
    2-2-2s ('Sharpies') – 47
    2201 Class 2-4-0s – 48
    3301 Class 2-2-2s – 50
    Dean 2301 (0-6-0) – 51, 70
    Dean Class 7 (or Armstrong Class) (4-4-0) – 56, 57
    Badminton Class (4100) – 58, 59, 62, 69
    Atbara Class (4100) – 52, 62-64, 102
    Bulldog Class (3300) – 52, 60, 69, 70, 121, 144
    Bird Class (3300) – 60, 61, 62, 121
    Duke Class (3252) – 52, 57, 60
    City Class (3700) – 52, 62, 64, 102, 121
    Aberdare Class (2600) – 69
    102 France & sisters – 61, 98, 100, 101, 102, 105, 136, 168, 169, 172
    4-6-0 No. 36 – 66-68
    4-6-0 No. 2601 – 67, 68, 95
    2-6-0 No. 2602 – 68, 69, 121
    4-6-0 (prototype No. 100) – 97 – 99
    4-6-0 (prototype No. 98) – 97-99
    2900 (Saint) Class 4-6-0 – 98, 102, 102, 103, 120, 123, 129, 140, 169, 173, 176, 178, 182, 184, 185, 199, 205, 211, 216
    Steam Railmotors – 128-131
    2800 Class (2-8-0) + prototypes – 135-136, 140, 143, 148, 182, 201
    3100 Class (2-6-2T) – 137, 138, 141, 145
    5100 Class (2-6-2T) – 137, 138
    4400 Class (2-6-2T) – 138, 139, 140
    4500 Class (2-6-2T) – 139, 140, 201, 219
    4575 Class (2-6-2T) 140
    4000 (Star) Class (4-6-0) – 140, 168-174, 176-181, 182, 190, 191, 193, 196, 20-206, 218, 227
    3150 Class – 141, 145
    (Experimental) 0-8-0T – 142, 143
    (Experimental) 4-4-4 Passenger Loco – 142, 143
    3800 Class (4-4-2) – 142, 144, 145, 146, 160, 182, 201
    2221 Class (4-4-2T) – 142, 145-147, 182, 201
    6100 Class (2-6-2T) – 147
    Pacific (No. 111) – 185-200, 206, 210, 226, 236
    (Experimental) 2-8-2T – 201
    4200 Class (2-8-0T) – 201, 202
    4300 Class (2-6-0) – 213-215, 226
    4600 Class (2-4-2T) – 217, 219, 220
    4700 Class (2-8-0) – 229
    4073 (Castle) Class (4-6-0) 198-200, 206, 230, 231, 235
    6000 (King) Class (4-6-0) – 200, 236
  South Devon and Cornwall Railway –
    2129 2-4-0ST – 32, 33
    2137 2-4-0ST – 32, 33
    0-4-4 'Tiny' – 33
    2-4-0 'King' – 33
    0-6-0 goods engine – 33
    4-4-0ST passenger engine – 33
    0-4-0ST shunting engine – 33
  London & North Western Railway
    Experiment Class – 204, 205
  London & South West
    Railway 4-4-2 – 204

Locomotive Exchanges – 203-204
London, Brighton & South Coast Railway – 58, 128
London & South West Railway – 49, 128
London & North Western Railway – 203, 204
Longbridges – 31

Maffei – 96
Margary, Peter – 30, 34, 35
Marillier, Frank – 86, 87, 127, 224, 228
Master Mechanics Association – 78
Mechanics Institute – 37, 157-163, 228, 238
Merryweather – 34
Midland Railway – 35, 213, 214
Mildenhall, Lot – 232

National Union of Railwaymen (NUR) 211, 224, 226, 227
New Jersey Railroad   213

New Zealand Railway – 185, 186
Nock, O S – 194
Norris Loco Works (USA) – 66
Nord Railway – 61
Northover, Frederick – 232

Ocean Mail Express – 104

Pearson, G H – 83
Peck, Alan – 207, 210
Peel, Robert – 41
Pellow, William – 89-94, 229, 230
Pennsylvania Railroad – 95, 133, 134
Penny Satirist – 12
Philadelphia & Reading Railroad – 66
Plaister, Ted – 231
Pole, Felix – 228
Pope, Tom – 232
Powning, Rev James – 23, 24
Prussian State Railway – 82, 134, 173
Purdue University – 174

Ragged Schools – 12, 14
Railway Executive Committee – 220
Railway Magazine – 184
Raven, Vincent – 185
Rea, Charles – 24
Regulating the Gauge of Railways Act – 42
Riddles, Robert – 62
Robinson, H J – 184
Rolls Estate – 16
Row-Martin, Charles – 65, 66
Rowes Farm, Stoke Gabriel – 16-18
Royal Commission 1846 – 43
Royal Horse Artillery – 155
Rinciman, Walter – 220
Russell, Charles – 42
Russell, John – 42

Sara & Co – 33
Science Museum – 20
Schenectady/Cole Nos 1 & 2 Superheaters – 174-176
Schmidt, Wilhelm – 82, 173-176
Scrivens, Mabel – 232
Severn Tunnel Project – 28, 36-40
Sharp, Stewart & Co – 67
Shatford, Matilda – 212
Slaughter Grunning – 33

Slaughter of Bristol – 31
Snell, F N – 83
Societe Alsacienne de Construction Mecaniques (SACM) – 61, 98, 102, 102
Solacroup, George – 186, 187
South Devon Railway – 24-35, 56
South Eastern & Chatham Railway – 217
Spencer, Bert – 30
Spencer, Victor – 208
Standardisation Programme (Locomotives) – 131-134
Stanier, William – 62, 78, 83, 86, 149, 212, 228, 231, 232
Stanley, Albert – 220
Stephenson, George and Robert – 9
Stephenson valve gear – 57, 98, 132, 178, 201
SMAG Vulcan – 134
Stirling, James – 182, 183
Stirling Patrick – 75, 182
Stoke Gabriel – 16-18
Stoyle, F B – 23
Stroudley, William – 58, 182, 183
Swindon No 1 and 3 Superheaters – 198, 199
Swinhoe, Dr G M – 162

Technical Education Committee – 167
Test Station, Swindon – 122
Thomson, James – 9
Trades Unions Act 1871 – 162
Trades Unions – 153, 155, 156, 162, 207, 210, 211, 224, 226, 227
Tuplin, W A – 194

Union Pacific Railroad – 186

Vale of Neath Railway -56
Vulcan Foundry – 31

Walker, Thomas – 32
Wallace, Cuthbert – 232
Walschaert, Egide – 177
Walschaert Valve Gear – 177-199
Warwick, Ada – 232
Webb, Francis – 182
Webb, Sidney – 156, 157
Wenham, Francis – 128
Whale, George – 182, 204, 206
Wilkinson, Joseph – 54, 55, 61

Williams, Alfred – 149-155, 162, 238
Windeath, Edward – 22
Wiltshire Volunteer Rifle Corps – 160, 162
Woollcombe, Thomas – 33
Worsdell, Wilson – 57, 77

Workers Medical Fund Society – 160
Workhouses – 11-14
Wright, Frederick George – 53, 55, 56, 58-60, 78, 83, 167
Wright, John – 26, 28-35, 235